Masala & Other Mixes

A Journey into the Cultural Melting Pot of India & Nepal

Andy Hanlon

www.andyhanlon.co.uk

andyhanlon@hotmail.co.uk

© Andy Hanlon, 2022

The moral right of the author has been asserted

A CIP catalogue record for this book is available from the British Library

ISBN 978-1-80049-6286

Cover: Andy Hanlon

With special thanks to Tom Sykes for his invaluable editing of this book

Phelim Publishing 2022.

For my parents, and children: Claire, Daniel, Damien and Jasmin

Intro.

Indian food and curry in particular, have long been part of the UK mainstream diet. Way back in 2001, then-British Foreign Secretary Robin Cook had stated, 'Chicken Tikka Masala is now a true British national dish, not only because it is the most popular, but because it is a perfect illustration of the way Britain absorbs and adapts external influences.' I usually take what any politicians say with a pinch of salt...no culinary pun intended, but on that occasion the aptly-named Cook was spot-on. For quite some time I had been interested by the different ways British and Indian culture have fused and mixed and interacted with one another. I would argue that the continuing popularity of Indian cuisine is the most visible example of this phenomenon in Britain today.

My own first contact with anything or anyone Indian was with a family named Sharma. Whilst Mr and Mrs Sharma and their two young daughters were of South Asian origin, they'd in fact moved to the UK from Tanzania. It seems almost clichéd but the Sharma's owned the local newsagent shop in the Midlands where I worked as a paper delivery boy in my early teens.

The family were nominally Hindus. I say nominally because Mr Sharma once confided in me how he was partial to a juicy steak. He then pleaded with me to never mention this disclosure to his wife. Bespectacled with a moustache, Mr Sharma was avuncular and patently had very good business acumen. His wife, a petite and attractive woman, was equally astute.

Although they were the first people of Indian heritage I'd ever got to know, the Sharma's were actually remarkably Anglicized. I rarely heard them speak anything but English, they always wore fashionable Western clothes and they were avid fans of soaps like *Coronation Street.* On reflection, I would say they were the living embodiments of that intersection of British and Indian customs, habits and mores that has become a fact of life today. There were in fact wider historical reasons for the presence of the Sharma's and others of similar background in Britain at that particular time. Their ancestors had migrated from the Indian sub-continent to East Africa during the 19th and early 20th centuries to work for the British building railways, amongst other things. A South Asian diaspora had emerged in Tanzania and in neighbouring Kenya and Uganda. East Asians like the Sharma's had grown prosperous and this attracted resentment from the majority African population. After these countries had gained their independence in the early 1960s, government policies openly discriminated against the Asian minorities. In Tanzania, the nationalization policies introduced by President Julius Nyerere allowed the government there to seize Indian-owned businesses and properties. This was the reason why entrepreneurial Asians like the Sharma's had left.

That said, Mr and Mrs Sharma always spoke wistfully about the old country. They would often regale me with stories of the snow-capped heights of Kilimanjaro or the gleaming expanses of Lake Victoria and the big game seen wandering majestically around the Serengeti. What they never once mentioned however was India, simply because they'd never been there and knew little about it. Still, one aspect of their Indian culture that loomed large in the Sharma's domestic life was the food they ate. I recall the first time I smelled those exotic aromas coming from their living quarters beside the shop. I was intrigued but not adventurous enough to try the food, despite several offers from Mrs Sharma. I guess I just wasn't ready to leave my comfort zone of the standard meat-and-two veg diet I'd been raised on.

However, that all changed one day while I was waiting for the evening newspapers to arrive. I hadn't eaten since lunchtime and was feeling ravenous. Mrs Sharma asked if I wanted to try some of the curry she had cooked and, instead of politely declining as I had done before, this time I thought why not? She soon stepped through from the kitchen into the shop with a small plate of curry and rice. The only rice I'd ever eaten before had been in the form of a pudding, so the idea of it as a savoury dish was novel to me. I scooped some rice and a piece of chicken onto my fork and put it in my mouth. The combination of flavours was quite a revelation. The array of spices – intense, piquant, floral, both a little sweet but also with hints of bitterness -surpassed any stew or casserole I'd ever tasted before. The slightly fragrant rice – which I learned was the basmati kind – perfectly complemented the rich sauce. Indeed, I actually started drooling, which fortunately Mrs Sharma didn't notice.

5

With my taste buds going into overdrive I was bowled over by the realisation that food could be so exhilaratingly delicious, so complex and wide-ranging in its taste. Mrs Sharma asked me if I liked it, which I took it to be a rhetorical question given that I'd scoffed the whole lot in about thirty seconds flat. She then asked, 'Would you like some more?'...this offer being the only thing stopping me from literally licking the plate clean. So it was that my passion for Indian food was ignited thanks to Mrs Sharma-and my pangs of hunger- on that evening many years ago.

Ever since then I've eaten a lot of Indian food and experimented with cooking it myself. Whilst at university in Coventry, I lived in an area with a high South Asian population. There I soon became acquainted with the *ambala*, the Indian sweet shop, although I preferred the savouries they served: samosas and my favourite sheikh kebabs which I would douse in tangy condiments and enjoy wrapped in a chapatti. You could eat in or take away these tasty gems, and for much cheaper than the regular Indian restaurants thereabouts. In my second year of studies, a balti house opened close to where I was living, run by a Pakistani family from Kashmir. As the balti house didn't have a licensed to sell alcohol customers were welcome to bring their own. The food there was inexpensive and always delicious, prompting my housemates and me to become regulars. We befriended the owners to the point that, if the place was empty apart from ourselves, then they'd gladly allow us to bring a guitar from the house and have a sing-along after the meal. These happy nights combined three things I had come to enjoy greatly: beer, music and Indian food.

My love of Indian cuisine and my interactions with South Asian people in Britain stoked my curiosity about the wider historical, political and cultural forces that had shaped the sub-continent. At university, I studied a history module examining colonial India and the ramifications of British disengagement there. After learning all about Britain's lengthy involvement with South Asia, I grew more curious about the impact of British culture on India, particularly given the growing Indian influence on contemporary British life. Still, the more I studied the subject, the more I craved personal, visceral experience of it. A trip to India was the next logical next step if I was to understand the country beyond the abstract.

As a graduate of international relations living in a multicultural society, I was especially curious on my trip about any overlaps and connections between cultures, faiths, communities, societies and nations. These, I'd learn are evident in the complexities of Indian life, in: religion, sport, music, architecture, customs and cuisine, ethnic identities and social hierarchies. I would also end up visiting Nepal, a country never colonised by Britain and yet one that the British Army has been recruiting from for over two centuries. But cultural encounters, on both the personal and larger scale, do not always go smoothly, and so, besides the humorous and enjoyable incidents of my trip, there were moments of fear, confusion and life-threatening danger.

Chapter 1.

My first destination was Mumbai, that immense metropolis found on India's West coast in the state of Maharashtra. The cheapest flight I could find was with Air France which, unlike other airlines I had flown with previously, served small complementary bottles of champagne. I generally prefer beer but with an eight-and-a-half-hour window of opportunity to enjoy this high-end French tipple, it seemed daft not to partake. The more of the stuff I quaffed, the more amusing I thought the situation I was in: at the start of an epic trip to India and Nepal, here I was indulging in the very best of French culture!

I hoped that the in-flight meal like the alcohol might be some Gallic delight. I wasn't flying first class so obviously didn't expect *fois gras* with truffles, but disappointingly they served lamb curry. Despite my love of curried food, seeing how I'd actually be eating little else for the foreseeable future, I felt something European might have been preferable. I then began pondering how faintly ridiculous it was that here I was, a lover of Indian food on his way to India, regretting that only Indian food was on the menu.

During the flight I got chatting with a couple from Milan seated next to me. As we excitedly shared itineraries and expectations, the conversation flowed as freely as the champagne. By the time the aircraft started its descent, whilst speaking I was suddenly overcome mid-sentence by nausea; this admittedly induced by my over-indulgence in the bubbly. Not having time to excuse myself and flee to the toilet, I managed to utter 'excuse me one moment' before deftly grabbing a sick-bag and vomiting into it. It's true that a more sober individual might have found this moment socially awkward, but acting as though I'd simply sneezed rather than just thrown up, I then casually turned back to the rather embarrassed-looking pair and continued talking. Suffice to say upon landing we didn't exchange details.

By the time I'd cleared immigration and customs it was almost one in the morning and I was feeling a lot better if still a bit drunk. As I exited the refreshing coolness of the air-conditioned airport terminal through automated doors, I was hit by a sudden waft of hot air. The stark thought could not escape me, if it was this hot during the night what the hell would the daytime temperature be like? The lengthy taxi ride I took from the airport to the Colaba district of the city instantly exposed one sobering reality about Mumbai: namely its massive levels of homelessness. Sadly vast numbers of wretched souls can be seen sleeping in doorways and all along the roadsides... indeed in any spare corner they can find. India is of course notorious for its poverty, but witnessing so much destitution first hand still comes as a shock. No images I'd seen or descriptions I'd read could ever fully convey the scale of Mumbai's starkest social problem, but here it was, real and right in front of me. It was little wonder therefore that I spent the entire journey in silent depression.

It seemed ironic that my destination in Colaba was the Salvation Army Red Shield Hostel. After all Salvation Army hostels in the UK are generally associated with providing shelter for the homeless. In comparison this one in Mumbai; a city blighted by staggering levels of homelessness, was filled with relatively wealthy foreign backpackers taking advantage of its cheap rates.

Amidst the hordes, heat, and humidity I spent the next few days trying to absorb this frenzied conurbation. The traffic in Mumbai is proportionate to its large population, this making congestion of vehicles as big a problem as its congestion of people. Although ubiquitous elsewhere in India, three-wheeled auto-rickshaws are banned in downtown Mumbai, this restriction intended to ease traffic. Even so this leaves no shortage of taxis, private cars, buses, lorries, vans, scooters and motorbikes all producing endless noise and fumes. I marvelled at how, besides these modern modes of transport, there are ancient forms as well, like the occasional carts pulled by bullocks and the *tonga*, a type of two-wheeled, horse-drawn carriage. Whereas the large horns on a bullock obviously cannot be sounded, all motorists on the other hand constantly honked their horns to warn others of their presence. Basically a functioning horn is imperative when driving in Indian traffic, this the reason why most commercial vehicles have the words 'Horn Please' emblazoned across their rears, lest someone forget to blast theirs every twenty seconds.

In India as in the UK they drive on the left-hand side... and there any other similarities between the rules of traffic end. Judging

9

from the number of people packed on to any manner of transport clearly safety is not paramount on Indian roads. Be this a cycle-rickshaw carrying seven schoolchildren, or indeed both parents with up to three or four of their children all riding aboard just one scooter, evidently the notion of overloading does not exist. Even public transport seems to operate on the premise that there is always room for just one more passenger, whether this is inside, hanging on to the outside or indeed perched up on the roof. As in London, lots of Mumbai local buses are red double-deckers. Here however they are regularly overloaded beyond anything London Transport would ever permit. In astonishment I even watched one bus so laden with passengers on its one side that it only narrowly avoided tipping over whilst navigating a traffic island.

The city struggling to cope with all this traffic isn't an old one by Indian standards, but it had long been a crossroads where diverse peoples have met and interacted with each other. Originally an archipelago a short distance from the mainland, for centuries the indigenous Koli inhabitants of these islands had been the subjects of various Hindu and Muslim rulers. In 1534 the reigning sultan had ceded the islands to the Portuguese, the first Europeans to arrive in India by sea. Significantly in 1661 most, although not all of the islands, were gifted as a dowry to English monarch Charles II when he'd married the king of Portugal's daughter, Catherine of Braganza. Although they were possessions of the English Crown, the islands were soon being leased by the privately owned East India Company. In due course the commercial endeavours of this company were to have a profound impact on the sub-continent.

Marking the genesis of a great commercial centre, in the late 1660s, the East India Company began trading on the island known as Bombay, hence the city's former name. As its colony developed by 1775, the Company had found itself at war with the Maratha Empire, a major power ruling a vast swathe of India at that time. The Marathas were victorious but nevertheless, as part of a 1782 peace treaty they had ceded to the Company the largest island of Salsette, which had been captured from the Portuguese earlier. As trade through the port steadily increased along with the size of its population, by the 1840s, engineers began building causeways and reclaiming land from the Arabian Sea. This was an ambitious project which had eventually transformed the archipelago into the present-day single island also known as Salsette. With only a river and two creeks separating the north of Salsette Island from the mainland, the British had also built road and rail links to connect Bombay to the rest of India.

The city's economic fortunes really took off in the 1860s during the American Civil War, when India replaced the United States as the principal source of Britain's cotton and Bombay became its main export centre. Within a few decades the opening of the Suez Canal, which drastically cut the sea journey time between Britain and India, further boosted prosperity. With a booming economy and an ever growing-population Bombay soon established itself as the financial and commercial powerhouse of India, a position that the city has steadfastly retained ever since.

The popular tourist area of Colaba sits at the southern end of Salsette Island and is spread around the tip of a peninsular. I spent much of my time there on Colaba Causeway, this being a main thoroughfare close to the hostel which runs through the south of the peninsular. With masses of shops, stalls, street vendors and eateries, it is as chaotic and claustrophobic as any other street in Mumbai. Memorably along one section the noxious fumes of the traffic were alleviated by scents emanating from the numerous perfumeries. Further south along the causeway I'd be longing for the fragrance of these perfumes again, as the less desirable odour of fish from the nearby docks would fill my nostrils. Unpleasant as the stink may have been, it was nonetheless a pungent reminder that whatever else might have changed since Mumbai's humble beginnings, fishing still went on pretty much as it always had. If you wanted 'real' Mumbaikars then this Koli fishing community are about as authentic as it gets, having been casting their nets in the surrounding sea for countless generations.

Whatever perils and misfortunes befell such communities they were usually shielded from the misery of hunger and starvation by the very nature of their livelihood, a not inconsequential fact in a land that suffered several famines throughout its history. In an urban environment which constantly attracted people from across India, the longevity of this indigenous fishing community is quite something really. They are in a sense like the Cockneys of Mumbai

11

the original working-class inhabitants of the city who'd long since become some almost invisible entity. Indeed the fish market at Colaba docks is their Billingsgate, supplying fish and seafood for the surrounding shops, restaurants and hotels whose appetite for the fruits of the sea never diminished.

The Koli community in Colaba and elsewhere around the city's shoreline may appear to be an immutable part of Mumbai life, but their future is under threat from falling fish stocks. The causes of this decline are not natural. Human impact on the environment through overfishing and pollution has depleted fish numbers, as has continued land reclamation from the sea which has destroyed the mangroves where fish breed. It's a sad thought that Mumbai's oldest community – one who'd historically seen their island life morph into India's most populous city – could eventually dwindle away along with the fish they so depend upon.

India had gained its independence from Britain in 1947 and yet the city's colonial past still resonated at the time in the names of several Colaba thoroughfares I visited. Roads called Henry, Barrow and Mereweather and Walton all echoed the days of British Raj or rule, as do the neighbouring districts known as Churchgate and Fort. It stood to reason that many of the impressive buildings seen hereabouts also dated from the colonial period. Amongst them is the Prince of Wales Museum located on Colaba Causeway next to a traffic roundabout known as Wellington Fountain. Opened in 1922, in nationalist spirit, the museum had since been renamed in honour of Shivaji, a former Indian royal rather than a British one. Fronted by a picturesque lawned garden and palms, this three-storied structure is a combination of typical English brickwork with the hallmark arches, spires and domes of Indian architecture. It is an intriguing fusion of European and traditional Indo-Islamic designs, a style of architecture which came to be known as Indo-Saracenic. In fact, this hybrid aesthetic came to characterise the design of many municipal buildings, railway stations and other structures built by the British in India.

Another British era construct which caught my eye is the former High Court building located about a kilometre north of Wellington Fountain in the Fort district. Having opened in 1879, this particular imperial structure was built in a more recognizable Gothic revival style of architecture. As the centre of Bombay's colonial judiciary its courts had witnessed several major trials, including those held against Bal Gangadhar Tilak, who'd been the first leader of the country's independence movement. Interestingly Bal Gangadhar Tilak had instructed the city's first Muslim barrister Mohammed Ali Jinnah to defend him, this of course the man who would later become the founder of Pakistan. A relatively unknown Mohandas Gandhi had also practiced law here in this historical building.

For all the grandness of this court building the administration of justice under the British had been far from...well just! In the eyes of the law some facing colonial courts were indeed, to quote one Indian born writer...'More equal than others'. Regardless of its supposed impartiality the legal system had been one which was harsh on Indians, whilst unduly lenient on Europeans. It was a staggering indictment of injustice, that in over three centuries of British involvement on the sub-continent only *three* cases can be found of Englishmen executed for murdering Indians, while the murders of thousands more at British hands went unpunished.

From the old High Court building I took a five-minute stroll east to St Thomas' Cathedral. In what was to me an unfamiliar city, this construct presents an all too familiar sight. Opened in 1718, St Thomas' was both the city's first Anglican church and indeed its oldest British-era structure. The fact this building had outlasted all other early British residential and commercial structures, just went to demonstrate the importance the colonists had placed on Christianity. Moreover, as it still functions as a place of worship, evidently an Indian Anglican community had been established here in Mumbai. I have to admit that the presence of the Church of England in India was only one of many colonial introductions I'd never considered before visiting.

A kilometre west of Wellington Fountain, British-era constructs give way to the modern skyscrapers of the Nariman Point business district. These and many other towering edifices found around the city, not only symbolise India's economic power, they are also a reminder of the great wealth which co-exists alongside the great poverty. I must confess that in such an affluent area it was all too easy to forget about the surrounding endemic poverty, hunger, homelessness and unemployment.

Nariman Point is a centre of political as well as economic power being home to the Maharashtra Legislative Assembly. It convenes in a strange-looking circular building which had opened in 1981. From here more than 112 million people are governed in India's third largest state covering over 300,000 sq. km. I read that those elected to this parliament are voted in under a first-past-the-post electoral system, this an example of British influence in modern Indian politics.

Stretching northwards in an arc from Nariman Point is the shore of Back Bay, this lined for much of its length by a wide promenade and the eight-lane Marine Drive. A taxi ride along Mumbai's best-known highway reveals some of the most desirable properties in the city spread along its way. At the northern-end of Marine Drive sits Chowpatty Beach, a favourite recreational-spot for countless people, although the sea there was pretty polluted ruling out any safe swimming.

As well as the beach, there are also a number of large sports grounds or *maidans* offering respite from the relentless noise and fumes of Mumbai's downtown traffic. These urban green spaces are proof that the city had been planned out, even if it does feel more like a random sprawl at times. It was on these very playing fields that the English had once played cricket. As they had done so, little could the colonists have realised that cricket would one day become India's favourite sport, one excitedly followed by millions. Without a doubt no other aspect of English culture has been so wholeheartedly embraced in India as cricket. It makes the game one of the most important and lasting legacies of Britain's colonial involvement in India, this much to the detriment of many an England team.

A more glaring reminder of British colonialism is the city's most famous landmark, which happens to be just a couple of hundred metres from the Salvation Army hostel. Designed by the same architect responsible for the Prince of Wales Museum, Mumbai's Gateway of India is an enormous waterfront arch constructed of concrete and light-coloured basalt. Situated along the delightfully named Apollo Bunder, it had been completed in the 1920s to commemorate a 1911 visit by King George V, the then emperor of India. I was impressed by its mammoth rectangular form, turreted archway and vast hall attached to either side of the archway. The Indo-Saracenic design is evident from the typically Indian floral and geometrical patterns carved into the stone and the intricate lattice work around the architraves of the arched entrances to both side halls. While it seems highly unlikely that such an extravagant monument would be commissioned for a modern Indian head of state, historically European rulers and victors had often been honoured with such grandiosity. Still, whatever colonial glory it may have once represented, like the remnants of many a former empire today it's a tourist attraction, and for me a conveniently situated one at that.

With most people arriving in India by sea back in those days, this statement of imperial eminence had been purposely erected near the harbour entrance. Within 25 years of its completion, the very last British troops departed the country through the Gateway of India, reportedly as a band played 'Auld Lang Syne', although I am sure very few if any watching had been singing along to it! No other edifice I saw during my trip was a more powerful symbol of the changing relationship Britain had with its Indian colony. When constructed, the huge Gateway had signalled pride about Britain's domination of India's land and seas, whilst later it represented humility and perhaps even humiliation when the deposed British had made their final exit from the sub-continent through it.

Not far from the Gateway of India lies another famous Mumbai landmark: the exclusive and expensive Taj Mahal Intercontinental Hotel. Its room tariffs are certainly beyond my limited finances, but the bar is open to non-residents and I was curious to see how the well-heeled enjoy Mumbai. The 'Taj', as it's affectionately known, had been founded by an Indian industrialist, purportedly after he'd been refused entry into a 'whites only' luxury Bombay hotel. Since opening in 1903, this spectacular building had attracted affluent visitors from around the world. Everyone from rock stars to US presidents have stayed there.

As I went to enter the Taj I was stopped by the doorman who informed me that collared shirts had to be worn in the bar. I then offered him a tip...or bribe, in the hope that he'd let me in with my sweaty T-shirt, but to no avail. The dress code was strict hotel policy. I sulked away annoyed at this requirement which given the oppressive heat, seemed a little bit formal. As I did so, I mused on the irony that, as a white person, I had just been denied entrance to a hotel founded by someone...because they'd supposedly been refused access to a 'whites only' hotel!

It is sad to think that whatever positive interactions might have taken place between British and Indian culture historically, racial segregation had been an uncomfortable reality of colonial life. Signs reading 'Europeans only' hadn't just been displayed in hotels but in many shops, restaurants and reserved railway carriages. Other public venues such as waiting rooms, theatres and hospitals had separate sections for Europeans and Indians. It is upsetting to think that the British operated a form of apartheid long before it ever became official policy in South Africa. Still on a positive note, things have progressed since then and in the 21st century, Indian hotels now discriminated on the basis of a person's attire rather than their skin colour.

Still, whatever gulf might have existed between my own modest accommodation and the opulence of a luxurious hotel like the Taj, even a Salvation Army hostel was relative luxury compared to the squalor endured by so many Mumbaikars. Colonial architecture, apartment-blocks, gleaming skyscrapers and business districts are one part of the cityscape, tragically though so are the sprawling-slums. I had seen Dharavi, Asia's largest slum, on my drive in from the airport which spreads over 2.1 square kilometres and is home to 100,000s of people. Lacking any adequate infrastructure and sanitation, its impoverished masses; who are themselves at least a step up from the homeless, live in makeshift shacks constructed from second-hand materials.

Many slum-dwellers depend on begging, a very visible social ill. Lots of this is run by organised criminals, furthermore reportedly children are even mutilated or blinded in order to elicit sympathy from the public and maximise donations. Given their prevalence, the only beggars I personally ever gave money to were those who were either blind, limbless or suffering from leprosy. Clearly such disabilities are difficult to cope with anywhere, but especially so in a country lacking a welfare state. The widespread impoverishment created by an absence of any state help is an unsavoury facet of

Indian society and fuels begging, theft, slavery and prostitution. Worst of all it leads to the sexual exploitation of children. Mumbai's combination of endemic poverty, overpopulation and high unemployment creates a massive surplus of human labour. People undertake work normally done by donkeys, horses, water buffalo or oxen, and I'd often see heavily laden carts being pulled by humans. Remarkably advertising billboards are hand-painted rather than printed. Another example of this cheap labour force was one chap I noticed sitting by a roadside, mundanely breaking rocks into smaller pieces with a hammer. It, like so many sights in India, is unimaginable in the West where such things are done by machinery.

The rock-breaker was most likely a member of the *Shudra* caste, the lowest of the four *varnas* found in the Hindu social hierarchy. According to Hindu belief each *varnas* respectively came from the: mouth, arms, thighs and feet of the god Brahma at the moment of creation, the *Shudras* obviously emerging from the latter. If the lot of the *Shudras* seems harsh in Hindu society, then spare a thought for India's *Dalits*, a group at the very nadir of this social system beneath even the *Shudras*. Their ranks are condemned to do the worst menial labour no-one else wants to do, work such as toilet cleaning or dealing with human and animal remains. In fact, the English word 'pariah' meaning outcast is derived from a *Dalit* sub-group that had traditionally been ceremonial drummers, which frankly seems like a preferable job to wiping up faeces. Regarded as polluting in Hindu culture, the *Dalits* are so marginalised, that in the past they'd even been forbidden from entering Hindu temples under pain of death. Truthfully one shuddered to think which part of Lord Brahma's anatomy the poor *Dalits* supposedly emanated from!

India's most celebrated *Dalit* was the academic and politician Dr B R Ambedkar, who having studied in Bombay was honoured with a statue near Wellington Fountain. Despite his lowly beginnings, Ambedkar rose to become Minister for Law in India's first post-independence government, framing the new nation's constitution whilst in office. Never forgetting him roots, he had been a fierce-champion of India's *Dalit* communities campaigning vigorously for their social and political rights. Shortly before his death in 1956

Ambedkar converted to Buddhism and in so doing had persuaded large-numbers of other *Dalits* to do the same. One of his greatest legacies had been the introduction of government policies aimed at helping the *Dalits* and other underprivileged minorities. Even so, in reality the hierarchical nature of Hinduism makes such social reforms difficult to attain.

Being in a country where around 80 percent of the population identify as being Hindu, a visit to a Hindu temple seemed almost inevitable. Located a thirty minutes' taxi ride northwest of Colaba and reputedly worth visiting is the Mahalaxmi Temple. Taking its name from the surrounding neighbourhood, the temple dates from the late 18th century and is crowned by a fifteen-metre-high curvilinear spire. All Hindu temples, or *mandirs* as they're properly known, are dedicated to a specific deity either male or female; whose image is found enshrined inside an inner sanctum. The Mahalaxmi Mandir happens to honour the extremely popular female deity Lakshmi, who is both Lord Vishnu's consort and the goddess of beauty and prosperity: two things desirable to most people I'd say.

Non-Hindus are seen as polluting and therefore not permitted into the sanctuary where apparently statues of Lakshmi and two other goddesses form a shrine. Nonetheless the rest of this lively temple complex was fascinating to walk around and observe. In parts it felt more like a marketplace with stalls selling all kinds of religious paraphernalia including the coconut, sweets and flowers offered by devotees at the shrine. I could not get over just how noisy and animated the temple environment was; quite different to the generally quieter atmosphere normal in Western Christian places of worship. It was at this temple that I first spotted *sadhus,* devout Hindus who renounce their worldly possessions to pursue an ascetic life of mendacity and meditation. *Sadhus* tend to wear orange-coloured garments; while some of them forsake clothing altogether such is their desire to abandon all material belongings. Distinguishable by their long or dreadlocked hair and frequently smeared in ash, these holy men are the embodiment of ultimate Hindu piety.

Along with the sadhus, I saw the more familiar sight of beggars around the temple complex. I guess even a sacred site could not offer sanctuary from this bane of everyday Indian life. At various images positioned around the temple walls, I watched devotees bring their hands together and bow as they approached. Like bowing the head and making a sign of the cross in Christianity, such gestures of respect show similarities in ritual worship. The smell of incense burning, even if it was a very different aroma to that used in churches, was another commonality I could not help noticing. When close to the inner shrine I heard *pujaris* (priests) chanting mantras as part of the prayer ceremony known as *puja*. Priests and monks often chant in Christian services too, so again it is not a custom unique to Hinduism, although Hindus have been practicing it a lot longer than Christians.

Such mantras along with other sacred texts are recorded in the substantive body of Sanskrit literature called the *Vedas*. Dealing with philosophical concepts, principal amongst the *Vedas* are the *Upanishads*, these scriptures having influenced Hindu spiritual thought more than any other. A historical context for Hinduism is provided by the poems the *Ramayana* and the even more epic tale titled the *Mahabharata*. In a section of the latter called the *Bhagavad Gita*, Lord Vishnu asserts *'Now I am become death, the destroyer of worlds'*. Famously, US physicist Robert Oppenheimer chillingly recalled this passage upon helping to create the world's first atomic explosion during WWII.

When it came to the fluidity and diversity of culture in India, I was interested to learn that the tenets and rituals of hundreds of millions of Hindus don't conform to any one creed, philosophy or doctrine. With no founder, prophet or central authority Hinduism has evolved as a very broad system of beliefs, which in turn had enabled it to accommodate other existing religious practices and traditions on the sub-continent. This was why thousands of lesser gods and goddesses can be found in Hinduism, although many of these are either incarnations of the three main-deities Brahma, Vishnu and Shiva, or linked with them in some other way as their consorts, offspring or animal avatars. In short India's main religion can best be understood as a collection of various sects, with the devotees in each following particular deities.

Today Hinduism is associated primarily with India but it had in fact once flourished right across South East Asia, this prior to the establishment of Buddhism there. A fine example of this is the temple of Angkor Wat in what is now Cambodia, built by a Khmer king in the 12th century CE in honour of the Hindu deity Vishnu. Hinduism had similarly been followed in many parts of West Asia before the arrival of Islam in that region. Over centuries several million Hindus on the Indian sub-continent had converted to other faiths, Islam in particular. Some had been forced conversions but many had embraced Islam willingly. Even so, Hinduism endured as the majority religion of the Indian masses and that is unlikely to change any time soon.

Illustrating the trans-cultural nature of Hinduism is the fact that many of its adherent believe that the Buddha is a manifestation of Vishnu, even though Buddha had founded a completely separate religion. Other followers of Vishnu go even further claiming that Jesus Christ was yet another aspect of their favoured deity. I took one Mumbai taxi which highlighted perfectly this kind of syncretic spiritual belief. Adorning the car's dashboard was a green sticker containing Quranic script, whilst alongside it were also images of Jesus and the elephant-headed deity Ganesha. When I queried the driver about his eclectic mix of religious imagery he replied quite gleefully 'All from the same God sir'. This was hardly a compelling theological argument but I quite liked his simplistic sentiment all the same.

It is fair to say that Hinduism is not usually a religion that seeks converts and few Westerners follow it. There is however one facet of Hindu philosophy which has gained popularity far beyond the sub-continent itself, including Britain. This is yoga, the well-known practice of meditation and exercises long used in Hinduism and other Indian religions for both spiritual and physical benefits. Like the Hindu religion, yoga is not a unified discipline and exists in a number of forms and traditions with equally varied approaches. Some schools of yoga will advocate celibacy and sexual restraint, while by contrast those following the tantra tradition believe sex plays an important part in yogic exercise. In a religious context, practitioners of yoga in India, share the ultimate goal of attaining self-liberation from the soul's endless cycle of death and rebirth. Although the exact origins of yoga are unknown it had certainly developed by the 6th century BCE. In the 20th century, a number of yogis introduced techniques based upon *hatha* yoga combined with elements of Western gymnastics to the Western world. Using postures, breathing control and mental exercises, this hybrid approach popularised in the West, places emphasis on fitness and relaxation rather than a quest for spiritual enlightenment. Today this type of yoga is taught and practiced in countries right across the world and remains an ever-popular keep fit activity. It's not an exaggeration to say that no other aspect of Indian culture has had the global reach of yoga.

Unsurprisingly a vast city like Mumbai is home to a number of different religious communities, all of which have absorbed local influences. India's second largest religion Islam, itself evolved as Sufism, a branch reflecting aspects of the spiritual contemplation common in Hinduism and other indigenous Indian faiths. Sufism is a mystical expression of Islam and emphasises personal closeness to God through meditation and a life of abstinence from material pleasures. Many of the early Sufis became saints and their shrines are venerated; this, a custom anathema to mainstream Islam, as indeed is the singing and dancing also associated with Sufism. Such worship is however acceptable to Hindus, many of whom attend celebrations at Sufi shrines. The devotional songs of Sufism known as *qawwali* are immensely popular on the sub-continent, even gaining an international audience thanks to singers like the late legendary Nusrat Fateh Ali Khan.

Sizeable Christian, Buddhist, Jain and Sikh populations are found in Mumbai too. However much older than any of these religions is Zoroastrianism, a faith practiced in the city by a small community. Originating in Persia; modern-day Iran, approximately 1,500 years before the birth of Christ, it had been the official religion there for a thousand years before Islam arrived. Named after its founder Zoroaster, it was the first religion to stress the duality of human nature and the inherent struggle between choosing good or evil in life. In Zoroastrianism there is a single God who is manifest not only in animals and plants but also in the elements: earth, water, sky and fire, in fact prayers are offered to a fire which symbolises God's purity, truth and order. A number of 'fire temples' as they are described exist in Mumbai, but alas non-Zoroastrians are not allowed to enter these.

The first Zoroastrians had arrived in India in the 10th century CE escaping persecution after the Arab conquest of Persia and the establishment of Islam there. The fleeing Zoroastrians eventually settled in what was then Bombay and to this day their community of less than 80,000 people are still referred to as Parsis, meaning 'Persians'. There is no easy way to identify Parsis as they have no distinctive appearance or dress. This small Parsi community are nevertheless quite prominent in commerce and politics and form an interesting minority on account of their unique funeral rites. For Zoroastrians neither bury nor cremate their dead, preferring instead to place corpses outside, high up and exposed on a so called 'tower of silence' in order to be devoured by vultures. This tradition stems from the belief that burying or burning a person's body will pollute either the earth or the flames involved, both of which are regarded as sacred. These towers of silence are located upon a large hill in a secluded part of the city to the west. I have to say this struck me as a slightly macabre funeral practice; albeit a natural one appreciated I'm sure by the well-fed local vultures!

Just as the corpulent might be conspicuous in a land of famine, here it didn't take very long to realise that being a non-Indian acts like a magnet for attracting people. Whenever I was approached the standard opening line was 'which country sir?' Whatever your reply, the person asking would allegedly have a family member or good friend residing there. Whilst many Indians were genuinely friendly and merely sought your acquaintance, many others had far less noble intentions. It would very quickly transpire that they were either begging or trying to sell something which you neither needed nor wanted. For example, on my first day of exploring the city I'd been offered the services of a woman by some desperate looking chap. The pimp had somewhat amusingly declared that she would perform a 'sex dance' for me, by which he presumably meant a striptease. As tempting as such a proposition sounded; particularly for anybody having an interest in choreography, I had politely declined.

The woman in question was likely driven to prostitution by an oppressive combination of poverty and patriarchy. Poverty was unquestionably a key factor when considering the issue of gender equality in Indian society. The fact that India had its first female prime minister 13 years before Britain did is misleading, after all Indira Gandhi had been the daughter of the country's first Prime Minister Jawaharlal Nehru, and part of a wealthy family still very prominent in national politics today. In light of this, her privileged background had hardly made her representative of Indian women in the main.

Although affluent women in Indian society may enjoy a degree of autonomy and independence, life for the majority of females is one tightly governed by inviolable codes and customs. From being daughters to becoming wives and mothers, the social position of women is strictly defined within a culture which is unquestionably male dominated. This reality is reflected by the fact that many Indian women can only achieve respect and acceptance from their husband's family by bearing sons rather than daughters. Although male attitudes regarding honour claim to be protective towards females, in truth they are often driven by chauvinism and help to maintain the sexual inequality inherent in Indian society.

The normal practice of arranged marriages further exposes this discrimination against women through the tradition of the bride's family paying a dowry to the groom or his family. The dowry can be given in cash, gold or any other types of valuables including land and livestock in rural areas. This system of dowry is actually illegal in India and had been since 1961 although it is a law very rarely enforced. It is a tolerated custom which has had horrible consequences, resulting in female infanticide, child marriages and even brides being burnt alive by their own husbands and in-laws! It's a grotesque reality that annually thousands of married women throughout India became the victims of so called 'bride burnings', these usually being committed when attempts to extort additional dowry payments from the woman's family fail. In such murders the husband, often in connivance with his own relatives, will pour kerosene on his wife and set her alight, afterwards claiming she'd fallen foul of a 'domestic accident'. Since the mid-1980s all such deaths are treated as suspicious, even so, as kerosene is widely used in India for cooking purposes, it makes these claims difficult to disprove in a court of law.

Such murders are a truly heinous form of domestic abuse, one that is perpetuated by a dowry system operating in an essentially conservative, patriarchal society, this despite all the economic and technological achievements of India in recent years. Much like the *varnas* system, the tradition of dowry giving is firmly entrenched in Indian society, although it's a cultural not a religious practice. In light of this prevalence, in my mind it is unlikely to end meaning the problems highlighted will continue. The national crime records show that in recent years more than 20 women were killed in such 'dowry deaths' every day, most of the victims burnt to death. In fairness domestic killings are a universal problem, and the bottom line is, the acquisition of material wealth will always motivate some people to commit murder. Unfortunately however, in India the dowry system readily provides that motivation, whilst the common usage of kerosene stoves easily provides the means.

One area where women do appear to enjoy equality with their male colleagues is in film. Mumbai is of course famously home to the Bollywood film industry. Productions in Hindi out of these studios are often blockbusters enjoying audiences of hundreds of millions, not just in India, but in Pakistan as well where these films are equally adored. In a similar way to religion, these Bollywood films invoke tropes and structures which can transcend regional identities and unite disparate audiences. Normally any Bollywood feature will be: a drama, thriller, romance, fantasy, comedy and musical all rolled into one. Such multi-genre productions have warranted the humorous nickname 'masala films', masala being a word used across India for a mixture of spices. Thin on plots but typically having a good versus evil theme, plus plenty of action, singing and dancing; it's a format with mass appeal.

As I would soon discover the loud playing of Indian movies was pretty much mandatory on long coach journeys, a bit of escapism for passengers existing in what seemed to me a pretty surreal land already. The massive popularity of film, hints that entertainment rather than religion is arguably the opiate of the masses in 21st century India. When it came to the stars of these Bollywood epics- many run for three or four hours- I personally had never heard of cinema legends like actor Shan Rukh Khan or the actress Shidevi. But then again, Robert De Niro and Meryl Streep are not exactly household names to millions of Indians either. Sometimes the films being shown on coach trips were sub-titled, albeit done so in the local language rather than English, thereby making them no less comprehensible to me. That said, I did understand occasional bits of dialogue as this was spoken in English. Hearing these films I became aware of 'Hinglish' the common practice of people mixing English with Hindi and other regional Indian languages.

Equally as popular as the actual Bollywood films are their songs and music which also tend to become big hits. Given that songs are a standard component of Bollywood cinema, it is surprising to learn that the starring actors and actresses hardly ever actually perform the songs themselves. Instead they mime to tracks pre-recorded by so called playback singers, artists who have become major stars in their own right. One of them had even inspired a UK number one song in 1998 by the Leicester based British group Cornershop. The track 'Brimful of Asha' eulogizes the legendary playback singer Asha Bhosle, with singer Tjinder Singh describing her as 'saddi rani' meaning 'our queen' in Punjabi. Her cultural significance is understandable when you consider that, over a six-decade period; she recorded thousands of film songs. The slower album version of 'A Brimful of Asha' also references two further famous playback singers, Lata Mangeshkar, who just happens to be Bhosle's elder sister, and male vocalist Mohammed Rafi.

India's multiculturalism evident in Bollywood, religion and other things, had one of its greatest exponents in the famous Mohandas Gandhi. Towards the end of my stay in Mumbai, I visited the two-storey *Mani Bhavan* where Gandhi had stayed whenever he was in the city. Located around seven kilometres north of Colaba, the building today contains a library and a collection of photos and personal memorabilia. I was touched by Gandhi's room which was sparsely furnished and lacked even any chairs. A mattress on the marble floor had provided seating and a bed, whilst, positioned around it were a small desk and tables all with shortened legs. Notably, the room contained the wheels upon which Gandhi had spun cotton. As part of the campaign for Indian independence, Gandhi had encouraged his compatriots to spin cotton with which to produce their own clothing rather than buy imported British garments. With a telephone being the only concession to the 20th century, this was simple, modest accommodation for an incredible man who'd lived a simple, modest life.

After Gandhi had arrived there in 1915, Bombay as it was then called became a major centre of anti-colonial resistance. Amongst those prominent in the long struggle against British rule had been Bhikaji Cama, a Parsi woman after whom a major Colaba road is today named. She'd travelled around Europe speaking up for the revolutionary cause and was instrumental in pushing for gender equality as a part of the post-independence settlement. Madame Cama like lots of independence activists from that period remains largely unknown outside of India, this something which certainly couldn't be said about the movements' leading-light Gandhi.

Even though Gandhi's famous Hindu-based philosophy of non-violence against the British ultimately delivered independence, his pleas for religious tolerance on the other hand proved to be less successful, alas failing as they did to prevent communal slaughter during the partition of British India in 1947. The mass transfer of population resulting from partition, as millions of Hindus and Sikhs made for India and an equal number of Muslims for Pakistan, was tragically accompanied by bloodshed which claimed a million lives possibly even more.

Partition provoked India's worse religious-bloodshed but sad to say not its last, as it's a problem which has continued to resurface intermittently. In no small part this was down to the willingness of less high-minded political figures than Gandhi, to incite communal hatred in their pursuit of power. As such, sectarian divisions had inexorably spilled over into Indian political-life. In the early 1990s Bombay as it still was then, had been plagued by rioting between Muslims and Hindus which over a two-month period left more than 800 people dead! Just as shocking was the fact that much of the violence was orchestrated by Hindu extremists in government. This unrest in turn sawn Mumbai rocked by a series of explosions in one day which killed around 250 people.

Throughout the early- and mid-2000s, more bombs in Mumbai killed 260 and injured over a thousand people. Then in 2008, ten Pakistani Islamist terrorists embarked upon a prolonged shooting and bombing spree which claimed around 175 lives and injured about 300 people. These bloody attacks took place in six locations around downtown Mumbai, three of them happening in Colaba, including one at the Taj Hotel which had been badly damaged by fire. Thankfully things appear to have quietened down since these turbulent years, even so such violence was a stark reminder that Mumbai's; and India's, cultural pluralism has generated negative as well as positive outcomes. I just hoped that, on my trip, I would experience the positives rather than the negatives. Luckily I would not encounter anything quite as terrifying as a bomb going off, but I would nonetheless come uncomfortably close to a gun battle and witness violence on more than one occasion.

Chapter 2.

I bought a coach ticket to the popular holiday destination of Goa, India's smallest state located south of Maharashtra further down the coast. When my coach pulled in at the Mumbai Central Bus Depot, I soon discovered that people don't queue to board public transport in India, but rather make a frantic rush for it. This was certainly a difference between British and Indian habits. I watched with surprise as people desperately began pushing and shoving each other in order to get on the vehicle, as though its departure was imminent and they were all in danger of being left behind. In fact once everyone had boarded, the coach had then remained stationary for the next 15 minutes. Furthermore, with only half of the seats on the bus full it wasn't even as if the scramble had been for limited space. It was risible behaviour and just one of the many absurdities about India I would observe on my trip. I could only conclude that commuters in India seem to enjoy these moments of frenzied activity as a reaction to the monotony of waiting for public transport. I'd soon realise that train and bus delays were routine occurrences in India making patience a necessity rather than a virtue.

After sixteen hours and over 500 kilometres the bone-shaking bus, having exacted its toll on my kidneys arrived in the Goan city of Margao. It was then only a short taxi ride to the relaxing coastal village of Colva. As beach resorts go, Colva wasn't overdeveloped and remained at heart a fishing village, evidenced by the regular sight...not to mention smell, of fish being dried out in the sun. The accommodation I found in Colva had a restaurant attached, albeit one which at times resembled some farmyard with chickens, goats and even pigs, wandering freely around the veranda area among the guests as they dined.

Incredibly, one evening when I went to use the toilets located at the rear of the kitchen, I saw a pig trussed up ready for slaughter. I assumed from this unexpected sight that the premises served as an occasional abattoir as well as a veritable menagerie. Seeing the contents of the next day's pork *vindaloo* in this manner certainly took the dining out experience to a whole different level, even if it did prove that the meat used was fresh and sourced *very* locally. In addition to pork, I was surprised to find beef on menus in Goa. After all, neither of these meats is eaten much elsewhere in this country with massive Hindu and Muslim populations.

It turned out that these meat ingredients were a legacy of the Portuguese, who'd arrived here in Goa decades before they did on the Bombay islands. Aiming to command the valuable spice trade along the coast, in 1510 the Portuguese with the aid of local allies captured Goa's capital Panjim. It was a victory which would mark the beginning of four and a half centuries of occupation. Besides turning up on the sub-continent a century before the English, the Portuguese had been in no particular hurry to leave there either, not even after India had gained its independence from the British. Together with the state of Goa, Portugal had also governed an island and a coastal enclave further north in the state of Gujarat up until 1961. The Portuguese only left then after an exasperated Indian government, which initially tried blockading the territories, resorted to military action to drive them out. Obviously, where European colonialism in India was concerned, for the Portuguese it was very much a case of *first* to arrive and *last* to leave.

The Portuguese had brought tomatoes and potatoes to India, now both used as everyday ingredients in cooking all over India. Without a doubt though, the most vital Portuguese introduction, not only to regional Goan cooking but to food across the whole sub-continent, had been the chilli pepper, a plant native to the Americas. For sure, it would be pretty hard to imagine most Indian food – whether consumed in India or Britain- without the flavour and heat of chilli whether fresh or powdered.

My favourite accompaniment to the spicy cuisine of India was Kingfisher lager, it's a familiar brand of course, also being found in many curry houses and off licences across the UK. When served cold it's a half-decent beer, being quite smooth and light in taste, if perhaps a touch metallic. Unfortunately, in India it was all too often served lukewarm, thereby making the slogan on the label – *'most thrilling cold'* – sound somewhat tantalizing. That said, this struck me as a slightly strange advertising claim because, while I've enjoyed plenty of cold beers in my time, I don't recollect any; kingfisher included, ever managing to thrill me! The company that brews Kingfisher had branched out into the mineral water market, meaning I was able to drink their products all day long. Indeed the Kingfisher empire had even expanded to include an airline, with their aeroplanes bearing the same logo as the beer and the water. That said, if I ever flew on a Kingfisher aircraft, I'd prefer the pilot to be sipping the latter rather than the former.

Besides exhilarating lager other slightly stronger alcoholic drinks are also available, amongst them Indian spirits like *feni, arrack* and *desi daru,* the latter a type of rum distilled, often illegally, from sugarcane molasses being the most popular. A further option for shorts is so called Indian Made Foreign Liquor or IMFL, domestic imitations of Western spirits such as brandy and above all whisky. Even with tempting brand names such as: Aristocrat Whisky, Best Choice Whisky, and Gold Medal Whisky, this stuff is assuredly no single malt. In fact, it's mostly distilled from sugarcane molasses to produce a clear spirit which is more usually associated with rum than whisky. Furthermore, flavourings and colouring are added to IMFL as there's very little or no ageing involved in their production process. Even when blended with traditional grain-based whiskies it is still debatable whether a number of these brands could be described as true whiskies.

To be fair some of the better Indian whiskies are distilled from grain and a popular one called Officer's Choice which I tried was drinkable. When it came to cultural appropriation another brand suggests a Scottish connection by naming itself Bagpiper, its label depicting a turbaned Indian holding the musical instrument. If that projected an insufficiently Scottish image for some Indian whisky drinkers, then McDowell's is another domestic brand whose name is far more likely to evoke Glasgow than Goa. Perhaps one of the strangest sights I noticed when it came to alcohol was the sale of whiskies in tetra packs! I know wine comes in boxes-well more accurately foil sacks-but what reputable spirit in the West was likely to be marketed in such a form? Unbreakable and lighter yes, but also guaranteed to instantly cheapen the brand it contains. Somehow, I think it'll be a long time before scotches like Johnnie Walker or Grants become available in milk cartons.

One non-alcoholic beverage I tried was *lassi,* a creamy blend of yogurt, water and spices which is served either sweet or salted. Other soft drinks include Limca, a lemonade-style soda universally available even if it isn't clear exactly what the stuff is made from. I mention this because I actually spotted hand-painted billboards proudly advertising that Limca 'contained no real fruit'. Initially I thought it was perhaps an error before realising it was in fact a candid admission that artificial additives rather than any natural ingredients provided the flavour. Equally popular is the Indian-made cola Thums Up which uses an approving upright thumb as its logo. It was difficult to know whether this misspelling was a deliberate marketing ploy or actually a semi-literate oversight on the naming of a national brand. Then there were the perennial US favourites, Coca Cola and Pepsi, *which* had once been banned by the government to protect domestic drinks manufacturers. Even so, an aggressive business strategy by Coca Cola, meant that the American company by now has pretty much bought out all its soft drinks rivals in India, ironically a form of economic colonialism in a post-colonial globalised economy.

Another lasting impact of the lengthy Portuguese occupation of Goa is that around a quarter of Goans are Roman Catholics. As was generally the case with European colonisation, missionaries shortly followed the traders to establish both churches and the congregations to fill them with. Between them, Jesuit, Franciscan, and Dominican Orders had converted large numbers of Goans to Catholicism. In truth however many of the locals had adopted the religion for social advancement or even simply to receive food from the Portuguese. The success of these early missionaries is the reason why lots of Catholic churches can be seen around the state. Nowhere was this more so than in the onetime Portuguese capital of Old Goa found an hour's bus ride north of Margao. A trip there one day revealed churches which are named: St Anne's, St Cajetan's, St John's, St Francis of Assisi, Our Lady of the Rosary and Our Lady of the Mount, there was also a cathedral and a basilica. Even by European standards it was a large concentration of churches and went to show the emphasis the Portuguese had placed on Catholicism in their colonies.

Notable amongst the churches of Old Goa is the Basilica of Bom Jesus as it contains the mortal remains of Spanish born missionary St Francis Xavier. A co-founder of the Jesuit religious Order, Xavier had helped spread the Catholic faith in Eastern Asia, particularly in the Portuguese colonies. Amongst his saintly contributions to the people of Goa, Francis Xavier had requested an Inquisition there, this intended to preserve Catholicism and weed out any heretics and apostates. Thus, in addition to exporting produce from India, the Portuguese simultaneously imported religious intolerances to the sub-continent. It's fair to say that this hadn't been one of the more peaceful or positive aspects of European-Indian interaction.

Similar to its European counterparts, the Inquisition held within Portuguese India was administered by zealots who weren't averse to engaging in torture and killing in the name of their God. Those hauled up before the tribunals were overwhelmingly Indians, both Christian converts but also plenty of Hindus and Muslims. Really unlucky individuals had found themselves sentenced to what was euphemistically called 'relaxation to the secular arm'; or in other words to be burnt alive at the stake. Even an actual execution of a victim was innocuously described in Portuguese as an *auto de fe* or an 'act of faith'. With mercy deemed a Christian virtue those condemned to be burnt to death did have the option to repent, in which case they would be killed by garrotting instead and *then* cremated! Not very much of a choice then. Ostensibly carried out in order to maintain Catholicism, in reality the Inquisition had also sought to eliminate Hinduism and Islam in Portuguese India. Little shock then that a Jewish minority in India had also found itself targeted by these ecclesiastical excesses, just as they had been by previous Inquisitions conducted in Spain and Portugal.

Catholicism isn't the only discernible reminder of Portugal's long tenure in Goa. I was amazed to learn that Hispanic surnames, such as Fernandes, de Souza and Rodrigues are pretty commonplace amongst Goans. This is positively akin to visiting somewhere like the Algarve in Portugal, only to discover that a lot of the locals are named Patel, Khan or Singh. Not what you would expect really. Portuguese had formerly been the official language spoken here whereas nowadays it was Konkani, a regional tongue spoken by the majority of Goans. Another language commonly used in Goa is Marathi from neighbouring Maharashtra, whilst tourism means that English is also fairly widely spoken.

Goa is an ideal place to laze around on sandy beaches. Here, unlike Chowpatty Beach in Mumbai, it was at least safe to swim in the Arabian Sea without fear of contracting some faecal-borne illness. The landscape of this small state is undeniably scenic being somewhat isolated from the rest of the country by the foothills of the Western Ghats, a mountain range which runs parallel to the South-West coastline of India. Sitting between these Ghats and the coast of the Arabian Sea is a fertile, verdant countryside, one with an observable abundance of coconut trees and rice paddies. Indeed, the endless paddies seen constantly in Goa and elsewhere in India illustrate the importance of this staple crop, one which crucially sustains millions of people across Asia. Rice seedlings are of course usually grown submerged in flooded-fields or paddies, this something I believed necessary for its cultivation although it actually isn't. Instead this is done more as a measure to protect the crop from both competing weeds and any vermin; however rice plants do require lots of irrigation, making them well-suited to the often wet tropical climate of southern India. It is little wonder really that after China, India is the largest producer and consumer of these grass seeds in the world.

I found that one of the cheapest and most fun ways of getting around the beautiful Goan countryside was by hiring motorbikes, including on one occasion a classic model known as the Enfield Bullet. With its 1950s design the Bullet holds the record for being the world's oldest model of motorcycle still in production. Initially British made, the Bullet has been manufactured under licence in India since 1957. Even though the front brakes on the one I hired were decidedly unresponsive, the bike still looked cool with its sturdy, classic design; moreover its 350cc engine was pretty loud. Even in relatively traffic-free rural Goa, riding a motorbike called a 'Bullet' paradoxically involved constantly trying to *miss hitting things* on the roads, be they potholes, cows, water buffalo, goats, dogs or more usually people walking.

Old motorbikes were not the only classic vehicles I spotted on India's roads. One of the most widespread types of car in Goa and beyond is the Hindustan Ambassador, affectionately nicknamed the 'Amby'. This too was of 1950s British design, namely that of a Morris Oxford Series III saloon. With the introduction of a new model in the late '50s, UK car maker Morris Motors had sold the tooling for the older-style Oxford car to an Indian company. With some modifications being made to the original UK model, in 1958 the Ambassador thus became the very first car to be built on the sub-continent. Millions have been manufactured in total and the vehicle remained in production for an impressive *fifty-six* years, remarkably with few alterations made to its basic design during that period. With their front bench seats and robust suspension making them ideal for overloading, it's small-wonder that so many taxis across India are still Ambys.

The most iconic of all Indian vehicles simply has to be the three-wheeled auto-rickshaw taxi. Basically a body shell attached to a scooter engine, for the masses they provide cheap transportation over short distances. The bulk of these mainly green and yellow-coloured taxis are manufactured by Bajaj, a company based in Maharashtra who unsurprisingly had once produced Italian Vespa scooters under licence. The main flaw of these three-wheelers is that their cabs have a roof but no doors, leaving passengers fully exposed to fumes from surrounding traffic. Incidentally, the auto-rickshaws had themselves once been a massive contributor to this same pollution because earlier models had two-stroke petrol and diesel engines that produced higher emissions. In order to address the problem, less polluting four-stroke engines were introduced, plus most the auto-rickshaws now run on more environmentally friendly compressed natural gas. Battery powered versions are also now manufactured although it will be some time before the familiar buzz of the auto-rickshaw engine disappears from Indian traffic.

Thankfully noise and pollution from traffic in Goa is negligible compared to Mumbai. What's more, life in Goa naturally operates at a more leisurely pace than it does in India's most populous city, and Colva is a seductive place to spend time in. It has a laid-back friendly atmosphere and I got to know plenty of other foreigners there: British, Irish, German, Dutch, French and Australian. I would soon come to discover that one of the highlights of travelling in India was meeting others doing the same thing. There is a natural connection between kindred spirits who explore places and this makes for easy conversation and friendship. We foreigners were usually all drawn towards the same sites, so meeting those who'd already visited them provided a useful network for information and advice. My conversations with other travellers would typically centre on the humour of the contrasts and bizarreness of Indian life. It was a welcome distraction from some of the less amusing aspects of travel there.

The enjoyment I got from interacting with other foreigners was matched by the high level of irritation caused by being frequently accosted by Indians. Still, those who approached weren't always unwelcome as occasionally they'd sell me hash or *charas* as it's called in India. Indeed, within the first hour of exploring Colva, I'd managed to purchase a sizable piece off an auto-rickshaw driver. India is a sizable producer of cannabis resin and its use seemed fairly widespread to me. For example, it is very popular in religious rituals with many *sadhus* smoking it in order to get closer to Shiva. It was safe to say that some of the *charas* I smoked in India was sufficiently potent to connect with not only Lord Shiva but Vishnu and Brahma as well! For all its availability and regardless of the fact that *sadhus* openly smoke *charas*, possession of even very small amounts by foreigners is illegal and punishable with imprisonment. Still, if caught with *charas,* reportedly you could usually pay the police off in order to ensure that the matter would go no further. Ordinarily, I would not condone corruption but it is patently better to pay an unofficial 'fine' than to end up in some prison.

Be that as it may, bribery was not always a viable option in such scenarios, this something I learnt in Colva from an Australian chap named Owen. He came back to my room for a joint one night and told me how he and his best friend had worked and saved for a couple of years to go travelling, eventually intending, via Asia, to visit Europe including London. It was a well-trodden path for many Antipodeans and, following the virtually obligatory stays in Bali and Thailand, they'd arrived here in India. In Delhi they purchased a *tola* of *charas*, a *tola*, which equals about ten grams, being a pre - metric Indian weight still used to measure gold... and obviously hash. They left most of this fair chunk in their room while out and about sightseeing, taking with them only a few joints' worth. One day whilst they stood outside a store, a car pulled up alongside them. Two men got out and approached the pair. Although their car was unmarked and they wore no uniforms, the men produced identity cards whilst announcing that they were officers from the

Narcotics Control Bureau. They then asked to see the Australians' passports and questioned them about where they'd just been and where they were heading. Next the officers searched Owen and his friend, which may have been legally dubious, but this was Delhi not Darwin and the authorities in India do as they liked.

Unfortunately, they had found on Owen's friend a bit of charas wrapped up in a piece of plastic. As he was being placed into their vehicle, Owen in disbelief looked his friend in the eyes and gently shrugged his shoulders. Whist telling me this, Owen commented rhetorically with a croak in his voice: 'What could I do or say?' The officers found nothing on Owen himself and told him to leave as they continued to detain and question his friend in their vehicle. Walking away in a total daze, the dreadful gravity of the situation began to slowly dawn on Owen: for his best friend and travelling companion was now under arrest for the possession of *charas*.

Owen raced back to the hotel and immediately deposited the remaining *charas* in a plant pot located on a communal balcony. A couple of minutes later, there came a knock on the door. Opening it, one of the bureau officers from earlier was standing there, this time accompanied by a uniformed policeman. Entering they made a search of the room including the pair's luggage, before leaving when their efforts yielded nothing. It had certainly been a close shave and pretty quick thinking on Owen's part; otherwise, he too would have been joining his hapless friend in custody. The upshot was his friend subsequently pleaded guilty to possession of the charas. Even though there hadn't been very much on him, he still received a shocking five-year prison sentence.

Owen started crying as he acknowledged that the *charas* had belonged to them both and yet his friend had taken the rap and ended up in prison as a result. I guess that his survivor's guilt was compounded by the fact that they were best friends. In an effort to offer comfort, I pointed out that his friend would understand how it was just bad luck that he had been carrying the *charas* on that occasion, stressing that it could easily have been the other way around. I asked if his friend had tried to bribe the police. He had according to Owen, but these were members of the Narcotics Control Bureau and they were looking for convictions rather than cash.

The only minor note of conciliation in this woeful episode was that his gaoled friend had a brother who worked at the Australian High Commission in Delhi, this at least providing him with support and regular visits. Hearing this cautionary tale first-hand certainly made me understand the potential risk involved when indulging in Mother India's finest. Here it wasn't only drug smugglers and dealers who risked lengthy custodial sentences; the bleak reality was hundreds of foreigners like Owen's friend were languishing in prisons for possession of quite small quantities of soft drugs. If nothing else, it irrefutably proved that unlike colonial times, the law was applied equally in modern India and as such white people no longer received any special treatment from the courts.

Chapter 3.

My journey onward from Goa to Kerala involved auto-rickshaws, trains and buses. It took 23 hours and one change of train at 4am to travel over 750 kilometres down the coast to the city of Kochi. Just travelling by train in India is an adventure in itself, providing fascinating opportunities for visitors to observe the transit of the masses along with all the corresponding confusion, bustle and noise. While by and large the trains were crowded and often late, the one thing they could not be faulted on was their cheapness. This was especially true of the excellent value second-class non air -conditioned carriages.

India prides itself on its extensive railway network even if it is largely an inheritance of British colonial rule. The railways, which were nationalized after independence, operate over a vast 67,000 km network making it the biggest in Asia. As an indication of just how important rail transport is to the country's infrastructure and economy, only the Indian military receives more in annual budget funding from the national government. With 1.4 million people required to run the state-owned Indian Railways, it is one of the largest non-military employers in the world. With jobs for life, its workers enjoy benefits such as subsidized meals and housing, healthcare and pensions. These provide crucial incentives to the massive workforce, and are one of the reasons why there has not been a major strike since 1974.

During my time riding trains in India, I didn't notice any trolleys or buffet cars for food and drinks. Instead hawkers boarded at the stations to ply their wares with their chants of 'chai, chai' (tea, tea) reverberating down the carriages. This refrain was a tad more animated than the dull announcements for refreshments heard aboard many British trains.

One thing about the non air-conditioned rolling stock that did concern me slightly wasn't so much the absence of any glass in the carriage windows, but more the addition of metal bars across them. I worried if the bars, intended as a safety measure to stop people leaning out of the openings, were themselves a potential danger. Despite each side of every carriage having one emergency window with a removable grille, bars across all the other window openings meant that, in the event of derailment, passengers were much more likely to get trapped inside. Although such an accident sounds improbable, I was well aware that rail crashes were in fact all too common in India, claiming on average around 100 lives per annum between the years 2013 and 2018. Moreover, out of these accidents responsible for hundreds of fatalities and injuries every year, more than half were a consequence of derailments!

Kochi railway station is located in Ernakulam, the modern core of the city found on the mainland. Formerly known as Cochin, this port city sits on the Malabar Coast which extends along much of south west India. A number of islands and peninsulas lie west of Ernakulam and it was right on the tip of one such peninsula, in the historic Fort Cochin area, where I found accommodation. Long before Kochi existed, this coastal region had been trading with the outside world for millennia; all the way back to Greco-Roman times. Kerala was ruled by the Chera at that period, a dynasty that grew prosperous on this form of proto-globalisation enduring until the 12th century. It is little surprise that Arabs were amongst the very first foreigners to trade with this region of India given Kochi's location beside the attractively-named Lakshadweep Sea, which is part of the Arabian Sea. These Arab merchants had dealt in spices, gold and precious stones, spreading their commercial operations through-out the Middle East and on into Africa and Europe. One enduring consequence of this early interaction with Arab traders was the introduction of Islam into the sub-continent, with the first Muslim converts in India being those along the Malabar Coast in the 7th century. India's first mosque had been built 45 km north of Kochi as far back as 629.

Other early foreign traders along this coast were the Chinese, who introduced something now considered emblematic of Kochi: its fixed-cantilevered Chinese fishing nets, clusters of which I saw along the shoreline of Fort Cochin. Widely found here in Kerala and requiring quite a few people to operate them, these rather cumbersome-looking contraptions use levers, ropes and weights to lower and raise nets suspended from arced poles into tidal waters. An ancient but effective method of fishing, these nets add significantly to the more than half a million tonnes of fish which is harvested annually in Kerala.

The Portuguese navigator Vasco de Gama and his men were the first seaborne Europeans to reach India when they landed on the Keralan coast in 1498. This historical arrival took place only about a 150 kilometres to the north and within a couple of years the Portuguese had arrived in Kochi. Reactions towards such foreign incursions had varied amongst different indigenous rulers with some seeing them as a threat. Others however had been more welcoming and the ruling *maharajah* in Kochi signed a treaty with the Portuguese. With a sea route between Europe and India now discovered, in due course the Dutch, English, French and Danish had followed the Portuguese. All went on to establish their own trading posts around India's coastline from where they imported spices, sugar, textiles and indigo amongst other commodities. This had created Intense competition and sparked conflict between these rival European states, which saw the Portuguese lose some of their footholds in India, although as I knew from my time in Goa by no means all of them.

One stark reminder of the former Portuguese presence in Fort Cochin was St. Francis Church. Built by Franciscan friars and dating from 1503 it's the oldest European church in India. Vasco da Gama had died in Kochi in 1524 and been buried here for a number of years prior to his body being re interred in Portugal. The famous seafarer had evidently succumbed to malaria, which following the endless mosquito bites I'd suffered in India myself wasn't exactly surprising to learn. Originally constructed as a Catholic place of worship, St Francis was later rebuilt as a Protestant church by the Dutch after they'd kicked the Portuguese out of the city in 1663. It looked decidedly Dutch with its prominent gable and a relatively unadorned exterior and interior. The Dutch themselves had been eventually ousted from Kochi by the East India Company in 1795 and the church has been Anglican ever since. It occurred to me that very few sites in India could have been consecrated by three different denominations of European Christianity. Still, as a taxi driver in Mumbai had recently put it, they're ultimately 'All from the same God'!

The Europeans might have brought their different strands of Christianity to India, but they hadn't introduced the religion itself. Rather, in Kochi and elsewhere along this part of the coast, some of the oldest Christian communities in the world were already well established when the Roman Catholic Portuguese first arrived in India. According to legend the apostle St Thomas came to Kerala in the 1st century CE. The bible knows him as 'Doubting Thomas', which is quite apt given that this story of Christianity's origin in India is itself doubtful. Apocryphal though it may be, many Keralan Christians believe their ancestors were converted by St Thomas. What is more provable is that there were Christian communities in the region from the 3rd century. Christianity continued to expand, spurred on by the arrival of missionaries from the Church of the East centred in Persia. Also identified as the Nestorian Church, this early branch of Christianity successfully converted many Keralites. Despite schisms and the impact of both European Catholicism and Protestantism, this ancient version of the Christian religion, one which traditionally uses a dialect of the biblical language *Aramaic* for worship, still survives in India.

Like many Westerners I tended to see Christianity as a religion which evolved in Europe. This Euro-centric view is the reason why I was surprised to learn that Christianity existed in India even before Buddhism, Jainism and Sikhism had. I guess it was revealing about Western perception generally and certainly exposed my own misconceptions regarding Christianity and India itself. Based upon those church buildings I'd seen in India; I'd come to regard Christianity as an imported European religion. Whereas in reality, it had of course, actually been an Asian religion introduced into Europe. Presently slightly over eighteen percent of Keralites are Christians of varying denominations. In fact Christianity in India is practiced countrywide and the current three largest faiths in the world: Christianity, Islam and Hinduism, happen to be in reverse order the three religions with the most adherents in the amazing mosaic of Indian multiculturalism.

One of the more curiously named districts of Kochi – Jew Town – came from yet another religion I did not readily associate with India. No one knows when the Jews first came to the west coast of India; it may have been after Jerusalem fell to Nebuchadnezzar in 587 BCE, perhaps it was even earlier. Known as Malabar Jews they became active in the lucrative spice trade and their community expanded by intermarrying with Indians and converting locals to

Judaism. During the 16th century, Christian persecution in Europe led to a further influx of Jews into India. Settling mainly in Kochi, a lot of them had been exiled by the Catholic Inquisitions conducted in Portugal and Spain. These 'Paradesi' or foreign Jews had built their first synagogue in 1568, on a plot of land bequeathed by the local Hindu *raja*. Unfortunately for these local Jews, in 1662 the Roman Catholic Portuguese, in keeping with their intolerance to all other religions, had destroyed the original synagogue.

By contrast, the Dutch, who'd soon supplanted their European rivals in the region, took a far more enlightened attitude towards religious diversity, even if the Netherlands had expelled its own Jews in the 14th and 15th centuries. With Dutch approval another synagogue – the Paradesi – was constructed on the site a couple of years later. Believed to be the oldest still functioning synagogue in India, I found it by taking a short walk south of Fort Cochin. As the exteriors of synagogues don't conform to any specific design, aside from a three-storey clock tower, the white-walled building looks pretty unassuming from the outside. The synagogue's clock tower is topped by a cupola and has dials on three of its sides. Unusually, one clock face displays numbers in Hebrew, a second are in the local Malayalam language whilst the third has Roman numerals. None of this made any difference whatsoever as none of the clocks actually worked, at least not while I was there. At the entrance, iron gates depicting Jewish candlesticks or *menorahs* and Stars of David in their design offered the only real clue that a synagogue existed within.

It was not until I entered the main sanctuary inside the building that it finally resembled a place of worship. Here were coloured lanterns, chandeliers and a fancy central podium with decorative brass railings around its front and sides. Known as the *bimah* and found in all synagogues, it is from this podium that services are conducted. The Paradesi synagogue is particularly notable for its fine floor composed of hundreds of 18th century Chinese willow-patterned tiles, each individual tile having a slightly different design. Benches along the walls and around the *bimah* provide seating for the male congregation, whereas the women attending services assemble in a separate gallery. The *bimah* faces towards both Jerusalem and the most sacred part of the synagogue, the

42

ark, which is an ornamental cabinet housing the scrolls of the holy Jewish scriptures the *Torah*.

When the synagogue wasn't being used, the intricately carved teak *ark* was normally kept closed and covered with a curtain. As luck would have it however, some government dignitaries also happened to be visiting at the same time as me and it was opened for their benefit. Inside the *ark* we got to see the silver-encrusted wooden cylinders crowned with gold which contained the *Torah* scrolls. As he showed us these, the elder in charge explained how on its 400th anniversary, the then Indian Prime Minister Indira Gandhi had visited the synagogue. During the ceremony marking this occasion, Mrs Gandhi had addressed the congregation and ended her speech with the Hebrew words *'mazel tov'* meaning good luck. Impressed by this the elder, who at the time had obviously been more of a younger, later asked the Prime Minister where she had learnt to say this in Hebrew. A smiling Mrs Gandhi had answered 'From my Jewish room-mate when I was a student in New York.'

After the tour ended and the officials left, I got chatting with the elder, who kindly invited me to join him for some tea at his home within the synagogue complex. I found it fascinating as he talked more about the history of the local Jewish community. More so considering that the last thing I'd expected to see whilst in India was a synagogue. He even showed me a video clip of himself as a child partaking in a religious ceremony. As a minority one might expect the Jews of Kochi to be united community, yet sadly the pervasive caste system has also impacted their numbers as well. In fact, on account of their European ancestry, Kochi's Paradesi community are also described as 'White Jews'. Moreover, they'd kept themselves separate from other local Jews, ones descended from either the slaves of Iberian Jews who'd converted to Judaism or from local Indian converts.

While India's Jews may have practiced discrimination amongst themselves, paradoxically enough in a country often plagued by religious tensions, they'd escaped the rabid persecution suffered by Jews elsewhere. Despite this absence of anti-Semitism, most of the country's Jews had emigrated to Israel back in the 1950s, drawn there principally by better economic opportunities. In light

43

of the huge levels of poverty in India, it was understandable why they had sought a better life in a country which would offer them things like welfare, housing and healthcare. Consequently, Kochi's Jewish community has dwindled to only a few dozen people and will likely disappear completely in the future.

A short way west of Jew Town in an area named Mattancherry, I visited another religious building, this one a Jain temple. Jainism is a religion concentrated in western India, from the neighbouring state of Karnataka northwards up to Rajasthan. There are nearly 4.5 million adherents of Jainism in India which sounds like a lot but still only represents less than one percent of the country's total population. Their faith is based upon the teachings of Mahavira, believed to have been the 24th and last in a line of great teachers or *tirthankaras*. Born in northeast India in the 6th century BCE, Mahavira's life appears to have mirrored the Buddha's, the two were possibly even contemporaries.

Amongst many other concepts, Jainism shares with Buddhism and Hinduism common beliefs in karma and a reverence for living beings, known as *ahimsa*. The three religions also believe in the eventual goal of *moksha* in its sense of self-liberation from the cycle of life and death. Jains believe that all life forms have a soul and therefore one should avoid harming any living entity. This is part of *right conduct*, one of three guiding ethical principles Jain's follow to attain *moksha*; the others are *right faith* meaning seeing and understanding things clearly and truthfully, whilst lastly a good understanding of the Jain scriptures will bring *right knowledge*. Jainism discourages the possession or use of anything which isn't really needed, it even advocates sexual restraint. What's more the strict Jain diet eschews not only meat, fish and eggs, but any fruit or vegetable which when harvested might kill the plant bearing it, thus ruling out vegetables like onions, garlic and potatoes. In light of these religious precepts, Jainism is in many respects a far more rigorous and demanding creed than Hinduism or Buddhism.

A Jain community, whose ancestors came originally from the north-eastern state of Gujarat, has existed in Kochi for at least a couple of centuries, although the Sri Dharmanath Jain temple was not built until 1960. Dedicated to the 15th Jain *tirthankara* and occupying a fairly large complex, this carved pinkish-hued *mandir* is roofed with ornate domes, many of these tiered. The most prominent section of the exterior is the large decoratively-carved mound tower or *shikhara* which extends above the sanctum at the rear of the temple. This type of tower, whose name translates as 'mountain peak' in Sanskrit, is a familiar architectural feature on Jain and Hindu places of worship earning such temples the name *Shikharabandi*.

As is customary when entering any temple, I removed my shoes before going inside Sri Dharmanath. The interior has white marble flooring, walls and ceilings, none of which is overly decorated. The place was not too dissimilar to the Mahalaxmi *Mandir* I'd seen in Mumbai, with the innermost shrine being likewise off limits to non-believers like myself. Where the Sri Dharmanath Jain complex seemed to differ from the Hindu temple at Mahalaxmi was that it was far less busy. However, this may have simply been due to the time of my visit or the fact that Mattancherry is not exactly as densely populated as Mumbai. Still, whatever the reason was, the quieter environment definitely lent the temple building a more spiritual and meditative ambience. Just before leaving I watched as hundreds of pigeons were fed rice in the grounds, which quite frankly as far as my travel experiences went was pretty banal and prosaic. I mean let's be honest about it, when compared to the manner in which Mumbai's Zoroastrians fed their local *vultures*... it was positively boring!

The very last place I explored in Kochi is also in Mattancherry, a palace that had once been home to the Hindu rulers of the former Kingdom of Cochin. Dating back to the mid-16th century this one-time royal residence had been built by the Portuguese as a gift for *Raja* Vira Keralavarma. Later on, the Dutch added to the building which explains why it is known locally as the 'Dutch Palace'. As royal palaces Dutch or otherwise went, the two-storey structure is pretty plain looking, although the interior was decorated with some interesting murals. There are 300 square metres of detailed colourful friezes inside the palace, these painted in an eloquent but basic animation style. A considerable number of the paintings depict scenes from the epic Hindu poem the *Ramayana*, which recounts the incarnation of Vishnu as Rama, and in particular his struggle with the demon god Ravana.

The Hindu potentates who had once resided in this palace had not been alone in surviving European intervention in India. Such dynasties had lasted because they cooperated with the Europeans and benefited from the pragmatic policies of foreign powers, to leave any existing local and regional power structures in place wherever possible. These indigenous heads of state were known as: *maharajas, rajahs, nawabs, nizams, sultans* and other titles, and their numbers had included Hindus, Jains, Muslims, Sikhs and Buddhists. It's something frequently overlooked but around half of British India had actually consisted of these semi-autonomous princely states. Indeed, more than 550 of them had been headed by traditional rulers who had continued to exercise power, albeit under overall British sovereignty.

In reality, many of these so called 'states' had been fairly small entities which amounted to estates rather than principalities, their heads wielding only limited powers. The larger ones nevertheless did function as states having their own governments, judiciaries and armies, raising taxes and even issuing their own currencies and postage stamps. Overall the British maintained responsibility for India's foreign policy and controlled communication across the sub-continent, otherwise these monarchs were free to run their own affairs. It had been a mutually beneficial arrangement, one which allowed most of these Indian rulers to survive up until the time of independence.

Chapter 4.

After Cochin I took a 200km bus trip south along the coast to the state capital of Kerala, Thiruvananthapuram. With the exception of a windscreen for the benefit of the driver, the bus I travelled on had no glass in its window frames. Like Indian railway carriages this helps cool the interior in the absence of any air-conditioning, although minus the bars across these openings. Believe me; whilst we were moving, the refreshing breeze produced by having no glass in the windows was really appreciated in the humid heat. Be that as it may, a far less desirable consequence of this natural air-conditioning was the large amount of dust I was covered in by the journey's end.

Still, a bit of grime was the least of my worries when compared to the general danger presented by Indian traffic. Alas, even using public transport could not guarantee safe driving as my bus trip to the Keralan capital confirmed. To put things graciously, our driver was frighteningly reckless when at one point he unwisely decided to overtake another bus. Nothing inherently wrong in that you may think, only the bus that we were trying to pass was already in the process of overtaking a third bus! With three buses lined across the width of the road all desperately sounding their horns at each other, the drama intensified even further when a truck appeared on the road ahead coming straight towards us. In what seemed to be some deadly game of chicken involving three bus-loads of passengers, luckily we just about managed to get past the two slower buses and pull out of the path of the oncoming lorry.

It was a scary moment which typified the sort of manic driving I was witnessing all too often in India. The blunt reality is that road accidents are unnervingly commonplace across the country with a large number of them fatal. It was staggering that in the decade preceding 2018, over 1.5 million people had died on India's roads, a very high percentage of them pedestrians. When it came to road safety in Britain we have two kinds of pedestrian crossings: zebra and pelican. Judging from these statistics, India also has the two sorts of pedestrian crossings: in this instance, those who make it and those who don't!

After four hours of travelling through the Keralan countryside, I eventually arrived in Thiruvananthapuram. Its bus station, like the adjacent railway station, is logically located in Station Road just a short distance from the city centre. Rather than stay in the city itself, I jumped on a bus to the resort of Kovalam, twenty-minutes ride south of the capital. Having the requisite warm climate, palm-fringed beaches and clear, shallow waters, this Keralan fishing village, like many further north in Goa, is something of a holiday hotspot. Still, for all the tourist charter groups there was still lots of budget accommodation to be found along Lighthouse Beach, a sandy cove unsurprisingly overlooked by a lighthouse.

Whenever seeking accommodation, the heat and humidity of the Indian coast made it advisable to ensure hotel rooms had ceiling fans. Rooms with air-conditioning were expensive, though thankfully cheaper ones with ceiling fans were usually available. That said, obviously air-conditioning and electric fans are only able to function if electricity is available to power them and in India it frequently is not. Officially termed as *load shedding,* disruptions to power supplies are in fact deliberate and necessary, with demand for electricity far outstripping the capacity of the grid to provide it. The failure of the system to cope is hardly helped by the immense number of properties connected to any available electricity supply massive numbers of them I suspect not actually paying for it. This was very apparent from the indeterminate number of cables to be seen emanating from virtually every pylon, electrical junction box and distribution point.

Night time power cuts were always worse as they made sleep extremely difficult. Once the ceiling fan had stopped working, the soaring temperatures combined with the humidity, would cause me to wake up sweating torrents. What is more, once the noise of fan blades spinning stopped the dreaded buzzing of mosquitoes was often heard. No longer deterred by the waft of the fan, any mosquitoes in the room would move in looking to feed on me. I say feed, but these insects don't actually ingest blood for nutrition but rather use the protein in it to produce eggs. Hence why, only female mosquitoes bite. Furthermore, unlike mosquitoes in other parts of the world, those found in Asia use only human blood for this purpose. Besides leaving those small itchy lumps on the skin, their bites of course carry the risk of infection from malaria and other diseases which are easily transmitted through the insect's saliva. Malaria is prevalent in India so being one of those blighted individuals prone to mosquito bites, it was imperative I took anti-malarial tablets.

While no-one knows exactly why mosquitoes are attracted to some folk and not to others, all I know is that they love me, and not only during the night-time power cuts. The liberal application of chemical repellents had limited efficacy determined by both their strength and how much I perspired. Whilst sleeping, a net does afford some protection but even then, if any part of your body makes contact with the netting whilst asleep, a mosquito is able to push its proboscis through the mesh and bite. For sure, what-ever precautions I'd take somehow these infernal insects would still manage to bite me making them a massive downside to my travels.

At my accommodation in Kovalam I befriended a bloke named Martin, a Scotsman from Inverness now living in London, who I'd end up travelling with for a while. One afternoon we took a stroll to a pink mosque or *masjid* further along the coast on a headland just to the south of Lighthouse Beach. Joining us were a couple of German girls from our hotel, both of whom dressed modestly for the visit, their hair and bodies covered so as not to offend Islamic sensibilities. Though the mosque looked historic, a dated plaque showed that it had in fact been built in the 1970s. After we loudly announced our presence there appeared to be no-one about so we removed our shoes and entered the building. The cool marble interior was carved with some ornate Quranic inscriptions. Equally decorative was the *mihrab*, a niche located in the wall indicating the direction of Mecca towards which the congregation faces to pray. The most immediate visual difference between the mosque and the average church or temple was the absence of any images, human or godly. In other religions, statues, carvings and paintings commonly depict a mixture of human and divine forms, while in Islam such things are deemed idolatry and therefore forbidden.

Upon exiting the mosque and whilst we stood in the courtyard admiring the architecture, a man appeared from across the other side and hastily approached. Whilst speaking no English he clearly seemed irritable and started shouting and gesticulating. Alas our Malayalam had not progressed beyond more than a few phrases, meaning all we could do was look at each other baffled. Realising we did not understand he resorted to mime, pointing at both girls and then at the entrance before making a walking gesture with his fingers. With this, it immediately became clear he was expressing concern that the girls had entered the mosque through it. The fact of the matter was, from his agitated tone I got the impression that an admission that they had done so wouldn't be well received.

Surmising that women probably weren't permitted to use that entrance into the *masjid*, I offered assurances, declaring with an extended hand the conventional Muslim salutation of '*As-salaam Alaikum*' meaning 'peace be upon you'. By saying this I hoped to infer that I was myself a believer and as such would be aware of the protocol. Thankfully, this seemed to assuage him. He smiled and shook my hand as the situation was immediately defused. I gave a donation towards the mosque and we were able to leave as friends rather than disrespectful foreign tourists, unintentional though it had been. Ultimately, I'd like to think that an incident of cultural misunderstanding was alleviated by my quick thinking about cultural understanding.

The mosque served a nearby fishing village and, feeling slightly adventurous, we decided to head there and see if any fishermen might take us out in their boats. A road to the village followed the shoreline whereas a shorter, more direct route lay across a sandy beach. We chose the quicker course. As we proceeded along the beach, it gradually became apparent from the unfolding sight of human waste that this stretch of sand served as the village toilet. Relying on the tides for sewerage disposal meant that this toilet only got flushed away by the sea once a day, something which had clearly yet to happen. Thus cautiously, the four of us navigated a path through what was essentially a turd minefield. It made us all realise that one didn't need to venture that far from beach resorts to find communities lacking basic sewage or sanitation. Evidently the benefits of tourism hadn't bought much development to these villagers, and yet how many of the restaurants in Kovalam made a handsome profit from serving the fish they supplied to wealthy foreigners? It was a sad awareness to gain, but then again, in India so much was.

As we traversed this sandy latrine, in order to minimize the risk of stepping in any unpleasantness we walked close to the water's edge. Despite this precaution, at one point a piece of excrement was carried in by a wave and lapped against my boot. I shouted 'ahhh' as though the victim of some real mine detonating; only my scream was one of utter disgust rather than agony. At this the other three started laughing, which admittedly is what I would have done had it been one of them having this gross encounter. Thankfully I was wearing boots and not sandals, had I been, this would have doubtless raised the volume of my scream by a few decibels. I guess if nothing else came from this amble, by now I'd at least added the words *scheisse*, *mist* and *puh* to my German vocabulary. Revolting though the experience was for us, I suspect the spectacle of four clueless tourists walking through the middle of their communal toilet must have amused the perplexed locals in the village we now approached.

Following an offer of cash, some of the fishermen took us out in a large canoe. At first I felt quite relaxed as the crew of eight paddled us through the calm waters of the harbour. However that soon changed once we were out on the open sea and the canoe began to feel like a cork bobbing in choppy waters. Being so low and close to the water we really felt the effect of the waves hitting the boat and it was pretty scary. In the event of any of us going overboard we'd have been in danger from some strong currents and rip tides, which from Mumbai south to Kovalam claim many victims every year. For good reason these drownings aren't widely publicised in the glossy tourist brochures promoting this part of the world. Then of course neither were the less sanitary stretches of 'sunny, palm kissed tropical golden sands' promised to visitors.

With no life jackets, I for one would not fancy the chances of anyone aboard if the canoe capsized. We were easily a kilometre from land with little hope of swimming ashore in this swell. My sudden anxiety was a shame as I normally enjoy being on boats, although ideally ones which are marginally more than six inches above the water. I suppose it's a bit like flying, some people may enjoy hang-gliding but personally speaking give me a large aircraft every time. The canoe felt vulnerable and gave a real appreciation of just how difficult and potentially dangerous it is trying to earn a living from the sea. The waves were pretty large that day but I'm sure conditions out here on the water could get much worse for the fishermen. When we eventually moored up back in the fishing village, drenched but safe, we were all relieved that the trip was over. Prudently when leaving the village, the four of us went via the road and not the beach this time, as put bluntly by then we'd all been through enough shit for one day!

On a few occasions Martin and I headed out from Kovalam and into Thiruvananthapuram. The city was doubtless much older, but its first recorded rulers were the Ay dynasty from neighbouring Tamil Nadu who'd controlled the port until the 10th century CE. Thiruvananthapuram then become a part of the Venad kingdom whose monarchs had been based in the port city of Quilon lying further to the north. Following the foundation of the Kingdom of Travancore by a descendant of the Venad royal family, in the mid-18th century Thiruvananthapuram became its capital. Thereafter the Venad kingdom went on to survive European encroachment, emerging as one of the princely states existing in British India.

When the British Raj ended in 1947, all of India's princely states including Travancore technically become independent and some monarchs had toyed with the idea of remaining so. Realistically though the formation of national governments in both India and Pakistan had heralded the end of these dynasties, if not an end to their great wealth. Within a couple of years of independence, the sub-continent's princely states had all but one acceded to either India or Pakistan. The one exception had been the north-eastern Kingdom of Sikkim which managed to retain its autonomy right up until 1975 before being absorbed into India.

In 1949 the Travancore kingdom merged with the neighbouring Kingdom of Cochin, acceding to the Indian Union as a new state with the less than original name of Travancore-Cochin. Despite India declaring itself a socialist-republic in the following year, the former Travancore *maharaja* had continued to wield power by becoming governor of this state right up until 1956. It was then that the country began reorganizing its states along the lines of language, rather than on the actual lines of former princely state boundaries. Most of the Travancore-Cochin state territory became Kerala, a state created from the Malayalam speaking regions of Southern India.

During the decades following independence, the Indian National Congress Party had pretty much dominated political life in India. I was intrigued therefore to discover that in 1957 the world's first democratically elected communist government came to power in Kerala. In spite of several splits amongst their ranks, communists had formed numerous governments in the state since that time. For decades, the political administration of Kerala has alternated between coalitions dominated by communists and coalitions led by Congress. Kerala's communist governments have a reasonable track record in achieving land reform and providing health care and education. As such Keralites are rightly proud that their state consistently boasted the highest literacy rate in India.

As religion appeared to be such an integral part of life in India, it seemed something of contradiction that godless communism was so popular. The electoral success of communist parties in Kerala and other states suggests that not all Indians are prepared to wait until death for their lot to improve. I found it interesting how communist ideology was being used to challenge traditional Hindu hierarchy. This was an unexpected example of the way European ideas had impacted Indian political culture, although somehow, I doubt if they came via the British. In one Thiruvananthapuram market I saw posters of Karl Marx and even Joseph Stalin for sale alongside others depicting Ganesha and Gandhi. Now there was a juxtaposition I could never have predicted before coming to this part of the world! That said, Joseph Stalin, the one-time ruthless dictator of the Soviet Union, who had been responsible for the suffering and deaths of millions, seemed a strange choice as the literal poster boy for communism in Kerala! Further proofs of the state's communist leanings are the hammer and sickle emblems displayed in numerous public places. An even more unexpected symbol seen regularly not only in Kerala but throughout India is the swastika, which has been used in Hinduism, Buddhism and Jainism for centuries now. A swastika even forms part of Jainism's official logo. It also appears in several different cultures beyond the sub-continent, including in European Christianity. Obviously a certain German fascist political party had once usurped the image, making its use taboo in Europe. By contrast, in India, you can find it on anything from a simple box of matches to a temple complex because it represents good luck, divinity and spirituality. Needless to say, these weren't exactly associations the millions of victims of Nazism would have made with the swastika. Whenever I saw the swastika in India, the grim irony couldn't escape me that a symbol of peace and purity, one which originated amongst non-European religions in a non-white society, had found itself appropriated by European white supremacists!

The former royal and now state capital Thiruvananthapuram is an agreeable place to wander round, containing as it does acres of parks and plenty of palms. The major commercial thoroughfare is Mahatma Gandhi Road, this a fairly common road name in India usually abbreviated in speech to simply MG Rd. On that note, as the name Thiruvananthapuram hardly rolls off the tongue, I had taken to calling the city TP.

The *maharajas* of Travancore had left their mark on the Keralan capital with some outstanding buildings, amongst them the state government Secretariat which nowadays houses several Keralan government ministries. Completed in 1869, this white plastered structure had originally been a *durbar* hall, a ceremonial *durbar* being when Indian monarchs held court to meet their ministers and on occasion the public. To assert their hegemony the British had also adopted *durbars*, reversing the roles so that the heads of princely states themselves became subjects paying homage to a monarch. These very public displays of subjugation by the British had been extravagant affairs which combined European pageantry with Indian *durbar* rituals. Such was the manner in which British colonialism hijacked and subverted Indian traditions at that time.

Although this *durbar* hall had been built for Indian royals, the building's columns, pediment and domed clock tower were of a characteristically European design. Such obvious departure from more traditional Indian architecture demonstrated the fervent admiration some princes had for European culture. A much more typically Indian-style construct of the former *maharajas* is the Shri Padmanabhaswamy temple, which even today is still controlled by the former royal family. Standing in the historical Fort area of TP, it was built by the founding *maharajah* of the Travancore kingdom in the 18th century on the site of an older shrine. Surrounded by high walls, not only is the inner sanctum out of bounds to non-Hindus in this particular *mandir,* but disappointingly non-believers like us are prohibited from entering any part of the complex.

Our trips into TP happened to coincide with *Thiruvonam,* one of Kerala's main Hindu festivals. Generally shortened to *Onam,* this is an annual event eagerly celebrated with parades, music, singing and performances of traditional Keralan dancing and theatre. In essence, *Onam* is a festival marking the rice harvest intertwined with Hindu mythology, much of it centred round the deity Vishnu. According to Hindu mythology, Kerala had itself been a creation of the god Parashurama, an incarnation of Vishnu.

One evening whilst in a large park at the north end of MG Road, Martin and I first heard then watched a procession of drummers arrive as part of the *Onam* celebrations. On a lawned bank in the park I could see a massive, intricate floral design easily 10 sq metre in size. At first glance it looked like a flowerbed, but was in fact a *pookkalam,* a decorative pattern which is entirely hand-made from flower blossom. As we listened to the assembled drummers frantically playing their beats, the excitement of the occasion then intensified when half a dozen caparisoned elephants were ridden into the park. Lined up and resplendent in their finery, these huge tusked beasts made for a surreal spectacle as the light faded and the coloured-lights festooned across tree branches lit up. With the hypnotic rhythm of drums filling the warm night air and throngs of excited revellers surrounding us, it created a totally mesmerising atmosphere. The gathering could best be described as a carnival atmosphere with an underlying spiritual vibe about it; the mix of the two making the experience quite magical.

Chapter 5.

No Indian festival is ever complete without food and there was no shortage of choice. One popular Indian meal I came to really like was *thali*, a selection of different vegetable curries, pickles and dips, which here in the south is always served with boiled rice. It's eaten by mixing the rice and accompanying dishes to form mouth-sized balls. What I particularly enjoyed were the variety of flavours a *thali* offers in one meal. *Thali* means 'plate' in Hindi as they are typically served on a platter elsewhere in India, although in Kerala memorably they are regularly served on a banana leaf. Thankfully Kingfisher lager was usually available for me to wash down any thali or other spicy foodstuffs. Many restaurants that didn't have a licence to sell alcohol humorously listed the tipple as 'special tea' on their menus and discreetly served it in cups.

As with *thali*, meals in South India are generally served with the country's staple grain rice, eaten both sweet and savoury boiled or steamed. This cheap source of calories is commonly consumed together with *dal* or *sambar*, types of curried sauce both made from lentils. Rice is also mixed with a kind of bean known as black gram and ground to make a fermented batter. When steamed this batter produces spongy rice cakes named *idlis*, a favoured option for breakfast in the south of India, which is also normally eaten with *sambar* or chutney. The same batter mix is used for making *masala dosa* too, a light pancake stuffed with a spicy potato filling. A cheap and tasty repast, *masala dosa* too comes with pickles or sambars and is definitely one of my favourite Indian vegetarian dishes. Another comestible I often relished was *malai kofta*, fried dumplings of potato and a cheese known as *paneer*, which is then coated in cream and served in a spicy sauce. Delicious as they are, I have never been able to find either of these dishes on the menus of UK Indian restaurants.

Still, a couple of foods I came across in India were familiar to me as items from starter menus in most British curry houses. One is those appetizing deep-fried triangular savouries *samosas*, these being filled with either meat or vegetables. Another is *bhajis* also known as pakoras in many parts of India. Created by deep frying onions and other vegetables such as potatoes and spinach in spicy chick-pea flour, batter, they are a much-loved street food across India. Sometimes these *pakoras* can also contain red hot chillies encrusted in batter, this something I unwittingly discovered after biting into one and almost choking as my mouth began to burn!

The meats I ate most in India were chicken and water buffalo, which is frequently described as 'buff' on menus. Given the Indian penchant for 'buff', obviously the water buffalo is one member of the bovine family many Hindus don't consider sacred. There are risks however in consuming any meat, largely due to issues of cleanliness and bad storage conditions. What especially put me off was seeing one butcher's stall displaying unrefrigerated slabs of nondescript meat covered in flies. If this wasn't repulsive enough, a mangy-looking dog then began licking one piece of meat before being nonchalantly shooed away by the vendor. In all honesty such a lack of basic hygiene would likely explain why a great number of Indians are vegetarians.

Roaming dogs were not the only health risks when it came to food. In one restaurant unbelievably a waiter's thumb was firmly inserted into the bowl of *dal* he placed on my table. Naturally I remonstrated with him and demanded a fresh serving, but it went to highlight further the problem when it came to food hygiene standards. Surprisingly many dishes I consumed in India were very poor quality compared to the Indian food I was accustomed to in the UK. To emphasise this point, I would sometimes reply when asked if I was enjoying my visit to India that I couldn't wait to get home. 'Oh, why's that sir?' the person enquiring would usually ask in a concerned tone, at which I would quip, 'So I can have a decent Indian meal! '

Indeed, I believe that one of the great blessings of British life is the wide availability and popularity of Indian food. It is a love affair rooted in the Raj and Britain's very first Indian restaurant had been established in London way back in 1810 by a Bengali Muslim businessman. Even so, until the 1960s Indian food in Britain was generally only available in cafes or canteens catering for South Asians. By the 1970s though the UK had really started to embrace Indian cuisine and Bengali Muslims had once again been at the forefront of the curry house trade. These were those Bangladeshi refugees fleeing the 1971 war in what was then East Pakistan. Key to their success was richly flavoured, cheap food and a willingness to stay open late in order to satisfy the appetites of those leaving pubs and clubs. In fact, the serving of alcohol itself by many of these restaurants further broadened their appeal and, within a generation, curries were as familiar as cod and chips to people in Britain.

The majority of UK Indian restaurants and takeaways are still owned and run by Bangladeshis, almost all of whom have links to the city of Sylhet. Back when Sylhet had been part of British-ruled Bengal, many Sylhetis had found work on merchant ships. During the age of steam travel, Indians had especially been employed in ships' engine rooms, being better able to cope with the fairly high temperatures generated by the boilers. A few of these mariners from Sylhet later settled in Britain where they established small communities, their numbers swelling in the wake of the 1971 war. Concentrated in places like the East-End of London, subsequent chain-migration further increased the size of Britain's Bangladeshi diaspora.

Bangladeshis may have cornered the Indian restaurant market but the food they offer originates from many regions of the sub-continent beyond their native Bengal. As a generic term *Indian food* as used in the UK, is a reference to the colonial definition of what was British India which today constitutes India, Pakistan, Bangladesh and Sri Lanka. By popularising South Asian cuisine to the point that Indian food is now a regular part of the British diet, the Bangladeshi diaspora has made an invaluable contribution towards British culture. It is very easy to forget in today's age, but by bringing the cuisines of the sub-continent to the British masses, they had achieved a remarkable change in national eating habits. Undoubtedly, no other cultural import from its former colony has impacted Britain more than the cuisine of the sub-continent. I'd say for most Britons the adjective 'Indian' is more likely to conjure up thoughts of spicy food than anything else.

As I knew from my student days a later development UK Indian dining experiences had been the emergence of the balti house. Originating amongst Birmingham's Pakistani community during the 1980s, its roots are rumoured to be in the Pakistani province of Baltistan. Balti houses of course specialise in curries cooked and served in a wok or balti, this type of metal pot commonly known as a *karahi* on the sub-continent. Whereas curries in South Asia are traditionally simmered, balti dishes are flash fried over a high temperature using a technique more usual in Chinese cooking. Normally eaten with naan bread rather than rice, balti dishes are an inexpensive, fast food-take on traditional Indian cooking and the reason why balti houses became so popular. In spite of the success of balti houses in Britain the concept hasn't taken off on the sub-continent. What's more the word 'balti' means bucket in Hindi, so requesting a meal in one in India would undoubtedly cause confusion. While it is true that a famous fried-chicken chain may tempt customers with 'bargain buckets' of their fare, serving food in buckets certainly isn't a normal practice in India.

Britain's affinity for Indian food has grown so great that plenty of non-Asians nowadays routinely cook their own. Let's face it, in today's instantaneous society it's no harder than adding a jar of ready-made sauce to fried meat or veg and microwaving a sachet of rice. The more adventurous like me make their own curries from scratch, with hundreds of recipes for preparing and cooking Indian food only ever an internet search away. Furthermore, the spices and fresh garlic, chillies and ginger which abound in India are nowadays readily available in most British supermarkets. It is a sign of how multicultural modern Britain has become that many supermarkets will now stock popular Indian vegetables like mooli, dudhi and bindi alongside traditional staples like carrots, cabbage and potatoes.

Like all good food the joy of a decent Indian meal whether it's in South Asia or Southall is partly olfactory. I have to confess that if I'm feeling particularly ravenous, the tantalising spicy aroma of Indian food often makes me salivate like a Pavlovian dog. Unlike many types of cuisines, ingredients in Indian cooking tend to not have overlapping flavours which accounts for its distinctive taste. Scientific research in India has analysed thousands of recipes and around two hundred ingredients to prove this. Each ingredient in a recipe possesses on average fifty flavour compounds formed by certain chemicals, in Western cuisine; ingredients normally share the same flavour compounds. The opposite was found to be the case in Indian food, where less flavour sharing produces a greater combination of compounds for our chemical sensors to react with at a molecular level.

Beyond the renowned heat of much Indian food, which can vary in intensity, different flavours might be detected in the same dish ordered in different places. For example, one might have a slightly sweetish, warmer taste and another sharper and sourer, while yet another could possess a faintly bitter or nutty quality to it. The flavour is mostly determined by the proportions and types of spice used in the recipe; with the way they are cooked also making a difference. Some spices are first roasted to release the flavour and aroma whereas the commonly used *tarka* method involves frying spices quickly in hot oil. Ultimately the mix of spices, whether they are fresh, dried or powdered, is more important than any other ingredients used. These spice blends can be both homemade and commercially produced, with *garam masala*-meaning 'hot spices'- a really popular type of mix in India.

An integral part of the Indian diet is yoghurt and curd, both of which are combined with spicy dishes either directly in cooking, or as marinades and side dishes. I discovered that eating these dairy products alongside curries not only tones down the heat of many spices, they also provide an exciting clash of flavours. Apart from the yoghurt and mint dip *raita*- which in Britain is used mostly as a dressing poured onto meat and salad-this Indian eating habit isn't one generally adopted by diners in UK curry houses. Some Indian dishes in Britain may be slightly adapted for a western palate, with perhaps less chilli or a greater amount of turmeric added, but the general flavours I think are similar to those experienced in India itself. Admittedly this may be a somewhat controversial opinion, one that runs contrary to the view held by 'purists' who may claim that Indian food in Britain is a shoddy imitation of Indian food in India, and that the two bear little similarity. I would argue that this depends on the particular dish and where exactly in the UK it's being eaten. It's obvious the quality and choice of South Asian cuisine in Southall or Wembley is better than it is in say Sterling or Wrexham. Likewise, Belfast probably could not compete with say Birmingham or Bradford when it comes to Indian food. I cannot deny that the range of food in India is a lot more varied. In Britain fewer than ten basic varieties of Indian curry sauce are generally available, whilst in India less standardisation of recipes resulted in more variation in the flavours of dishes I ate there. Even so, I can't malign the high standard of so much Indian food I've enjoyed in places like London and the Midlands. One key difference I noticed however was that in the UK curries are usually off the bone, which I preferred to India where bones are typically left in.

I've always struggled to understand why English meals appear on the menus of Indian restaurants in Britain, usually dishes like chicken, steak and omelette all naturally accompanied by chips. I mean would somebody attending a classical Indian music concert don headphones during the performance and listen to Elton John downloads? On that note, one English girl I met in Colva had without any hint of irony at all decried the lack of English food available in India, to which I could only comment how bang out of order this was. After all, how dare people in India eat Indian food!

In Britain, mainstream Indian food is focused entirely around the savoury, with spicy heat being the defining characteristic. On the whole, dessert options are limited in UK Indian restaurants with little in the way of authentic dishes beyond perhaps some mango; India's national fruit, or Indian ice-cream *kulfi*. You could be forgiven for thinking that sweets don't figure largely in the South Asian diet, but as the *ambala* I'd so often used whilst at university proved, nothing could be further from the truth. The most common *and* healthy dessert consumed by Indians is fruit, otherwise there's a whole range of afters available from *kheer*, a type of rice pudding to *ras malai*, a dessert made from balls of cottage cheese steeped in a sweetly spiced clotted cream. Many Indian sweet dishes are produced by using different sorts of flour but unlike the sponges and pastries relished in the West; these mixtures are normally fried rather than baked.

One of the most widely used ingredients in the making of Indian sweets and desserts is milk, which is first boiled for several hours and reduced down to a semi-solid consistency called *khoya*. For sweetness sugar, syrup or honey are added to these milk-based preparations, whilst flavouring comes from nuts such as cashews, almonds or pistachios, fruits and spices, in particular cardamom. When it came to confectionery there is a notable absence of the milk chocolate so beloved in Britain and elsewhere. Instead, there are things such as *gulab jamun*, fried milk balls soaked in syrup and the popular fudge-like *barfi*. Two of the most common flour-based sweets are *jalebi*, fried strands of usually chickpea flour steeped in sugar syrup, and *ladoo,* small sugary fried dough balls often filled with nuts. Given the British fondness for Indian cuisine, it's indeed food for thought that the many sweets and desserts of the sub-continent have never really caught on in the UK. Most British cities with a sizable South Asian population have *ambalas,* and yet non-Asians are rarely enticed by their sweet and often colourful offerings. When it comes to confectionery and puddings, I guess ultimately the British sweet tooth is just more content with traditional choices.

Cuisine across the north of India is quite strongly influenced by Persian food; this introduced by both the Zoroastrians who fled Persia and later the Mughal rulers. Many well-known dishes that Britons might think are typically Indian are actually Persian in their origin, examples being korma, pilau and biryani. The spice saffron and dried lemons are also both classic Persian additions to some Indian recipes, as is the use in meat and rice dishes of nuts like almonds and pistachios, or dried fruits. Sausage-shaped lamb or mutton kebabs were another Mughal introduction into India and the spicy version we know as *seekh* or *boti* kebabs, are virtually mandatory listings on the starter menus of any half-decent UK Indian eatery. Wrapped in a chapatti, they had of course been an *ambala* staple of mine at university.

Along the south west coast of India are Muslim communities who eat traditional Arabian foods like *mandi*, an originally Yemeni style of meat and rice containing the same spices routinely used in Indian curried dishes. In parts of Kerala, even the Middle Eastern standard *kibbeh*, this a preparation of spiced minced lamb coated in bulgur wheat, has found its way onto the dining tables of some Muslim families. One instance of a decidedly Arabic food seen right across South Asia is *halva*. Usually made with semolina flour in India, its name is derived from the Arabic word *halwá* meaning 'sweet' and like most Indian foods, there are regional variations although nuts and dried fruits are customary in recipes. The best-known Portuguese input into the cuisine of India, well apart from chillies of course, is vindaloo, an adaptation of the Iberian culinary practice of marinating meat in wine and garlic (*vinha d'alhos* in the Portuguese language), to both help preserve it and to improve the flavour. In India, wine is substituted with palm vinegar and chillies are also added to the recipe. In mainly Muslim-owned British Indian restaurants it's a dish served with chicken or lamb, unlike Goa where I knew from my own personal encounter with a pig awaiting slaughter, pork is the meat of choice for vindaloo.

In addition to these Persian, Arabic and Portuguese influences, had British cooking made any impact on the cuisine of the sub-continent? Whereas British traditional fare such as roast beef and Yorkshire puds or bacon and eggs were never likely to tantalise the taste buds of India's many Hindus and Muslims, you'd think that centuries of British colonial involvement might have had some bearing on Indian gastronomic habits. The reality was, this had only amounted to some fusions of the two cuisines plus the British introduction of vegetable ingredients like cauliflower and carrots. In the main cities where the British presence had been greatest, an Anglo-Indian population had naturally existed and it was from these communities that well-known dishes like jalfrezi emerged. In the former Calcutta, leftover beef or lamb from their traditional Sunday roast was used to make jalfrezi, a curried dish which in many recipes includes Worcestershire sauce as one of its ingredients. We may think of Worcestershire sauce as being a very British condiment, but its origins in fact lies in an Indian recipe for a fish-based sauce. Although the exact recipe for Worcestershire sauce is a closely guarded secret many of its known ingredients such as pepper, garlic and tamarind are very popular in Indian cooking. In point of fact India is the world's largest producer of the legume tamarind.

Another meal accredited to the Anglo-Indians is kedgeree, this being a curried mixture of rice, smoked haddock and hard-boiled eggs. Kedgeree is actually based on *khichdi,* a dish made of rice and lentils. People returning from colonial India made kedgeree a fashionable breakfast meal in Victorian Britain. In India itself it had limited appeal beyond the colonial centres like Calcutta, Madras and Bombay. One culinary creation of the Anglo-Indians which still remains popular in Britain today is mulligatawny soup. The idea of soup as a meal is a British one rather than Indian, and this spicy tomato variety, which originated in the city of Madras, famously derives its name from a corruption of the Tamil word for 'pepper water'.

The general blandness of British food could never compete with the rich, spicy flavours that define Indian cooking, and these days I reckon many Britons would say the same thing! Still, there is one thing consumed in copious amounts all across the sub-continent which had come via the British, namely their introduction of the plant *camellia sinensis* more commonly known as tea. Although the consumption of tea or *chai* amongst Indians is prevalent this had only come about after independence. A shrub native to China, its commercial cultivation in India was started by the East India Company to sate British not Indian, demand for the beverage. In the post-colonial era, an attachment to tea has therefore become another aspect of British culture adopted by Indians. Globally only water is drunk more than tea and India and China are the world's biggest producers. Whether in Manchester or Mumbai, Cardiff or Kochi, Dundee or Delhi or indeed Belfast or Bengaluru, the mass everyday ritual of infusing tea into water and enjoying a cuppa is something that unites the peoples of the UK and its former Indian colony.

In India however the tea drinker has no choice about whether they would like milk and sugar, as *chai* is normally made by boiling both of these together with the water and tea leaves all in a pan. If you like your tea sweet and milky it's perfect; if like me you do not, then it's tough. The typical milk and sugar options are not the only additions, as *masala chai* prepared with: cardamoms, cinnamon, cloves ginger, pepper and various other spices is also extremely popular. While this concoction is loved by Indians I never took to it myself. On a more personal level, one further type of beverage popularised in India by the British is equally significant. Without stating the obvious, the bestselling brand in India today is named after a feathered *monarch angler*, it being a drink that reputedly thrilled when chilled!

Chapter 6.

Having reached the southernmost part of Kerala it was now time to start heading back north. Martin and I took a bus from TP to Kollam around 70 km up the coast, enjoying the lush beauty of the Keralan countryside en-route. As the state's sandwiched between the Lakshadweep Sea and the Western Ghats, its landscape and seasonally wet climate enables a diverse range of flora to thrive. Foremost were the innumerable coconut trees seen from the bus, unsurprising then that the state's historical name Keralam means 'land of coconuts' in the Malayalam language. Personally, I think coconut palms, with their distinctive long thin tapering trunks and pinnate shaped leaves convey the essence of the tropics more than any other tree. Able to withstand salinity and easily taking root in sandy soil, they commonly grow along beaches and are naturally pollinated by sea currents. This would explain how these trees have successfully managed to colonize the coastal regions of the world's tropics... an achievement matched only by Europeans!

India is the world's third largest-producer of coconuts with over 11 million tonnes of them harvested annually, that's an awful lot of *Bounty bars*! As well as providing edible kernels, famously coconuts are also a source of liquid refreshment. In southern India I often enjoyed drinking the delicious natural water contained in green unripe coconuts. The sap of the palm is regularly consumed in India too, either as a soft-drink or when it's fermented into a traditional alcoholic beverage called *toddy*. Not that I drank either during my trip. Besides providing food and drink, coconut palms have from their roots to their fronds an impressive range of uses. Their hardwood is suitable for construction or fuel, furthermore thatch for roofing, doormats, sacks, rope, baskets and medicine and dye can all be obtained from the tree. With such versatility of uses it is understandable why coconut trees are such a defining feature of the Keralan landscape.

Apt though the name 'land of coconuts' is, other commercially valuable trees are also plentiful in Kerala, amongst them those producing cashew nuts and rubber. Extensively cultivated as well are banana, guava, papaya, mango and jackfruit trees, the latter bearing the largest fruit of any tree as mature jackfruits can easily weigh over 20 kilograms. With their green dimpled skin and sweet yellow flesh, these large exotic fruits are few and far between in the UK but a common native species in South India. Eaten raw and used in curries, jackfruits are so popular they are in fact the state fruit of Kerala, this being no mean accolade in such a fruitful land. By coincidence, one type of fruit I had always thought came from trees I actually saw growing in the ground, namely pineapples.

Other trees abundant in Kerala yield spices like cloves, nutmeg cinnamon, mace and tamarind, as do plants producing the likes of cardamom, ginger and pepper. In terms of what chefs christen the 'master spice' the state in fact grows some of best quality pepper or peppercorn in the world. Coming from the drupe of a flowering vine native to India, it has been used as a spice since the second millennium BCE. India's best-known spice had in the past been the main ingredient for heat in Indian cooking until the Portuguese introduction of the chilli. It was once considered to be a luxury commodity affordable only to the wealthy, now in modern times peppercorn has become one of the world's most common spices and used second only to salt for seasoning food.

After a couple of hours driving through this fertile land our bus terminated in Kollam, a city formerly and still frequently known as Quilon. This former capital of the Vanad dynasty had historically been at the heart of the regional spice trade. Indeed, by the time the Portuguese arrived in Kerala in 1498, Quilon had long been a major port of the Malabar Coast. Its spice heyday may have been in the faded past, but Kollam remains the centre of the country's cashew nut industry. Just like tomatoes, potatoes and of course chillies, cashew nuts had been introduced to India from South America by the Portuguese. Cashew nuts nowadays are principally grown in Africa and Asian, India being one of the world's largest producers.

An added bonus when growing cashews is that the nuts, which are actually the seeds of the tree, also sprout an edible fruit called cashew apples. In Goa juice extracted from this fruit is fermented and distilled into the spirit called *feni* which I'd sampled in Colva. Both this and another type of *feni* made from coconut toddy were so cheap in Goa it would have been *nuts* not to try them. Puns aside though, in all honesty they weren't the nicest tipples I've ever imbibed, which is a refined way of saying they were bloody disgusting. The smell of these spirits isn't pleasant either having a very unusual astringent aroma that's hard to describe. In fairness, the feni I tried perhaps wasn't the best quality. All I know is this stuff had a face-squelching harshness about it, making it nigh on impossible for me to appreciate any notes of cashew or coconut. I may have detected a slight earthy flavour but the overriding taste was more *nasty* that nutty!

I'm quite partial to cashew nuts themselves though and it's easy to understand their popularity whether for snacking or for use in cooking. While the actual nuts might be safe to eat, their shells contain acids which can burn the skin, which is the reason why they're always sold to the public in shelled form. Sure enough, for a labour-intensive economy like India's, the processing of cashew nuts is not automated but carried out by thousands of low-paid women workers. It's sad that they aren't generally provided with gloves as prolonged exposure to the caustic substances will cause permanently damage to workers hands. These are the deplorable conditions for unskilled employees in a harsh economic system that cares little for the wellbeing of those generating the profits.

Clearly we had not come to Kollam for cashew nuts; instead drawing us and other tourists is its location as an access point to Kuttanad. More commonly referred to as the backwaters, this is a fertile region which contains an interconnected system of canals, rivers and lagoons. Comprised of both fresh and brackish waters these waterways extend north as far as Kochi some 75 kilometres away. By all accounts, a boat trip through these backwaters is a must-do on any Kerala itinerary, albeit hopefully aboard a vessel substantially bigger than a canoe.

A suitably large enough boat boarded, Martin and I spent the day cruising through exotic countryside, one which ranged from verdant expanses of paddy fields to the lush vegetation of cashew plantations, banana trees and, naturally, the ever-present coconut trees. Even the water, which our boat navigated at a gentle pace, was variegated with hues of green, blue and muddy brown.

Visible from the boat in the passing landscape were villages and farms along with fishermen, farmers and other locals going about their business. Occasionally, on the banks it was possible to see the churches, temples or mosques of these picturesque waterside communities. With such scenic rural backgrounds, at times these buildings projected an almost magical appearance. It would be very easy to romanticize about life in this tropical setting, yet rural poverty in India was no less prevalent than its urban counterpart. Still, the beautiful surroundings were at least some compensation for those enduring hardship here in Kuttanad.

Plying the backwaters were other boats of differing sizes, from small canoes with two or three people aboard to larger fishing vessels with crews of twenty or more. Every now and again I spied large boats known in Malayalam as *kettu vallum*. Being at least thirty metres in length, these are floating homes that traditionally doubled as cargo vessels. Once indispensable for transporting the region's rice along the hundreds of kilometres of waterways, most of them today carry tourists.

Our own boat made a couple of stops along the way including one for lunch at a riverside restaurant. Here just one dish was on the menu, it consisting of ingredients found in abundance locally as we tucked into: fish cooked in a coconut curry sauce with rice. Continuing our sedate cruise through the backwaters of Kerala I felt pretty chuffed when I managed to spot a few kingfishers. This colourful bird with its bright blue and orange plumage is of course so well-known in India, a best-selling beer had been named after it. As it so happens, I never saw the national bird of India during my trip, not that I really needed to though as like most people I'd already seen a peacock.

After eight blissful hours cruising on the water we reached our final destination, the old trading town of Alappuzha. 'Backwater' is of course usually a word with a negative connotation but this had been an entirely positive experience. For sure, few journeys I have ever made have been quite as relaxed and enjoyable as this one. Alappuzha; which was previously known as Alleppey, proved to be a pleasant if unremarkable location to spend a night, given that it was just another Malabar port shorn of its former glory. From what we saw the town had a beach and the standard mixture of *mandirs* and *masjids*. What stood out though were the numerous interconnecting canals running through Alappuzha, these linking surrounding lakes and rivers.

The history of Alappuzha is a familiar one in this part of India. It was first governed by the Cheras followed by a succession of local and regional potentates. As might be expected, the Portuguese showed up later as did the Dutch and British after them. However, from the mid-18th century up until independence Alappuzha had been part of the Travancore kingdom. In one of the more unusual footnotes in Indian history, Alappuzha and the surrounding district was the scene of a communist-inspired uprising in 1946 against the monarchical government. It had been ruthlessly suppressed with hundreds killed in massacres carried out by the Travancore army. This bloody episode certainly revealed how these rulers of India's princely states could be every bit as repressive as their British overlords. Such brutal governance tends to be overlooked in nationalist versions of history that demonise the behaviour of foreign colonisers, whilst romanticising that of the native ruling elites. Still the uprising had shown – as did the hammer and sickle emblems *and* the posters of Stalin I'd seen – the extent to which communism had impacted the political development of Kerala.

Modern Alappuzha has more than 174,000 inhabitants, this a substantial number for somewhere only classified as a town. Then again, a village in India might be home to 20,000 people such is the vast size of the country's population. Today, like Kollam, it was backwater tourism that helped to keep the rupees coming into Alappuzha. At least there is one traditional sector of the economy continuing to thrive there, this unsurprisingly for Kerala coconut related. For Alappuzha is a centre for coir, a fibre obtained from coconut husks and used to manufacture rope, fabric, brushes and matting. Inheriting the properties of the tree it comes from, coir fibre is resistant to saltwater and thus also ideally suited for the making of fishing nets. The lucrative production of coir in the town alone highlights just how vital coconuts are to the economy of Kerala.

After a night in some mediocre hostel Martin and I bought bus tickets for Mysuru, a major city located in the neighbouring state of Karnataka directly to the north of Kerala. At times, I grew tired of the constant attempts to rip me off, as happened again on this occasion when the agent charged Martin and I almost double the fare. He attempted to conceal this fraud by having one of his staff retain the tickets and accompany us to the coach station. There, upon boarding, the driver took the tickets from our escort before then handing them on to Martin, which now allowed him to see the true cost of the fare clearly printed on both tickets.

At this, a visibly infuriated Martin immediately stormed off the bus and grabbed the chap before he was able to exit the scene. From the doorway I watched and listened as Martin then began to berate him, shouting that the agent was a dishonest man and had no right to overcharge us. The commotion prompted a mixture of surprise and admiration from onlookers. In fact, some of the more conscientious bystanders even slapped the man several times! It was summary justice Indian style and I appreciated their solidarity with us; we may have been foreigners but our cultural differences were transcended by a common sense of injustice and unfairness. Ideally if anyone deserved to be punished, it should have been the thieving agent himself. Even so, it was a justifiable demonstration of disapproval on Martin's part and quite honestly hilarious for me to witness.

Chapter 7.

Following another bone-shaking lengthy bus ride, accompanied by Bollywood films being played at the normal eardrum-perforating volume, we reached Mysuru. In an effort to shake off the colonial past, the Indian authorities had changed many place names over the years including Mysuru, which up until 2014 had been called Mysore. Located inland and elevated more than 750 metres above sea level, the climate here was less sultry than the coastal regions, this something I very much appreciated. The majority language in Mysuru and Karnataka state itself is Kannada, which together with Marathi and Malayalam make up the three key languages spoken along the west coast from Mumbai to Kerala. Because languages are so integral to regional identities in a large country like India, it made sense that state boundaries were eventually established on a linguistic basis. Having said that, there were limitations to this policy given that this is a land where dozens of languages have a million or more speakers.

Prior to India's independence, Mysore, as a part of the kingdom of the same name, had been under the sovereignty of the Hindu Wadiyar dynasty for the greater part of five and a half centuries. Their long reign was broken only during the last four decades of the 1700s, when a Muslim commander of the monarch's army by the name of Hyder Ali became ruler of Mysore. Whilst expanding the territory under his control, Ali had clashed with the East India Company, which at that point was attempting to consolidate its own power on the sub-continent. With French support, Hyder Ali and later his son and successor Tipu Sultan, fought a number of wars between 1767 and 1799 against the British and their Indian allies. The East India Company were ultimately victorious in these conflicts and restored the Wadiyar monarchy as heads of what then became yet another princely state. Be that so, the Wadiyar *maharajas* who resumed governing Mysore until 1947, had like all Indian rulers only done so under the suzerainty of the British. The British had thereby cleverly maintained the pretence of Indian self-government, even though all these princely states were ruled by unelected feudal elites, themselves ultimately subservient to their colonial masters.

A palace of granite and marble built for the 24th Wadiyar ruler stands as a monument to the status of the former *maharajahs*. If the royal palace I only recently visited in Kochi had possessed a rather unassuming exterior, the exact opposite was true of this extravagant palatial structure. Set in vast grounds and standing on the site of an earlier royal residence which was destroyed by fire, the sumptuous Maharajah's Palace had been designed by a British architect and completed in 1912. Constructed in the popular Indo-Saracenic style of that era, the palace is a striking edifice of domes and arches complete with a central tower topped by a gleaming brass-plated dome. If this place looked spectacular in the daylight, then it took on an almost fairy tale appearance when illuminated by tens of thousands of light bulbs on Sunday nights. We were fortunate enough to be there for this weekly spectacle and the palace including the gateway on its approach, looked just amazing when fully lit up. When one considered the frequency of power cuts in India such a display was even more incredible. After all, this enormous amount of lighting must have easily consumed half of Mysuru's nightly allocation of electricity!

Entering into the palace itself gave rise to one heart-stopping moment I hadn't anticipated. Beyond the reception, the entrance into the palace complex was manned by the local police. From what I'd noticed, in India police constables normally wore a beret with their khaki uniforms, whilst in Karnataka they instead sported a distinctive slouch hat with the brim pinned up on one side. As I went to enter, one of the policemen seated behind a table asked to look in a small cloth shoulder bag I had with me. Handing it to him I had expected only a perfunctory glance so was somewhat taken aback when he began to empty its contents. The problem was a small zippered pouch inside the bag contained a sizable chunk of *charas* inside it! To say that I was momentarily shitting it would be an understatement of some magnitude.

My heart was palpitating and the sweat began flooding down my face. All of a sudden I felt like I was in the opening scene of the movie *Midnight Express*. But this was assuredly no film set and the policeman about to bust me was no actor. I thought with dread of Owen's mate, the unlucky Australian chap who'd got banged up in Delhi for possession of hash. Immediately I saw in my mind's eye a

Westerner staring out miserably through the bars of some filthy, sweltering, overcrowded cell, with cockroaches the size of mice bumping up against his sandals, and the fetid smells of sewage and body odour making him want to vomit. This was a truly hellish existence of: routine verbal and physical abuse by sadistic guards, hunger, sleeping on bare floors and endless bites from fleas and lice. Adding to his despair would be the risks of illness and disease, plus the dangers of violence and rape from other inmates; all of this making him wonder how much longer he could cope before he cracked up.

Was I now too about to share Owen's friend's plight and end up incarcerated myself? I had seen how incredibly harsh everyday life is for so many Indians who have their liberty; it stands to reason therefore that things would be even worse in some hell-hole of a gaol. I started mentally preparing myself for such a nightmarish scenario of privation, suffering and despondency. This was a truly terrifying prospect as even the thought of enduring such appalling conditions seemed to me intolerable for hours, never mind years!

I snapped out of my horrific reverie as the policemen removed an inflatable neck pillow from my bag, and his eyes narrowed in confusion. Keen for any kind of distraction whatsoever, I instantly took it from him and blew the thing up, placed it around my neck and made a snoring noise. At this animated demonstration the policeman smiled as he returned my bag whereupon, with a huge sense of relief, I proceeded into the complex. It had been a scary experience and one that reiterated the need for caution where *charas* was concerned.

In keeping with its quite amazing exterior, the Palace interior is equally opulent, being a series of great marble halls with mosaic floors, chandeliers and intricately carved doorways. One huge doorway which had managed to survive the blaze in the former palace is elaborately embossed with silver. Along with the silver, a great deal of gold gilt, ivory and jewels can be found throughout the décor: an ostentatious display of Wadiyar affluence. Some of the palace ceilings are themselves outstanding examples of art being crafted from beautiful stained glass or finely carved teak. For me, the most unforgettable part of the palace is its stunning Public *Durbar* Hall. It's an immense area of ornate gilded colonnades and cusped arches, all crowned by white marble inlaid with gemstones to form floral designs. One side of the hall is open to the outside and has wide marble steps leading down to a parade ground, this where the public would have once assembled during *durbars*

Further adorning the remarkable palace interior is a medley of luxury furnishings, ceremonial objects, sculptures and paintings. Along with paintings of court life and royal portraits, many images of Hindu deities and scenes from Hindu scripture embellish the walls. One particularly memorable item on display is a ceremonial *howdah* –a wooden frame used as an elephant saddle-this one bedecked with an impressive *eighty* kilograms of gold.

Apparently, there is also a golden throne in the palace which is only put on display once a year during a festival known as *Dasara*. Whilst this immensely valuable seating wasn't on show when I visited, a couple of silver chairs were. In a country where much of the population even today don't possess chairs – never mind *solid silver* ones – this really did put the wealth of these former rulers into perspective.

The palace and its grounds have a number of temples of their own; however none are as significant as the Sri Chamundeshwari Temple which overlooks Mysuru. Sited a few kilometres southeast of the city, it sits on top of Chamundi Hill and reaching it involved climbing over a thousand steps. The ascent brought us past a low-gated plinth containing a huge statue of a seated bull decorated with many garlands and bells, the bull in question being Nandi the mount of Lord Shiva. The enormous statue, carved in 1659 out of a single piece of black granite, is five metres in height and over seven metres in length. In some parts of India, Shiva is worshipped as Nandi and, in the best tradition of Hindu idolatry; this imposing monolith attracts pilgrims bearing offerings. It even has its own priest in attendance.

Continuing we reached the impressive seven-storey pyramidal *gopura* that leads into the Sri Chamundeshwari Temple. Standing forty metres high this gateway tower is an astonishing work of art elaborately adorned with delicately carved patterns. The *gopura* dates from the 19th century whilst the temple itself originated as a shrine in the 12th century. Chamundeshwari is dedicated to the goddess of the same name who had been guardian of the Wadiyar dynasty. In this temple, as with the Mahalaxmi *Mandir* in Mumbai, monkeys can be seen all around the complex. These primates are in fact given sanctuary in Hindu temples as they are considered representatives of Hanuman, the monkey god avatar of Shiva who in the epic *Ramayana* assists Rama in his struggle. This presence of animals in *mandirs* was together with their lively atmosphere, another thing which readily distinguished them from places of worship in other religions.

Having invested in a type of clay pipe called a *chillum* used for smoking *charas*, I thought Chamundi Hill an optimum spot for us to relax and have a smoke while we watched the sun set over Mysuru. We were also safely well away from the prying eyes and hands of the local law. With the hill rising to a height of about 250 metres, it commands some fantastic views of the city unfurled beneath. Furthermore, being as stoned as a *sadhu* I could totally grasp the spiritual relevance of the site. I felt a euphoric sense of oneness with the world as I stared at a great masterpiece forming in the sky. I became transfixed as the blue firmament filled with a magnificent array of soft reds, vivid crimsons and golden yellows. Sunsets are frequently beautiful, but sat watching this one slowly disappearing into the horizon seemed to almost border on a religious experience. Its scale and beauty induced a mix of awe and serenity in me; it was a moment of connection not just with nature but also to a greater spiritual awareness and the cosmos beyond. The elation was wonderful, a sense of intense happiness and inner peace derived from the appreciation of a spectacular sight viewed from a sacred place. Feeling uplifted and full of joy, it was a sensation best expressed by Mahatma Gandhi who, upon admiring the exquisiteness of a sunset, once exclaimed, 'My soul expands in the worship of the creator.'

As yet a further example of India's religious diversity, Mysuru is home to the Roman Catholic St Philomena's Cathedral. Built in a perpendicular Gothic style with fifty-odd metre high twin spires and seating for a congregation of 800, it had opened in 1936. St Philomena's Cathedral stood out for me, as it was the first non-Portuguese Catholic church I'd seen in India, not that we bothered entering the place mind you, having by that stage had my fill of churches...being *churched-out* as it were. Instead, a slightly more stimulating place to look around is the city's Devaraja Market. This could be described as a microcosm of the country itself, offering a vibrant mixture of confusion, colour, noises and smells.

In the cooler evenings it's a delight to wander around this large market where together with fruit and veg all manner of flowers, spices and perfume oils can be bought. The market stalls generate some delightful scents and especially invigorating are the heavy smells of cloves, cardamoms and ginger. Reflecting the vegetarian diet of so many Indians, Devaraja is a food market that doesn't sell meat. On the other hand, there's no shortage of traders displaying conical mounds of the brightly coloured powder called *kumkum*; this being used by Hindus to make religious markings and also for other ceremonial purposes.

Mysuru is itself a large producer of something integral to Hindu religious ritual... incense sticks. Known as joss sticks or *agarbathi* and burnt in worship (*puja*), their distinctive smell permeating the air is a familiar one in India. Made by simply rolling a bamboo stick in a scented paste which is then dried, production in India tended as one might imagine, to be done by hand. The paste coating the stick is created from a natural adhesive mixed with a combustible, usually charcoal or sawdust, and then perfumed with any number of spices, fragrant woods, flowers, fruits and other plant parts. Take it from me; in a land where the traffic fumes and other less desirable odours are often pervasive, the aroma of incense could be a godsend... no religious pun intended.

By far one of the most popular scents used to make *agarbathi* is sandalwood, which comes from a tree native to Karnataka and the neighbouring state of Tamil Nadu. Known as *srigandhada* in the Kannada language, this local resource has made the city famous for sandalwood carvings, not that I saw any actual *sandals* carved from this yellowish-coloured wood being sold there! Still, for a couple of souvenirs I did buy one carving of the goddess Parvati, the consort of Shiva, and a second one of their elephant-headed son Ganesha.

Whilst it is not the only type of aromatic wood, sandalwood is unique in that it retains its fragrant sweet-scent for decades. It's a property that makes this wood one of the most expensive in the world, and Indian sandalwood is considered the best of all species.

The most prized parts of the tree are its essential oils which are highly valued for use in perfumes and other cosmetics. Besides its natural fragrance, sandalwood oil has been used for centuries in traditional Indian Ayurveda medicine for its natural qualities as a stringent, antiseptic and stimulant. Considered sacred in Hinduism and Jainism, sandalwood is utilized in ritual worship. For example, during *puja* a paste made from it is offered to the gods and also applied by Hindu devotees to their faces.

In recent years, high demand for the oil together with a limited supply has seen the price of sandalwood skyrocket. Only around 20 percent of the tree is made up of the heartwood from which the precious high-grade oils used in perfumery are obtained. The bulk of the tree is the less aromatic sapwood, this the outer layer between the heartwood and the bark, which is used for carvings, religious rituals and some cosmetics, its usage in soap a common example. The natural oils, which on average constitute about six percent of the heartwood, are extracted by steam distillation and a mature tree can yield between 600 ml and 700 ml during this process. Less than one litre per tree does not seem like a large amount, but remember this is a highly-prized aromatic essential oil not maple syrup, and back in 2018 it was selling for US $3000 a litre. Timber as a commodity is usually purchased by volume, but sandalwood by comparison is so valued that it's sold by weight.

Because of sandalwood's substantial commercial worth, illegal logging has left few wild trees in India's forests. Even the amount of officially produced sandalwood in India has been in decline for decades going from 4000 tonnes in 1970 down to 250 tonnes by 2016. India's status as the world's largest producer of sandalwood has now been superseded by Australia. Home to a lower-yielding indigenous species of sandalwood, Australia had begun large-scale cultivation of Indian sandalwood back in the early 2000s. India's decline in this sector can in large part be traced to the fact that, in the past, all cultivation and legal trading of the wood was carried out by the state governments in Karnataka and Tamil Nadu. Since the time of Sultan Tipu, when sandalwood was decreed a royal tree, any tree, even on private land had been classed as state property, a law which had continued even after independence. Eventually, illegal logging, combined with the absence of private cultivation or adequate reforestation policies, saw India's supply of sandalwood diminish.

To obviate this, the government changed laws in 2001 and 2002 bringing about an end to the monopoly of sandalwood production by state forest departments. Be that as it may, the official trade in sandalwood is still under the government's control. Many farmers cultivating sandalwood receive subsidies and nowadays the trees are commercially grown in other regions of the country beyond their native Karnataka and Tamil Nadu. This hardy evergreen tree can reach twenty metres in height, and requires low maintenance. Its saplings easily take root in a variety of soils, although being a partially parasitic species, a sandalwood tree does require certain nutrients from the roots of other plants, what are known as host crops. The host crops can include pigeon peas and fruit trees like pomegranate, mango and papaya, which themselves can generate a farmer income for about seven or eight years, after which time the growing tree will eventually kill them.

Whilst all this has encouraged private sandalwood cultivation, it does take fifteen years before a sandalwood tree can be viably harvested. This isn't long compared to say an oak tree which takes 500 years to mature; even so it is a long time for growers to wait for a return on their investment. Added to this lengthy delay in any financial remuneration is the issue of security, with the illegal felling and smuggling of sandalwood remaining a major problem. In spite of these difficulties thanks to the measures taken, India is now steadily increasing its production of sandalwood with more and more hectares coming under cultivation each year. It is now grown over an area of around 9000 square kilometres, the vast majority of this still being in Karnataka and Tamil Nadu. For all these developments, with a decade and a half growing period and an ever-expanding global demand for this fragrant wood, no-one is sure whether India can re-establish its former supremacy in the world sandalwood market.

Interestingly, ultimately the biggest threat to India's production of sandalwood is no longer from foreign competition, unlicensed harvesting or even disease anymore. In reality, the cultivation of sandalwood globally may be undermined by the development of sandalwood compounds in laboratories. By splicing DNA from a sandalwood tree with yeast cultures, its highly valued aromatic compounds can be cultivated in laboratory conditions in days not years. From the perspective of the perfume industry, whether its scents are derived from plant extracts or Petri dishes makes no difference to the final product, only to its cost. By commercially replicating the scent of sandalwood in a science lab, the natural product would unquestionably lose most of its value and end the cultivation of sandalwood at its current level. In the final analysis it would seem that the gifts of nature are no longer the preserve of the natural world alone; such are advances in modern science.

From the city of sandalwood and incense we travelled north-westerly in a 'Super Deluxe' bus heading back to the coast and the Karnatakan city of Mangalore. Our transport sounds luxurious, however from what I could tell the only extra this 'Super Deluxe' service appeared to offer was Indian movies being played in HD *stereo*! Our destination lies on the coast of Karnataka, which is located between Goa in the north and Kerala in the south. Unlike these two neighbours though, Karnataka extends much deeper inland bordering four further states. It's the country's 6th largest state in area, and much of its territory between the Western and Eastern Ghats, had formed part of what was historically known as the Carnatic region.

The state has one of the biggest economies of any in India, this largely being a consequence of its capital city Bengaluru, formerly named Bangalore, becoming the nation's hi-tech hub in the 1980s. These IT businesses today contribute billions of US dollars each year into the state's economy via their software and hardware exports. Other significant industries are also based in Bengaluru including biotech, communication and aeronautic companies, as well as United Breweries who make Kingfisher beer. Karnataka as a whole has benefited from these developments and some two-thirds of its economy is now related to the service sector. The state is indeed very much part of the new modern India, having transformed its traditional agrarian economy into one leading the country's hi-tech industry in the 21st century.

There is still of course an agricultural sector in Karnataka, this being a large producer of silk and ergo also of the mulberry trees whose leaves are necessary to feed silk worms. It is India's main coffee growing region too, coffee not a crop ordinarily associated with such a tea loving nation. The truth is coffee had been grown and consumed by Indians for a couple of centuries before tea ever was. According to legend, it was a Sufi saint returning from *Haj* who had introduced coffee cultivation to Karnataka in the 16th century. Allegedly the holy man smuggled raw coffee beans out of Yemen, which back then had strictly maintained its monopoly on coffee production by allowing only the export of roasted or boiled beans which could not be germinated. Coffee farming in India had remained small scale until the British established plantations in 1840 and although dwarfed by tea production, the coffee industry grew to become commercially important for the country. Figures vary, but today this land of *chai* drinkers is surprisingly the sixth or seventh biggest coffee producer in the world with in excess of 300,000 tonnes grown there annually.

The *arabica* species first brought to Karnataka from Yemen and originating in Ethiopia, nowadays accounts for less than a third of India's total coffee output, the rest being made up of the hardier *robusta* plant native to sub-Saharan Africa, which was introduced later. For all this high volume of coffee production it isn't Indians themselves driving demand as around 80 percent goes for export. It seemed somewhat bizarre but with Italy being the top importer of Indian coffee, you were actually more likely to drink a cup of it in Milan than Mumbai.

The caffeine naturally present in coffee is a favoured stimulant for much of the world, nonetheless a far more popular pick-me-up in India are areca nuts. White and red varieties of areca nuts are cultivated in India with Karnataka the country's largest producer, the state supplying nearly 68 percent of the total output in 2018 alone. Botanically speaking areca *nuts* are more accurately the berries from a palm of the same name, ones containing an oily compound called *arecoline* which is the psychoactive ingredient consumers enjoy. Whilst areca nuts are perfectly edible on their own, traditionally they're chewed together with *betel* leaves this mixture known as *paan*. In fact, the two are synonymous to the point where areca nuts are widely referred to as *betel nuts*, even though the two plants are unrelated. Betel leaves, which come from a type of native vine, primarily provide flavour although they themselves possess medicinal properties and can help create a feeling of wellbeing. The practice of chewing areca and betel leaf together is fairly common on the sub-continent and across the whole of South-East Asia, as it has been for centuries. In India a little calcium hydroxide known as slaked lime was normally added to the *paan*, this to help both digestion and absorption of the stimulants into the bloodstream via the mouth. Other varied *paan* preparations include seeds or spices for extra taste while in order to boost its overall effect, some people even mix tobacco with the *paan* they chew.

Those partaking in *paan* are instantly identifiable by their red stained mouths and teeth, this arising from a dye released when areca nuts are masticated. The residue created by chewing *paan* is usually spat out and even if digested, the red saliva generated is similarly expunged, meaning either regularly ends up as colourful, if repugnant blotches on pavements. If bits of red gob splattered on the ground seemed unhygienic, the actual use of *paan* itself is highly detrimental to health. Like the tobacco they're sometimes chewed with, areca nuts are not merely addictive but also highly carcinogenic and incidents of oral cancer are quite high amongst consumers of *paan*, as are those of rotting teeth and gum disease. Unfortunately it is a long-established habit and these, doubtless little publicised risks, fail to deter millions in India from chewing *paan*, as the 324,000 tonnes of areca nuts harvested there in 2018 clearly showed. On the question of sampling some *paan* myself, I just never really felt tempted, in all honesty why would I need to when India was basically one big stimulant itself!

It's not only the land in Karnataka which yields income but also what lays beneath it, for the state is home to India's biggest gold mines. Be that as it may, in 2021 India produced only slightly more than 1.8 tonnes of gold, which sounds a lot until you realize that neighbouring China churned out 420 tonnes of the stuff during the same year. Indeed, India's level of gold output comes nowhere near to meeting domestic demand, leaving the country to import over 500 tonnes of gold annually during recent years. Demand is so high because Indians have a particular attachment to the precious metal, one which extends far deeper than simply its universal intrinsic value. On a spiritual level, in Hindu mythology the very creation of the cosmos is traced to the existence of an oval-shaped golden womb called the *hiranyagarbha* the seed of all there is going to be. Furthermore in India it is customary for all brides, rich or poor, to be given gold jewellery by their families, the amount worn obviously dependent on their status. At least half of all the demand in India for gold rings, necklaces, bracelets, earrings and nose rings is believed to be for weddings, with the gold normally used being 22 karat, as pure 24 karat gold is too soft for jewellery purposes.

Indians also commonly purchase gold for other occasions such as anniversaries, births, religious ceremonies and festivals, and all but the most impoverished of families will possess some pieces of jewellery. Numerous days in the Hindu calendar are even deemed auspicious for buying gold, foremost being on the first day of the *Diwali* festival of light when jewellers see a real spike in demand. Throughout India in both rural and urban areas people basically want gold, not only the bling of jewellery but coins and bullion bought for security or investment. Farmers, whose profits are at the mercy of the weather, will for example often invest in gold when harvests are good in order to sell during leaner periods. Ironically in a country beset by poverty, such is the unfailing desire for the lustre of gold in Indian society, you could almost say it had a 22 karat culture!

Well after around seven hours of travelling through the exotic Karnataka countryside we arrived at the port city of Mangalore. This though was only a transit stop and we didn't hang around going straight to the railway station, there catching a train directly north to Goa. Upon returning to what had been one of their last enclaves, it occurred to me that pretty much everywhere I'd been in India thus far...had at some point in its history experienced a Portuguese presence.

Chapter 8.

Well, the familiarity of Colva with its palmed beaches and ample 'thrilling' chilled beer, somehow made the place more enjoyable than before. Moreover, most nights there was now entertaining ceremonies taking place on the beach, although it was not always clear which specific festival or occasion was being celebrated. One of these events we watched featured troupes of male dancers in matching clothing, performing their choreographed moves on the sand. Several of these dancers were wearing turbans as part of their costume whilst one group sported conical helmets made of flowers for headwear. The music for all this dancing, which mostly involved the participants forming circles, was provided courtesy of both traditional drummers and a military band. These drummers each played a *dhol,* this being a large double-sided wooden drum which hangs from the shoulder. A thicker skin over one end of a *dhol* produces a deeper bass sound, whilst the drum's pitch can be altered by adjusting the tension on ropes which secure the skins to the body. The *dhol* and the similar but smaller *dholak* are two of the most widespread types of drums played at these outdoor festivals; I had heard them previously in TP and knew just how hypnotic their rhythmic beats could be.

The assembled military bandsmen were smartly attired in blue and white uniforms, and included bagpipers, which came as a real surprise to me. Indian whisky brands were one thing, but I can say for certain that the drone of a bagpipe was the last sound I had expected to hear in India. After all, did military bands in Scotland play sitars? It was something I very much doubted and my Scots travelling companion Martin entirely concurred. From observing such festivities, I surmised by now that whenever the opportunity to do so arose, Indians seem to enjoy nothing more than a bit of music, dancing and singing.

Like in the West, Indian music varies in its genres and includes everything from folk songs to hip-hop and rock. Of course, Indian musical instruments like the sitar have occasionally featured in popular Western music, the 1966 Rolling Stone's hit song 'Paint it Black' being a classic example. In the 1960s Indian sitar player Ravi Shankar also found fame in the West after being embraced by the hippie culture. In fact this cultural musical exchange worked both ways. By the early 1970s traditional Punjabi bhangra folk music was being fused with Western instrumentation. What's more this new form of bhangra originated outside of India amongst Britain's Punjabi-mainly Sikh-diaspora. Such melding of Western and South Asian music had soon found its way into Bollywood film scores, thereby guaranteeing its popularity throughout India.

Classical Indian music nonetheless also remains popular across the country and falls into two categories: Hindustani and Carnatic. The former is specific to the north of India and is a style heavily influenced by the Persian music introduced historically by India's Muslim conquerors. Its most basic ensemble includes the sitar and percussion, the latter in the main being provided by small twin drums known as *tabla*. Although the sitar might be India's best-known musical instrument, few people outside the sub-continent realise that its body is traditionally made from a type of pumpkin.

Although strongly identified with India, the sitar is in reality only one of several stringed instruments; including the *veena* and the *sarod,* widely played in Indian classical and traditional music. In Carnatic music, a genre unique to South India, the *veena* rather than sitar is played and is quite often accompanied by a European stringed instrument; the violin. Be that so, in Carnatic music, the violin is tuned differently and played upright whilst seated on the floor. Actually, all performers in classical Indian music renditions are customarily seated on the floor. Delivering the main rhythm in any Carnatic ensemble is a double-sided *mridangam* drum. Often played in conjunction with the *mridangam* is a *ghatam*, this being a rudimentary percussion instrument resembling an earthenware water pot. Appearances aside, the *ghatam* is purpose made as an instrument using clay reinforced with metal. Although it lacks the tonal range of other drums, the frequently fast rhythmic patterns played on a *ghatam* provide an important contribution to many Carnatic compositions.

One instrument that's favoured in both Hindustani and Carnatic traditions is the sitar-like fretless *tampura.* Played by plucking its four strings, a *tampura* creates the harmonic drone crucial to so much Indian music. Carnatic is the more vocal of the two classical styles, although with both, music is regularly played in a way that emulates the singer's voice. Classical Indian music has a distinctly introspective quality and its component rhythmic patterns, drones and importantly *ragas* (these patterns of notes providing melodic structure) can be quite spellbinding. That said, most of the time during my trip, I heard hits from Bollywood film scores rather than classical music, although it all combined to offer a lively and often loud soundtrack to my travels.

Despite the occasional torrential monsoon rain, Goa proved to be the perfect spot to unwind before returning to Mumbai where Martin and I both had flights to catch. In due course we were back amongst the hordes and honking horns of India's most populous city. The next day as Martin returned to Britain, I was sad to see him go, my only consolation being the prospect of travelling on to the Indian capital Delhi. Nonetheless the pair of us would hook up again back in Britain and fondly reminisce about our adventures at where else; but an Indian restaurant over a curry and a beer.

Soon, I too was making my way to the airport as I shared a taxi with two English girls from the hostel. Now lots of things can delay traffic in India but none as extraordinary as the sight I witnessed that evening. 10 minutes into our journey, the traffic was brought to a sudden halt by a large crowd blocking the road a short way ahead. This hold-up immediately prompted our driver to turn off the engine. I then looked on in astonishment whilst a house-sized image of the elephant-headed god Ganesha was hauled across the road by hundreds of devotees towards the adjacent Chowpatty Beach. There, this clay figure of Ganesha; who is regarded as the remover of obstacles, along with thousands of other smaller ones, would then be ritually immersed into the sea. Being fashioned from clay, these Ganesha images will gradually dissolve and in so doing, symbolically any obstacles facing devotees would disappear with them. After gazing in silence upon this surreal spectacle, all I could do was turn to the girls sat in the back and joke somewhat disbelievingly, 'Did that really just happen?'

It was easy to form the impression that every other day in India was a religious celebration of some sort. The cab driver told me that this event represented the culmination of Ganesh Chaturthi, this the biggest annual festival held in Mumbai. Similar immersion ceremonies are performed all across India and amongst the Hindu diaspora, not only in the sea but in rivers, lakes and pools as well. Also a god of wisdom and intelligence, Ganesha is certainly one of the most popular deities in the Hindu pantheon; why even I had a sandalwood carving of him. To attain such prominence amongst India's multicultural Hindu population was akin to him being one of Jesus' twelve disciples in Christianity. Then again, he did stick out somewhat having the head of the world's largest land animal. Still for a god who supposedly removes obstacles, on this occasion Ganesha literally presented a giant obstruction to our progress to the airport. Without a doubt, this truly amazing spectacle seemed to perfectly encapsulate India's intriguing religious character.

Chapter 9.

I was soon aboard an Air India flight bound for the capital Delhi, a city located in north-central India some 1,000 km from the nearest sea. Flying-even sans champagne- obviously wasn't the cheapest way of reaching Delhi but it took just over two hours rather than two days by bus or even an entire day by rail. During my flight, I continued reading more about this amazing country. By the mid-3rd millennium BCE, the Indus Valley civilisation had settled parts of what is now northwest India. As one of the greatest civilisations of antiquity, it had appreciably advanced the region in terms of urban development, agriculture and trade. Following the decline of the Indus people probably as a result of climatic factors, came the Aryans invasion of North India. Their name might suggest an explanation for all those swastikas I'd seen; however, these tribes were very different to the blonde, blue-eyed myths of Nazism. Originating in Central Asia, the Aryans had introduced the sacred scriptures of Hinduism known as the *Vedas,* dating back to 1200 BCE and compiled over many centuries. Not only had the *Vedas* helped to establish Hinduism in India, they had also outlined the *varnas* caste-system still operating today.

The Aryan settlers, or Indo-Aryans as they came to be known, spoke a Sanskrit language from which Hindi and numerous related north Indian languages are derived. These include Gujarati and Punjabi in the west of the country and Bengali in the east. Urdu is another common Indo-Aryan language of northern India, one which is associated with Islam on the sub-continent. Spoken Urdu is basically a form of Hindi that is influenced by both the Persian language Farsi and Arabic. Urdu differs from Hindi and the other Indo-Aryan languages as it is written in a Persian script rather than a Sanskrit one. The common usage of the similar Urdu and Hindi languages is classed as Hindustani and acts as a *lingua franca* in North India and Pakistan. Of course, it's also the same name given to the classical musical tradition found in North India which-like Hindi Bollywood films- is widely enjoyed in Pakistan too.

All of the Indo-Aryan languages spoken in the north are totally distinct from the Dravidian languages used in Southern India and crucially divide the country in broad linguistic terms. This was why the implementation of Hindi as an official government language had created rancour in the south of country. In fact, such was this resentment that English, the language of their one-time colonial masters, is the preferred *lingua franca* for many in Southern India. English is one of 24 officially recognised languages and as I knew from watching Bollywood films, is often used in conjunction with Hindustani as 'Hinglish'.

The Dravidian speaking people of the south may have pre-dated the arrival of the Indo-Aryans; nonetheless they weren't actually the original inhabitants of the sub-continent. The existence of an isolated Dravidian language that's spoken in the west of modern-day Pakistan, strongly suggested that the Dravidian people had originally migrated to India from that part of West Asia. India's indigenous people are in fact the ancestors of the country's tribal populations referred to as Adivasis, a name roughly meaning 'first people'. The 2011 census recorded over a 100 million Adivasis spread throughout India with their distinct status being officially recognised by the government. Despite all the different historical influences over the sub-continent, the Adivasis have managed to preserve their own unique languages and still observed their own customs. Unfortunately in the past the Adivasis were subjected to persecution and discrimination, although nowadays at least their rights are legally protected under the constitution.

While the first Europeans to have a lasting impact on India were the Portuguese, they had not been the first Europeans to arrive on the sub-continent. Rather that claim went to the ancient Greeks who in 327 BCE, under Alexander the Great had conquered parts of what is nowadays North West India. Five years later, the great general and statesman Chandragupta Maurya overthrew the governors who had been installed by Alexander and founded the Maurya Empire in his name. At its peak in the 3rd century BCE, the Maurya Empire controlled all but the southern part of the sub-continent, it was a formidable achievement and no other power in India would match it for another 1800 years.

With the spread of Islam from the 7th century onwards, Muslim armies from western and central Asia repeatedly attacked North India. For centuries, various Muslim tribes had looted North India rather than settling it, something which did not happen until the foundation of the Delhi Sultanate in 1206. Ruled by a total of five different dynasties, all of these were either Turkic or Afghan in origin; the sultanate survived for more than three centuries being based in Delhi for most of that time. The extent of its territorial control varied, but all five dynasties; who uniquely for India even included a female sovereign amongst their numbers, ruled a large swathe of northern India beyond the actual city itself. The Delhi sultans not only battled indigenous monarchs, but had crucially defeated Mongol invasions of India during the 13th and 14th centuries. In 1526, the conquests of Babur, the warrior founder of the Mughal Empire, eventually brought about the end of the Delhi Sultanate.

The Delhi Sultanate had been significant in establishing Islam in North India with many *Shudras* converting to the religion. Given the enshrined hierarchy existing in the Hindu *varnas* system, the attraction for *Shudras* of Islam's egalitarian message, where all are deemed equal in the eyes of Allah was understandable. A further enduring impact of the sultanate had been the influence of their court language Persian upon the development of the Hindustani language spoken today across North India and Pakistan as a *lingua franca*.

The Mughal emperors who'd then succeeded the Delhi Sultans were also Sunni Muslims. The first of them, Babur, was of Turco-Mongol origin and born in what is today Uzbekistan. The Timurid dynasty from which he was descended were related to in-laws of Mongol emperor Genghis Khan, and the name Mughal, sometimes also spelt Moghul, is derived from this Mongol heritage. In spite of its Mongol linage, the Mughal royal court was essentially Persian in character, it like the Delhi Sultanate's using Persian as an official language. In order to form alliances, Mughal royals later married the daughters of indigenous Rajput rulers, this and other Indian influences on court life leading over time to the emergence of an Indo-Persian Mughal culture. So marriage and personal affiliations had therefore been significant factors in creating this multicultural society.

For most of the Mughal Empire's existence, first Agra and later Delhi were its capitals. By the early 18th century Mughal control of India had reached its zenith under the Emperor Aurangzeb, stretching as it did south as far as Karnataka and westwards from Bengal all the way across modern day North India, into Pakistan and Afghanistan. The administration of this large territory was centralized and operated via a framework of appointed regional governors, each one responsible for a province or *subah*. Whist the Mughal era consolidated Islam across the region, its emperors were tolerant of other religions and many Hindus had held senior positions in Mughal governments. The emperor Akbar even tried to introduce an official new syncretic religion comprising elements of Islam and Hinduism. Ostensibly a well-intentioned attempt to unify his subjects under a common faith, in reality it was more of a religious cult centred on Akbar himself. It remained confined to the royal court and soon dissolved on Akbar's death. As much as any indigenous powers had, the Mughals made a deep impact on the sub-continent, the era between Akbar and his great-grandson Aurangzeb spawning a golden age in literature, architecture and art.

In the wake of Aurangzeb's death, the Mughals grip on power weakened and their empire went into decline. Several factors had precipitated this demise, amongst them military defeats by both an invading Persian army and the emerging Maratha Empire. The Mughals were further undermined by internal feuding within their ruling dynasty, coupled with growing demands for independence from *subah* governors. Another major cause of disintegration was economic, for the high cost of administering and maintaining their empire simply became unsustainable. By the 1780s, their empire was reduced to an area of little more than Delhi itself. Thereafter, nominal Mughal emperors had continued as figurehead monarchs under the suzerainty and protection of first the Maratha Empire, and later on the British. The Mughal Empire managed to endure in name until 1858 when its last monarch was finally ousted by the British. Whatever failings the Mughals may have had, assuredly no other Muslim rulers on the sub-continent had made a mark quite like theirs. The cultural interchange arising from more than three centuries of Mughal involvement in South Asia resulted in Persian influences on many aspects of Indian life. In politics, art, literature, language music, architecture, cuisine, religion and horticulture the Mughal legacy is immense.

The British, who eventually came to control most of the former Mughal Empire, had initially established their presence on the sub-continent in the 17th century. They had arrived to set up trading posts for the East India Company, three of which would eventually become the cities of Kolkata, Chennai and of course Mumbai. In the latter part of the 1680s, the East India Company lost a conflict with Emperor Aurangzeb and was forced to pay considerably large reparations to the Mughals. Nonetheless the Company was later granted a *firman*, this being a decree given by the emperor which conferred trading privileges on the foreigners. Still, irrespective of having Mughal approval to trade there, the Company's economic activities in Bengal had soon provoked resentment from the local ruling nawab. Amongst quite a few other grievances, the Bengali monarch believed that the Company was abusing its trading rights and denying him duties revenue. Such had been his animosity that in 1756 the *nawab's* troops attacked and seized the British base at Calcutta. The Company sent in Colonel Robert Clive whose troops routed the Bengalis at the Battle of Plessey the following year. It was one of the most decisive military engagements in the British conquest of India and, by 1764, the Company had vanquished all opposition in Bengal.

Now in the ascendancy, the East India Company soon acquired legal recognition of its hegemony in Bengal from a weakened Mughal emperor. This marked a critical shift from the Company's purely economic involvement in India, to one of direct political control over a vast swathe of the sub-continent. With Bengal the major region for its commercial enterprises in India, the port of Calcutta soon became the East India Company's centre of power and in 1772, they declared it the capital of British India. In time, through a combination of forming alliances, coercion and military victories, the Company was able to exercise its paramountcy over pretty much the whole of the sub-continent.

Although officially titled the *Honourable* East India Company, as is evident from the MPs in Westminster, describing yourselves as being honourable doesn't necessarily mean that you are. For the Company's vast fortunes stemmed from its monopoly of trade, sharp practice, profiteering, corruption, looting and not least of all large-scale drug smuggling! From the late 18th century onwards, the Company controlled opium production in India and accrued huge profits from its illicit sale to China, where it had been banned due to wide scale addiction. While the opium business may have generated riches for the Company's shareholders, it also pushed countless Chinese into the misery of addiction. Furthermore this trade in opium sparked two wars between Britain and China. At one point, the revenues from opium even funded the Company's purchase of Chinese tea for export to Britain. You could say this was money laundering, a way of washing their profits from a dirty business.

Although commanded by Europeans, the vast army of the East India Company was overwhelmingly comprised of Indian troops known as *sepoys*. In spite of the army's multicultural composition, frequent racist contempt for sepoys from their European officers was one of several grievances behind a mutiny in 1857. There had also been widespread discontent amongst *sepoys* about pay and general conditions of service, in particular the requirement for Indian soldiers to serve abroad. Then of course there had been the notorious rumours that cartridges for a recently issued new model of musket were greased using cow and pig fat, something obviously abhorrent to Hindu or Muslim *sepoys*. The mutiny soon snowballed into a general rebellion against the British, when it spread in northern and central India. Supported by the heads of some princely states including the Mughal emperor in Delhi, the unrest took eighteen months for the British to crush. After they had put down the rebellion the British position in India might have appeared unassailable, even so resistance to their presence would continue only now largely along a more peaceful trajectory.

The crushing of the uprising had marked the end of the Mughal Empire; thereafter the British abolished its monarchy and sent the last emperor into exile. It also spelt the end of power for the East India Company, with control of India afterwards transferred to the British Crown. The rebellion highlighted the Company's failures on the sub-continent and after more than two and a half centuries of trading, in 1874 it was finally dissolved by Parliament. Helpfully for the British government, the apparatus and institutions needed for administering the sub-continent were already in place courtesy of the East India Company, this included everything from a legal and taxation system, to a vast civil service and military. By 1876 Queen Victoria had been proclaimed the Empress of India although real power resided with the Viceroy. It is extraordinary really to think that what had originally started out as a solely private speculative commercial-venture on the sub-continent, would in time become Britain's greatest imperial asset.

India would of course remain a part of the British Empire until 1947, during which period its infrastructure was developed with the British constructing railways, roads and canals. A degree of industrialisation also occurred with the manufacture of textiles, iron and steel. Despite the colonial narrative of a benign Raj that promoted the interests of all of its subjects, for any benefits India may have gained it had remained a subjugated colony and been fully exploited as such. Crucially for Britain's economy India had provided both cheap raw materials plus a huge market for British manufactured goods. For this reason, Gandhi had urged Indians to boycott imported British clothing by instead spinning cotton and producing their own.

Under British rule, Indian agriculture was seriously neglected in the face of an ever-growing population. Sadly this had resulted in several large-scale famines between the mid-nineteenth century and the end of the Raj. At the very height of one severe famine in 1877, the British had nonetheless chosen to lavish great expense on a *durbar*, thereby demonstrating indifference to the suffering of their subjects. Even as late as 1943, failures by the British were responsible for a massive famine in Bengal, in which four million perished. The shameful reality of the colonial era was that, whilst millions starved to death, Britain simultaneously extracted great wealth from the sub-continent.

It's true to say that not all Indians had fared badly under British colonialism, a reality illustrated by the emergence of an educated Indian middle class. One controversial British policy had been the introduction of a Western model of secondary education taught in the medium of English. By the 1830s, dozens of schools had been set up in Bengal which enrolled students on the basis of academic ability not caste. Depending on one's viewpoint these schools had been intended to either indoctrinate or bestow British ideals and culture through their curriculums. For the colonial ruling class it was patently seen as the latter, a way of moulding a workforce of Indian administrators inculcated with the same values and beliefs as themselves. In truth this enterprise amounted to a rejection of indigenous language, education and culture, a natural corollary of the Raj's paternalistic, racist attitude towards the Indian masses. In the colonial mindset the benighted *natives* could best achieve intellectual advancement through European knowledge, this being a mentality which denigrated all things Indian as inferior.

Justifiable though this criticism is, it does not alter the fact that today English remains the medium of instruction in many Indian secondary schools. As English is the modern international business language the ability of large numbers of educated Indians to speak it, is arguably of economic benefit to the country. OF course, along with Hindi, English has been implemented as the official language of government in India, making it like the game of cricket one of the most enduring legacies of the colonial era.

The new Indian middle class which evolved as a result of this British education system were exposed to radical Enlightenment ideas about national liberation. As they began to forge a sense of their own national identity, in 1885, this embryonic nationalism led to the foundation of the Indian National Congress, the first all-India political party. Initially Congress sought only modest reforms but was soon demanding *Swatara* or full self-governance and in time complete independence. As political agitation towards these goals gathered pace, understandably Muslim anxieties had arisen about the implications of a Hindu-dominated Congress, although Congress itself was always a secular party. These apprehensions had brought to prominence the Muslim League, a national party founded in 1906 in order to represent the Muslims who had made up a quarter of the population in British India.

Gandhi led a peaceful campaign of civil disobedience against the British, based upon the principles of *satyagraha*. This had involved strikes, boycotts and protests; although occasionally contrary to Gandhi's wishes there was some violent resistance. In 1919 British reforms brought limited autonomy for India, but by then not even the establishment of an Indian parliament could stem the growing demands for independence from British colonial domination. As the dynamic for independence had intensified, in 1940 hopes for a unified independent India diminished when the Muslim League, under the leadership of Muhammad Ali Jinnah, started lobbying the British for Muslim homelands in East and West Pakistan.

As the British tried to deal with these demands they were by then engaged in a devastating war against Germany and Japan. The Japanese, having defeated the British in Singapore, Malaysia and elsewhere in Southeast Asia, advanced into British-governed Burma on India's eastern border. Prepared to do whatever was necessary to oust the British from India, many Indian nationalists fought alongside the Japanese in Burma and other parts of Asia. Given such sympathies for the Axis powers had existed, perhaps the omnipresence of the swastika in India didn't seem so strange after all. However any collaboration by Indians with Japan was as nothing compared to the phenomenal two and a half million Indians who answered imperial Britain's call to arms during WWII. This massive contribution to the British Empire's war effort was the largest volunteer army ever raised.

The invaluable role played by Indian soldiers who had served in both the World Wars is something often overlooked in Britain. In contemporary India most nationalists would prefer to ignore it given that it undermines the narrative of universal opposition to British rule during that time. In truth the British had for a long time been capable of recruiting large numbers of Indians into their armies. As an example, when the sepoy mutiny broke out in 1857 the East India Company army had been a quarter of a million men strong, the largest standing army in the world at that time. There can be no doubt that British domination over the sub-continent could not have been achieved and maintained without these large armies comprised of mainly Indian troops.

By 1946, Britain much weakened by two world wars and with its empire now in terminal decline, was eager to disengage from the sub-continent. So it was that in August 1947, nearly three and a half centuries after the East India Company first began to trade there, the British finally departed the sub-continent. At the same time the two new sovereign, independent countries of India and Pakistan appeared on the global map, the latter created from the two regions of British India where Muslims had predominated. The partition that created both states was of course accompanied by untold violence which the British must take some responsibility for. Nehru, Gandhi and the leadership of the Congress Party had opposed partition and rightly predicted the death and destruction it would unleash.

In early 1948 'Midnight's Children' sadly lost their father when Mahatma Gandhi was killed by a gunman. The renowned political and spiritual leader, who'd done so much to further the cause of Indian freedom, was assassinated by a Hindu extremist angered at his defence of Muslims. Following the devastation of partition, it was left to the Congress party and first Prime Minister Jawaharlal Nehru to put in place a stable secular socialist democracy. Both industrial and agricultural development became an early priority for India's government as did implementing economic and social reforms.

During the first 45 years of independence, India had adopted a command economy which was planned and controlled by national government. Defined by central planning and state intervention in all spheres of economic life, it had created a massive public sector, restricted imports – hence the one-time ban on Coca Cola and Pepsi – and regulated commerce and business through licences. This form of socialism allowed governments to plan and protect the economy, albeit at the cost of low levels of economic growth. Set against this poor economic performance was an ever-growing population, which by the beginning of the 21st century had almost tripled in size since India gained independence in 1947. With an ineffective state-run economy compounded by huge population growth, this meant that few inroads were made into addressing India's acute poverty.

In 1991, an economic crisis triggered by unsustainable deficits in trade and governmental finances, initiated a major shift in India's economic policies. Thereafter the country started abandoning the protectionist policies of its socialist foundation and introducing market liberalisation. Decades later as the 21st century advances, comprehensive structural reforms have resulted in annual GDP growth rates averaging more than seven percent over the last few years. It's a trend predicted to continue with economic forecasts of between 7-8 percent GDP growth rates in the coming years. This may sound modest until it's compared with the less than 2.5

percent average growth rates in the UK economy during the same period.

In large part credit for this economic growth was attributable to Prime Minister Mohan Singh, who was head of the national government for a decade until 2014. As a gifted economist, Singh had been the consummate leader to preside over this transition from a heavily regulated state-planned economy, to a more free-market model open to foreign investment and operating in the global market. Over half of India's economy is now made up of the service sector and, let's face it; in this day and age your average call centre dealing with UK customers is more likely to be based in Mumbai than Milton Keynes. One successful area of development has been in the hi-tech IT and telecommunications industries with India now even pursuing its own space programme.

With sustained growth has come massive urbanisation as the rural poor move to India's cities in search of work and a better life. On a cautionary note, when overall annual GDP rates are divided by average population figures, the actual yearly per capita income of Indians is less than £1500. In global terms, this puts India right down in the bottom quarter of the world's poorest countries, not that any Westerners travelling in India need economic indicators to realise that poverty remains endemic. The pessimistic bottom line is that India in the 21st century, for all of its laudable economic successes, still has a long way to go towards eradicating the blight of widespread poverty and all the ills associated with it.

In addition to tackling socio-economic challenges, since gaining independence India has had military clashes with neighbouring China and Pakistan. It fought a brief border war with the former in the early 1960s and has taken on the latter in four conflicts. Of these hostilities it was the Indo-Pakistan War of 1971 that was to have the most profound consequences for the sub-continent. It was sparked by the refusal of West Pakistan to share power with its eastern wing, a political crisis that had prompted widespread unrest within East Pakistan. As the situation escalated a Pakistani army comprised almost entirely of soldiers from West Pakistan, had responded with a ruthless campaign of repression against the Bengali people of East Pakistan. The crackdown not only provoked armed resistance; it also drove millions of East Pakistani civilians to seek refuge across the border in India.

Faced with a mass influx of refugees India in turn had instigated attacks against both West and East Pakistan. In East Pakistan, the Indian military having support from the Muslim Bengali populous had soon been able to defeat Pakistani forces. In the wake of this surrender, East Pakistan went on to declare itself the independent country of Bangladesh.

Aside from these conflicts with foreign states, India has suffered its fair share of internal strife, whether political, ethnic or religious in nature. In the post-independence decades, militant separatist movements in the states of Mizoram, Assam, Punjab and Kashmir have all required substantive military interventions to quell them. What's more, civil unrest has frequently blighted the country with even the topic of language inciting riots in the past.

With so many potentially divisive issues for them to confront, both national and state governments have at times struggled to accommodate a multitude of competing demands. In an effort to clamp down on a plethora of political activists from revolutionary communists to far-right Hindu supremacists, Prime Minister Indira Gandhi had declared a State of Emergency in 1973. Alas in 1984, whilst in office, Mrs Gandhi was assassinated. Then Raji, her son and successor, met the same fate in 1991. For all this violence and instability, the country has remained a democracy governed by civilians; it also enjoys a free press and relatively fair elections. By interesting comparison, both Pakistan and Bangladesh had during various stages in the past been ruled by military regimes.

Communal violence remains an underlying problem across India. In the final decade of the 20th century, tensions were stoked by the rise of Hindu nationalism, as the Bharatiya Janata Party (Indian People's Party), came to prominence. Opposed to the secularism of the Indian National Congress, BJP ideology centres wholly upon the values and culture of Hinduism. Whilst the BJP accepts other indigenous religions such as Buddhism, Jainism and Sikhism, they explicitly reject those religions introduced from outside the sub-continent including Islam and Christianity.

In league with other Hindu extremists, members of the BJP had encouraged the 1992 destruction of a mosque in the North Indian town of Ayodhya. The vandals claimed that the mosque had been built on the site of Rama's birthplace. The orchestrated attack was widely televised and sparked communal riots in other parts of the country. Then in 2002, Hindu attacks on Muslims in the north-western state of Gujarat, led to the deaths of over one thousand people, nearly 80 percent of them Muslims. Communal unrest of this scale and intensity is mercifully rare, but sadly as the 21st century progresses India's longstanding propensity for religious violence remains a problem. The truth of the matter is, religious unrest continues because it is driven by an increasingly sectarian political landscape that at times threatens India's very foundation as a secular state.

One figure instrumental in the country's continuing shift away from secularism is Narendra Modi, who has been Prime Minister since 2014. Modi is a native of Gujarat as was Gandhi, however the India Modi and his BJP government want to create is radically different to the one envisioned by the nation's founding father. Slowly but surely the secular nationalism forged by Gandhi and the Congress Party is being supplanted by a new national identity which emphasises Hinduism at its core. Modi is a popular albeit controversial figure who, while serving as the Governor of Gujarat, had been accused of complicity in the 2002 outbreak of religious bloodshed there. In fairness, Modi has been absolved of all such charges and his supporters claim that, far from promoting identity politics, the BJP and Modi appeal to voters as individuals rather than part of any traditional bloc built around religion, ethnicity or caste.

With Modi re-elected as Prime Minister again in 2019, there is no denying the BJP's appeal. With a reported membership of over one hundred million, it is the world's largest democratic political party. In reality, however inclusive the BJP might claim to be, the party's underlying right-wing Hindu nationalist ideology damages India's multicultural polity. At its heart, the BJP advocates values that negate the diverse composition of Indian society in pursuit of a homogenized Hindu one. Given that even Hinduism itself in not a monolith, it seems very difficult to reconcile many BJP objectives with the reality of such a multicultural nation.

Chapter 10.

Arriving in Delhi a taxi ride took me to a cheap place in Paharganj, a fairly central area frequented by many foreign travellers. Unlike Mumbai, Delhi has a long history as an important urban centre and since the 8th century CE, a total of seven cities have existed at different times on the site of the Indian present-day capital. Built around the Yamuna River, nowadays the city is the capital of a predominantly Hindu country, but for many centuries it had of course been a centre of Muslim power for the Delhi Sultanate and Mughal Empire. The British took control of the city after the 1857 uprising and in 1931 relocated their Indian capital from Calcutta to the more centrally positioned Delhi.

The first place beyond Paharganj I checked out was the Mughal-era Old Delhi. Dating from the mid-17th century it had been the last of the seven historical cities constructed around the capital. Old Delhi had been built as a walled citadel by the Emperor Shah Jahan when the Mughals moved their capital from Agra to Delhi. Amongst its remarkable buildings sits the *Jama Masjid* or 'Friday Mosque', a quite outstanding example of Mughal architecture and craftsmanship. Built over a twelve-year period using both white marble and red sandstone, the *Jama Masjid* opened in 1656. If the last mosque I'd visited near Kovalam had been deserted, the same could not be said for this vast structure which covers an area of over 1,200 square metres.

With congregations of 25,000 on a Friday filling the courtyard, it is the city's largest mosque. The building boasts an impressive facade having a grand central portal with five symmetric cusped arches on either side, plus forty metre-high minarets at both ends. Topping the mosque and contributing to its beauty are three large white marble onion-shaped domes. Huge and busy as the *Jama Masjid* is, when compared to the Hindu temples I had visited it had a noticeably quieter more church-like atmosphere about it. Such a vast mosque is a vivid reminder of Delhi's-and India's- vast Muslim population. Indeed a third of the world's Muslims live in South Asia with India alone home to over ten percent of the global Islamic population. As most Westerners understandably equate India with Hinduism, it comes as a surprise therefore to realise the significance of Islam on the country. Even in the Dravidian south I'd seen no shortage of mosques, and the muezzin call to prayer, was as familiar a sound as was any temple or church bells ringing. From my visit, I now understood to what extent Muslims form a vital component of India's multi-culturalism, and have done for a very long time. Unfortunately, despite some thirteen centuries of cultural integration between India's Hindus and Muslims, tensions between the two can still arise. For the most part of course these divisions are fermented for political motives, but it remains a sad indictment of modern India nonetheless.

A short way from the mosque is another Old Delhi landmark I visited in the form of the mighty Red Fort or *Lal Qila*. It's so named from the deep-red sandstone used in its construction, and was the former palace of the Mughal emperors. With their turrets and bastions, the massive ramparts enclosing this citadel extend for over two kilometres above a dry moat once fed by the Yamuna River. Formidable as these fort's defences were, they had been breached by Persian, Hindu and Sikh forces at different points in history.

Within the mighty walls of the Red Fort and set amongst lawned gardens I saw the arched and domed palaces and pavilions of the onetime Mughal royal court. Most were built from white marble, including the *Diwan-i-Khas*, a hall in which the emperors had once conducted private audiences. This majestic pavilion in particular stood out having rows of scalloped-arches, which along with their pillars are ornately decorated and inlaid with gold, amber and jade.

In the centre of the *Diwan-i-Khas* I gazed at a marble pedestal which had once housed the Peacock Throne. Evidently this had been a priceless marble and gold Mughal work of art encrusted with jewels. The throne had been carted off as booty by Persian raiders in 1739, however by a historical turn of events its most famous diamond the *Koh-i-Noor* ended up in the British crown jewels. Given the Indian origins of the *Koh-i-Noor* and other British crown jewels, Disraeli's famous pronouncement that India had been the *"jewel in the Crown"* of the British Empire struck me as ironically fitting!

Despite its name, the city's oldest structures are not located in Old Delhi. Instead these can be found at Mehrauli, this a twenty-minute taxi ride south of Paharganj and my next destination. This designated archaeological park had been the site of one of Delhi's seven historical cities. Seen there are the ruins of the *Quwwat-ul-Islam* Mosque dating from the early 13th century. The mosque had been built with material salvaged from demolished Jain and Hindu temples. Although the mosque itself no longer stood, its gateways and a minaret tower remain intact, the latter naturally dominating the skyline. The minaret is the foremost attraction for those visiting Mehrauli, being not only the oldest in North India, but at 72.5 metres in height, also the tallest in the whole country. Known as the *Qutb Minar,* as with the mosque it had once served, construction of the tower started during the reign of the first Delhi Sultan Qutb-ud-din Aibak, founder of the Mamluk dynasty.

Besides its conventional use as an elevated platform from which a *muezzin* called the faithful to prayer, the *Qutb Minar* was also originally intended as a monument to Aibak's victory over a Hindu monarch, although he never lived to see its completion. Finished by his successor in 1230, it's an impressive tapering structure built predominantly from red sandstone bricks. White marble cladding was added later to the upper section after it had been damaged by lightning. Over 14 metres in diameter at the base, the exterior of the huge structure has both cylindrical and angular fluting and contains decorative bands of carved brickwork depicting Quranic inscriptions and floral motifs. Similar ornate carvings adorn the corbels, these supporting four balconies which ring the tower, the highest of these reached via some 379 steps inside. Sadly, public access to the interior wasn't allowed, although sadder still was the reason for this closure. In 1981 a blackout due to a power failure had caused hundreds of visitors inside the *Minar* to panic. Many of them thought that the tower itself was collapsing and, in the stampede that followed forty-five people were killed and a couple of dozen injured. Ironically, far from falling down the *Qutb Minar* has managed to survive the ravages of time and nature, including earthquakes, which was more than could be said for the mosque itself.

Positioned very close to the minaret is the domed Alai-Darwaza gateway, a southern entrance to the mosque added during the reign of Alauddin Khilji in 1311, a ruler of the Delhi Sultanate's 2nd dynasty. Standing around eighteen metres high, this square portal has a central arch in each of its thick walls, these archways having two perforated lattice windows on either side at the lower level. While its upper section is badly worn, the rest of the structure is ornamented with contrasting white marble and red sandstone, all carved with delightful lace-like floral tendrils, geometrical patterns and intricate Islamic calligraphy. This, together with the symmetry and proportion of the *Alai-Darwaza*, were certainly aesthetically pleasing and even its dome, an architectural feature we now take for granted, was one of the first successful examples built on the sub-continent.

In addition to building the gateway and enlarging the *Quwwat-ul-Islam* Mosque itself, Sultan Khilji also began building his own mighty victory tower only a short way north of the *Qutb Minar*. In order not to be upstaged by Aibak, this one, called the *Alai Minar*, was intended to be double the height of the *Qutb Minar*. It was certainly an ambitious project and the first storey was completed before the sultan's death in 1316. After then, his successors had abandoned the project. Today the base of the tower is basically a chunk of rubble, albeit a large one standing almost 25 metres high and with a circumference of over 77.5 metres. Badly weathered over the centuries, now it could be considered little more than an unfinished monument to the vanity of a bygone ruler.

Elsewhere on the Mehrauli archaeological site are the remains of a former religious school or *madrasa*, also built by Alauddin and containing his tomb. Other tombs around the complex include that of Mamluk Sultan Iltumish who'd died in 1236. Surrounding his white marble tomb is a square mausoleum of red sandstone with archways on three of its sides. Even though the mausoleum's roof is missing and its exterior walls are fairly plain, the archways and interior of the building are superbly detailed with a mixture of Islamic script and various geometrical and Arabesque patterns. From an architectural viewpoint the tomb, along with the other various structures located around the complex, are significant, even if some of them are now merely ruins. Here are the earliest examples of Turkic, Persian and Afghan architecture being used on the sub-continent. Furthermore, many of the designs and patterns decorating them are not Indian but Islamic. This melding of Islamic and indigenous building features marked the beginning of Indo-Islamic architecture, a style which would peak under the Mughal emperors.

Having explored parts of Old Delhi having a look around New Delhi was an obvious thing for me to do next. New Delhi applies specifically to that part of the city designed and built by the British and inaugurated as India's capital in 1931. Primarily the design of English architects Edwin Lutyens and Herbert Baker, it consists of the business and commercial-centre around Connaught Place and the larger governmental district to its south. I walked southeast from Paharganj to Connaught Place which was named in honour of Queen Victoria's son Arthur, the Duke of Connaught. I couldn't help thinking about the curious aptness of this name given that Connaught is a province of Ireland, itself a former British colony like India. The layout of Connaught Place is certainly magnificent, having a park at its centre and being ringed by three concentric circular roads, the innermost of these possessing a further eight roads radiating out from it. The inner circle itself is lined with neat Georgian style two-storey white buildings all having colonnaded verandas, these housing various shops and offices.

Unusually, the roads that run off the inner circle are numbered rather than named with the areas between them being divided into lettered sections. Connaught Place is the busy heart of the new city containing an array of restaurants, hotels, cinemas, banks and of course shops. I have to say that besides being newer than Old Delhi, the space and vast scale of Connaught Place make it an altogether less claustrophobic environment to walk around.

From the southern half of the outer circular road at Connaught Place, five broad thoroughfares link the rest of the new city. One of these avenues follows a south-westerly axis leading towards a large commemorative arch designed by Lutyens and called India Gate. Whereas another British-built archway I had recently seen in Mumbai commemorated an imperial visit, this one serves as a cenotaph to those Indian troops killed fighting for Britain in World War I and during the 1919 Anglo-Afghan War. Standing over forty metres high and about nine metres in width, India Gate is both an impressive memorial and a prominent landmark in New Delhi.

Walking under the India Gate archway, I noticed that a further monument had been added honouring those Indian forces killed since independence. Mounted on a three-tier pedestal and carved from black marble, this depicts an inverted rifle sticking up from a plinth with a helmet resting on its stock. Inscribed in Hindi on the four sides of the pedestal beneath are the simple words 'Immortal Soldier', whilst the tier below that has an urn at each corner, one of which burns permanently, the others lit only on certain special occasions. For all its simplicity the carved rifle and helmet design is thought provoking, and to me as poignant as the enormous war memorial under which it sits.

The hexagonal traffic roundabout circumnavigating India Gate has a total of eleven roads coming off it. Besides the one linking Connaught Place, these radiating avenues connect government and judiciary buildings, as well as several residential zones for government employees. The thoroughfares are wide, straight and tree-lined and pre-eminent among them is the Rajpath, this road extending westwards from India Gate for over two kilometres. It's a striking boulevard which has canals running parallel along each side and is flanked by trees and lawned gardens. As I walked along the grandiose Rajpath it was easy to see why the avenue serves as the capital's ceremonial mall for parades on state occasions.

Barely visible from India Gate at the time of my visit on account of the haze, the official residence of India's president stands at the opposite end of the Rajpath. Called the Rashtrapati Bhavan, it was originally constructed as a palace for the British Viceroys and has to be New Delhi's grandest building. Located atop a small hill, this absolutely enormous edifice covers more than 18,000 sq metres in area. Quite honestly its size would have been worthy of any British monarch themselves, never mind their chief representative in India the Viceroy. Little wonder then that to date it remains the largest residence of any head of state in the world.

Designed by Lutyens, the vast mansion had been constructed using red sandstone at the base and buff coloured sandstone on its upper part. Large steps lead up to the palatial front which is adorned with columns, whilst crowning the vast structure is a 55-metre high copper dome. Built as a symbol of imperial power, it is unquestionably a spectacular building, one intended to engender a sense of insignificance in the beholder.

In front of the huge Rashtrapati Bhavan and separating it from the Rajpath lays a vast square dominated by a central 145-meter high column. Situated on the north and south sides of the square are two further magnificent edifices in the shape of the identical Secretariat buildings. As with the adjacent presidential residence, they too were constructed using a combination of both cream and red coloured sandstone, which seems to work to greater effect on the aesthetics of these two buildings.

With numerous wings having columned balconies on their ends and both buildings topped by a central dome, the twin Secretariat blocks like the nearby imposing Rashtrapati Bhavan are essentially Neo-Baroque in their design. Although minimal in comparison to Indo-Saracenic architecture, these buildings do incorporate some Indian features, the most obvious being the decorative addition of small and domed pavilion-like structures known as *charismata* on the roofs

A short distance beyond the north Secretarial block sits yet another architectural wonder of the new city in the shape of the country's Parliament House. Known as the San sad Bhavan it is an enormous circular structure and, in keeping with the other grand buildings of New Delhi, has also been constructed from a mix of red and cream coloured sandstone. The dimensions of the San sad Bhavan are extraordinary its outer columned veranda boasting a whopping half-kilometre circumference and encircling an area of 24,000 square metres. The gigantic San sad Bhavan was purposely designed by Lutyens and Baker to house an Indian assembly after the British reforms of 1919 had granted the Indians a degree of self-governance. Inside the Sansad Bhavan, a circular, domed hall forms the hub around which are the three semi-circular chambers built to accommodate the three branches of this early parliament. The chamber which was once used by representatives of India's princely state states is today a library, whereas the, *Rajya Sabha* upper house and *Lok Sabha* lower house of India's Parliament still convene respectively in the other two.

Though the British had plundered and exploited India, as a small token of recompense they had bequeathed this rather astonishing cityscape. It had come complete with parks, gardens, ornamental ponds, fountains and broad tree-lined avenues: I guess the perfect backdrop for awe-inspiring architecture. What particularly wowed me about New Delhi was the sheer scale of it all, this vastness punctuated by its stark contrast to the tight confines of the Mogul era old city. As I had already seen the Mogul Empire also left some commanding monuments to their imperial power, nevertheless in New Delhi the British had done so on a much grander-scale. The most remarkable thing of all about the new city had to be that for all its splendour; and presumable expense, it had only served as the capital of British India for *sixteen* years. This quite short duration illustrated how rapidly empires could fall into decline. In the case of imperial Britain, this had largely been a consequence of fighting a financially crippling Second World War.

Chapter 11.

There's certainly no shortage of restaurants in the Paharganj area, although Connaught Place in the new city is only a ten-minute taxi ride away and has a much greater choice. There, can be found Chinese eateries, Middle Eastern restaurants, pizzerias, a Wimpy burger diner and a German bakery. For all that I knew, there was possibly even a delicatessen to be found there... a *Delhi deli* so to speak!

With a chance to eat non-Indian food for a change I decided to try the Wimpy, opting for a lamb burger as perhaps unsurprisingly beef ones were off the menu. Seeing how Wimpy are a Western chain one trusted that they had high standards. In this instance such expectation proved to be misplaced as the ensuing bouts of diarrhoea I suffered revealed. It wasn't the sole time in India when food resulted in me getting an upset stomach, but this time, the irony of a Western franchise being responsible did not escape me. In fairness, following this experience if I ever ate a dodgy meal in a British curry house, perhaps I might be a bit more forgiving.

Beef burgers may well be a rarity in India but the cows they are produced from certainly are not. There's probably no animal more associated with India and the breed mostly seen, have humps and long, downward pointing ears. The bottom line is, these generally scrawny-looking bovines wander unrestrained amongst the traffic and pedestrians throughout much of India, including in the capital city. I took a picture of one cow stood on the forecourt of a Delhi petrol station, an image surely unimaginable in Britain or probably anywhere else for that matter.

Hindus consider cows to be sacred creatures and, whilst they do not worship them as such, they are highly regarded symbolising amongst other things; the earth and strength, giving and wealth. Vishnu in his incarnation as Krishna is also identified as the deity Govinda, a name meaning one who protects cows. As I'd seen in Mysuru, Shiva too had bovine connections being associated with the bull Nandi. Another of his avatars is an ox. Hindus do not eat cow meat but they do consume dairy products and farmers often use cattle for ploughing land. After milk, another important cow product is its dung which is commonly used across rural India as both a fertilizer and a fuel. When burnt, the smoke produced by dried cow dung also has the added benefit of acting as a mosquito repellent. Cow dung apparently possesses disinfectant properties too, although personally I'd think twice about mopping the floor with any.

High up on the list of mind-boggling things I saw in India was a cow hospital! Here injured or diseased cattle were able to receive free treatment in a country where millions of humans lacked any adequate access to basic medical services. Apparently many of the animals treated become ill after digesting plastic as they forage around rubbish dumps. Unbelievably I read how cow ambulances could be phoned on toll free numbers, these vehicles staffed by vets and 'animal paramedics', the latter I suspect just a fancy job title for a veterinary assistant. There are a number of these cow hospitals scattered across this part of North India nicknamed the 'cow belt', this comprised of several states deemed the country's Hindu heartland. The slaughter of cattle is illegal in these states and anyone convicted of this offence faces a hefty gaol sentence.

There have even been some cases of Hindu mobs killing those accused of slaughtering cows, the victims usually non-Hindus. It is a perplexing mindset indeed which regards killing an animal for meat as a crime, whereas murdering someone who commits such a crime, is considered justifiable. Also found across North India are sanctuaries known as *goshalas* where cows and oxen can end out their days in care. I read somewhere too that 'stray and homeless cattle' are sometimes supported by temples, which appears to be equally bizarre given the massive amount of homeless people left unsupported on the streets. Maybe most astonishingly of all, cows in India enjoy full legal protection in quite a number of states and although they are found wandering on the busiest of city streets, accidently killing one in a road accident is punishable by gaol.

Of course the possession of a small amount of *charas* can also get you locked up in India and yet oddly *bhang*, a substance made from marijuana leaves is anomalously legal in most of the country. Sold in government licensed shops, *bhang* is typically ingested in foodstuffs such as *pakoras* and sweets or in milk and drinks like *lassi*. I guess it was inevitable that at some point I'd be tempted to try some which I did one night together with half a dozen others at the hotel in Delhi.

We all chipped in to obtain some edible paste rolled into small balls known as *bhang goli*. It didn't taste particularly nice but let's be honest none of us were exactly eating the stuff for its culinary properties. Then over a few beers we sat chatting around a table on the rooftop terrace as we waited for the *bhang* to take effect. After perhaps an hour or so, during what had thus far been a fairly lucid flow of conversation, I suddenly tried to speak only to find that I was totally unable to! The silent pause became permanent as I was rendered incapable of talking. Hence, I sat there amongst company, for all intents and purposes in a semi-comatose state. It is difficult to explain the sensation exactly but I felt a combination of being extremely high and heavily sedated at the same time. I would like to be able to say that whilst in a state of transcendental enlightenment, Vishnu entered my consciousness and I became one with the eternal Hindu cosmos. After all, taking *bhang* assists Hindus in connecting with the gods so why not me? Sadly if this did happen, I was far too out of my head to either realise or indeed remember it. I can only hope that in my *self-induced* stupor I didn't start dribbling at any point. It was one thing smoking *charas* and feeling relaxed but bhang certainly proved to be a lot more potent.

I've no idea how much longer I stayed up on the rooftop, but at some juncture during the night I had managed to navigate my way downstairs and to the comfort of my bed. Later the next morning, feeling decidedly rough and whilst delicately exiting my room, I bumped into one of the women who had shared the *bhang* the previous night. Having hardly been riveting company by the end of the evening, I awkwardly confessed to her about my inability to speak and general inertia once the stuff had kicked in. At this admission she started laughing aloud, before then explaining how she too had found herself unable to speak due to the *bhang*. Hearing this, I was relieved to learn that it wasn't only me who ended up in a vegetative state. Basically, I had been so out of it, I simply did not realise how wrecked everyone else had also been. Considering the *bhang* only cost about the same price as a bottle of beer and had succeeded in getting all of us utterly wasted, it was definitely great value for money.

Eating *bhang* isn't a daily event but obviously eating food is. One night as I dined in a Delhi restaurant, I got chatting with an elderly chap who turned out to be fascinating company. He told me how his father had often complained about the decline in standards after the country gained its independence. His father, who had evidently been in business, told him, 'When the British were here, if you made an appointment for 11.00 am, then the other person would always arrive promptly at the arranged time. Nowadays, if you make an appointment for say 11.00 o'clock, then the person you're meeting might turn up at 11.30, 12 o'clock or 12.30... if you are lucky!' According to the man's father, the British had been 'gentlemen' and since they'd left, values in general, but especially in the world of commerce had gone downhill.

One might think that ridding his country of the yoke of colonial oppression was hardly a cause for lamentation, even if people had become tardier as a result. However, the sentiment expressed by his father became easier to fathom when the man went on to explain how he and his family were Anglo-Indian. In other words his grandfather had been English, from Manchester in fact. As if to confirm this antecedence he then introduced himself as Richard rather than the name Reyansh or Rajesh I might have expected. It stood to reason that following over three hundred years of British involvement on the sub-continent, that there are many people in India of mixed Indian and British heritage like Richard.

Those who came to be identified as Anglo-Indians are in fact a well-known group within Indian society and their history had been very much one of changing fortunes. Their greatest concentration was perhaps understandably in those early British trading centres of Madras, Bombay and particularly Calcutta, these now renamed Chennai, Mumbai and Kolkata. During the earlier periods of British settlement, very few women from Britain had ventured to India meaning men employed by the East India Company would marry local women and raise families in India. The Company even went as far as to encourage such unions by offering a payment of gold whenever children were born. In marked contrast to later stages of colonial rule, there was no segregation or racism at this time, to the point that married settlers often assimilated completely into the local way of life, adopting Indian clothes and customs. These

East India Company men came to be nicknamed 'White Mughals'. By the end of the 18th century British apprehensions regarding this Eurasian population, as they were called, resulted in the Company banning their employment. Prompting this action were concerns about the role played by mixed race inhabitants in the French run colony of Haiti, who had led a successful slave revolt there.

Notwithstanding these strictures, with ever greater numbers of men from Britain arriving in India as members of the military, civil servants or engineers they had continued to marry Indian women thereby increasing both the size and distribution of this Eurasian population. In due course, people of mixed British and South Asian background could be found across British India, including in those territories which subsequently became Pakistan and Bangladesh. In neighbouring Burma, which was constitutionally part of British India up until 1935, a sizable Anglo-Burmese community had also evolved. It was only much later, when more women from Britain began to arrive in colonial India that these interracial marriages came to be frowned upon by the British, who had then started to distance themselves from the Indo-Britons, as they had also been called.

Despite being ostracised by the white ruling class, the Eurasian community had assuredly identified itself as British, as much so as the roast beef they ate for Sunday lunch. Their complexions may have revealed Tamil, Koli, Bengali and other Indian ancestry, but they nonetheless spoke English, had English names and dressed in Western clothes, practiced Christianity and liked a gin and tonic whilst attending the horse races or cricket matches. As mentioned previously, the Anglo-Indians- as they became officially named in 1911- liked to spice up their leftovers from a Sunday roast and were partial to mulligatawny soup. Still these culinary adaptations aside, their mindset had been decidedly British. What's more, as is common convention on the sub-continent they had married only within their own community. They had also set up local groups to promote Anglo-Indian interests including one in Bengal in 1876 which developed into the All-India Anglo-Indian Association, an organisation that remains active today. Whilst those with cultural affiliations to Britain constituted the majority of India's mixed race population, there were others with Portuguese, Dutch and French heritage.

Whatever disdain the British may have had towards the Anglo-Indians, their loyalty to the empire had been beyond reproach. As such, after the 1857 rebellion they became entrusted with jobs in the communication networks which were vital for administering British India, working on the railways and telegraph, customs and postal services. In particular, the fast-developing railways essential for the expanding colonial economy, were dominated by Anglo-Indians. So much so that their community were often dubbed the 'railway people'.

Understandably the British preference for allocating these jobs to Anglo-Indians created resentment amongst other Indians, who viewed their community as being very much part of the colonial establishment. Thus, the Anglo-Indians held an unusual position in colonial society, experiencing the dichotomy of having been both discriminated against by the British, but advantaged too relative to the majority of colonial subjects.

By the time the British departed in 1947 there was an estimated 200,000-300,000 Anglo-Indians, a figure based upon the census of 1931, the last to gather such information. Coincidentally, none of their community was offered automatic residency rights in Britain, despite their ancestral links to the 'motherland'. The early post-independence years proved difficult for their community, as the guaranteed railway, postal and customs jobs they had enjoyed for generations ended. Later, employment chances diminished even further for the English-speaking Anglo-Indians when Hindi became the primary language of Indian bureaucracy. So being faced with both uncertainty and a general mistrust from the wider society fostered during the days of the Raj, many Anglo-Indians decided to emigrate to Britain and other Commonwealth countries such as Australia and Canada, this contributing further to the dislocation of their community.

As had been the case since British reforms in the post-World War I decades, under the Indian Constitution those with any male ancestors of European origin are recognised as a distinct group, and are accordingly given political representation. George Baker, Ingrid Mcleod, Denzil B Atkinson and Neil O'Brien don't sound like names you'd readily expect to hear in the Indian Parliament, yet all of them have been members of the *Lok Sabha* representing the country's Anglo-Indian population. Unlike other constitutionally recognised minorities in India, the Anglo-Indians have no territory where they are preponderant, instead spread across the country from Delhi to Bengaluru and from Mumbai to Kolkata. There had been several historical efforts from members of their community to set up Anglo-Indian colonies in India, and even one plan after independence to establish an Anglo-Indian homeland in British New Guinea of all places, but none of these were ever realised. Due to their dispersed nature, if no Anglo-Indians are elected into the national Parliament, then the President is able to nominate two members of their community to the *Lok Sabha* to give them a political voice. Similar provisions exist for the state legislatures where one Anglo-Indian representative can be appointed by the state Governor if none already exist. When you think about it, such enshrined rights appear a generous political concession to a relatively small minority, one who are, after all, partly descended from the former colonial occupiers of India.

Although not a unique religious group like India's Parsis or Jews, similarly Anglo-Indians too cannot be visibly distinguished from most other Indians. As I could see from Richard, even lighter skin pigmentation wasn't necessarily a feature of their community. At any rate, this can vary immensely in Indians, from very dark skin to light. Nor were they the only Christians in India, with Kerala and Goa as I knew being home to much older Christian communities. The exact size of India's remaining Anglo-Indian population is not known as such details are no longer recorded in census statistics. Several estimates put the figure at around 150,000 with Chennai and Kolkata being home to the largest number. One thing widely acknowledged is that since independence India's Anglo-Indians have grown steadily less Anglicised. Even marriage outside of their own community is no longer that rare, as they become ever more subsumed into broader Indian society. This gradual integration means the differences between Anglo-Indians and other English-speaking Indians is ever more blurred, with all sharing common customs, dress and values. Realistically, this greater assimilation in both India itself and amongst the diaspora could erase the Anglo-

Indian sense of identity completely in the not too distant future. Still whatever happens long-term, as first-hand memories of the British-era slowly fade away, Richard's community remains a living link to the country's colonial past. In short, this intriguing minority represent the first, and the oldest, legacy of British settlement in India.

Chapter 12.

For all Delhi's historical architecture and manic appeal, the time came for me to move on. Martin had recommended that I visit the desert state of Rajasthan, so with this plan in mind I entered a travel agency in Paharganj to inquire about a bus ticket there. As I sat there waiting for the agent to finish a phone call, a big poster depicting snow-capped mountains and a beautiful lake caught my eye. This was the kind of stunning scenery that lures visitors and it advertised India's most northerly state of Jammu and Kashmir.

When the agent finished his call, I straight away pointed to the poster commenting how I would love to go there. 'No problem,' he responded with a beaming smile, 'we can arrange it for you'. I hesitated at his offer being aware that a conflict had been ongoing in Kashmir for a number of years. Prudently voicing my concerns to the agent, he insisted that any fighting was strictly between the Indian army and militants and as such there was no danger posed to tourists. Satisfied at his reassurance, I impulsively purchased a bus ticket for the Kashmiri capital city of Srinagar. In addition, as houseboats are a popular type of accommodation on several lakes around Srinagar, the agent booked me on one, explaining that he would contact the owner to meet my bus on arrival.

The next day I boarded a bus in Old Delhi, the station suitably located close to Kashmiri Gate. Four other Westerners were on the same bus and I was sat next to a chap named James from East Sussex. It was a relief to have someone to talk with for the 800km journey ahead. Heading north-westerly it took around half a day passing through the states of Haryana and Punjab before arriving in Jammu. This historic city doubtless has its attractions, but we were there just to change buses, only having enough time to eat something and pick up a copy of the English language *Kashmiri Times* newspaper to peruse.

I was somewhat alarmed to see the paper's headlines reporting that a bomb had gone off at this very same bus station only the day before. Reportedly Kashmiri terrorists were behind the attack which had killed seven people and wounded dozens. In case the text alone didn't convey the full horror of the explosion, a graphic photo showed a policeman at the scene holding a severed human head by its hair. The features of the face were sufficiently distinct that anyone who knew the decapitated victim would be able to recognise him. That such a gruesome image would be printed in a newspaper was pretty startling and a far cry from the somewhat more sanitised editorial policies of the Western media. With the newspaper report providing a frightening realisation of the gravity of the Kashmir dispute, James and I looked warily at each other. This indiscriminate bombing in a public bus station, also provided the first indication that the agent in Delhi might have downplayed any risk in visiting.

The violence in Jammu and Kashmir was nothing new. Starting in the late 1880s, the conflict had pitched the Indian state against several militant groups, most of them armed, trained and funded by neighbouring Pakistan. The uprising was in fact firmly rooted in the partition of the sub-continent in 1947. Uniquely, for an Indian state Jammu and Kashmir contains a Muslim majority population, much as it had done when a princely state before independence. Besides their shared religion, the inhabitants share a common language, Kashmiri, which along with Urdu is an official language there. Under the terms of the 1947 partition, Kashmir with its overwhelmingly Muslim demographic should in theory have been ceded to West Pakistan. Be that as it may, the Hindu *maharajah;* a member of the Dogra dynasty, procrastinated in the desperate hope that he might somehow retain his power in an independent Kashmir. Matters had come to a head when an invasion by Pathan tribesmen from the newly formed Pakistan forced the *maharajah* to plead for Indian military assistance. Congress agreed to help but only on the condition that his princely state joined the Indian Union, which the *maharaja* promptly consented to. By so doing he not only initiated the first Indo-Pakistan war, but over the longer term sowed the seeds of discontent amongst the Muslim majority of this now Indian state.

By the time hostilities between the two new countries ceased in 1949, India was in control of the central and southern parts of the former princely state, an area which includes the eastern Ladakh plateau bordering China. Pakistan possessed the smaller northern regions of the former state plus a 400km long strip in South West Kashmir, this tract of land proclaimed Free or *Azad* Kashmir by the

Pakistanis. Ever since this division, both countries have continued to assert their sovereignty over the entire territory once governed by the Dogra *maharajahs*. In recognition of its Muslim majority and the somewhat coerced circumstances of Kashmir's accession to India, the state was granted special status under the country's constitution, giving it considerable autonomy and uniquely within the Indian Union even its own constitution.

China too had territorial claims in Kashmir and, during the late 1950s, occupied the north-eastern Aksai Chin region, an area also claimed by India. In 1962, rising tensions between India and China over disputed boundaries led to a brief border war. Outnumbered Indian forces had been quickly defeated and Aksai Chin became a permanent part of China.

Enmity between India and Pakistan over Kashmir led to war for a second time in 1965, this ending inconclusively with a ceasefire. After the 1971 third Indo-Pakistan War, the ceasefire line known as the Line of Control, became the accepted de facto border by both sides. In 1999, with India and Pakistan by then both nuclear powers, a fourth war erupted between the two after Pakistani troops disguised as militants infiltrated Indian-controlled territory in the Kargil region of Kashmir. This conflict had ended in defeat for Pakistan when, after almost three months of fierce fighting, the Indian army retook the seized territory. Crucially, by the time of the 1999 Kargil War, Kashmir was no longer a struggle involving solely the Indian and Pakistani military. By then, over a decade of internal violence within Indian-administered Kashmir had seen a broader conflict develop, one where the police and military faced Kashmiri militants and a defiant radicalised civilian population.

Over the years, the UN and Pakistan have repeatedly called for a plebiscite to be held in Indian-administered Kashmir, one which would allow its inhabitants to decide which country should govern them. India rejects this demand and has in the past attempted to legitimise its sovereignty over the troubled Kashmir by conceding greater autonomy to its legislature. Alas neither this nor any other reforms have brought stability, as political corruption together with allegations of electoral fraud further fuelled resentment and insurgency in the state. Moreover, the situation has now grown more complex as, rather than become a part of Pakistan; many Kashmiris now wanted their independence from both countries.

Unrest in Jammu and Kashmir continues to this day and the two countries came close to war once again in early 2019. Tensions escalated after a suicide bomber killed 42 Indian troops in Kashmir with the BJP government in Delhi claiming that Pakistani military intelligence were behind the attack. Such incidents reiterated the fact that a permanent settlement to the problem didn't appear to be on the horizon despite repeated diplomatic efforts. It also demonstrated that after decades of wars plus scores of border clashes and stand-offs along the Line of Control, there was little realistic chance of a military resolution to this inveterate dispute between the two adversaries.

Following the 2019 attack, India's Prime Minister Modi and the BJP government took the controversial step of revoking the state's special status given by the Indian Constitution. Furthermore, the eastern region of Ladakh was split from Jammu and Kashmir, with both now becoming Union Territories rather than constituents of a single autonomous state. India's Union Territories are controlled by Delhi and have less autonomy than the country's 29 states. The BJP government rationalised these drastic measures by claiming that Kashmir's special status within the country had in fact only served to exacerbate divisions, encourage corruption and slow economic development. With Kashmir's autonomy already being reduced in recent years, in practical terms Modi's constitutional changes were largely symbolic and had very little impact on the everyday political administration of Jammu and Kashmir. Further to this, the Tibetan Buddhist population of Ladakh is one of India's most visibly recognisable ethnic minorities, so creating a separate political entity from the region was not an unreasonable move by the Modi government.

For most in Kashmir their real concern relates to the ending of a centuries-old ban on non-Kashmiris buying land or property there. Fears of a land-grab and large-scale settlement by non-Kashmiris have led to comparisons being made with Jewish settlement of Palestinian territories. Modi's attempts to fully integrate troubled Kashmir into a Hinduized vision of India are likely to radicalise a new generation of Kashmiris and perpetuate violent unrest there.

The reality is the people of Kashmir possess a particularly strong sense of separate identity from the rest of the country, a fact that no amount of government legislation or right-wing Hindu zealotry can alter. As the state now enters a new phase in its ever-fraught relationship with India one thing is certain: the security forces that have been stationed there for decades won't be leaving any time soon.

Our bus eventually entered the Kashmir Valley which runs for more than 130 kilometres through the Himalayas. This part of the trip was slow and arduous as our bus now proceeded along an ever more mountainous highway... with the emphasis being on *high*. As we gradually gained altitude, I could see the rivers cutting their way through the valleys down below getting smaller and smaller. Somewhat unnervingly, I also couldn't help noticing the occasional truck or bus wreck littered about the valley below, a forthright reminder of just how perilous the road could be.

The scenery was undeniably spectacular though, which made it difficult to understand why some seven-metre high, red lettering advertising 'Thums Up' had been painted across one rock face. To call this ad tacky and obtrusive was an understatement spoiling as it did the scenic beauty of the surrounding landscape. I guess this blatant disregard for the natural environment just went to show that advertising in India, much like newspaper reporting, appears to have few constraints on it.

Once into the Kashmir Valley, where 97 percent of the populous are Muslim, I noticed how the security became visibly tighter with numerous army checkpoints, bunkers and convoys along the road. Some reports claim that India had deployed upwards of 600,000 troops in this troubled region, a phenomenal number in a state which had an estimated eight million inhabitants back when the unrest had started. Whatever its current numbers are, the military presence in Kashmir remained huge and demonstrates just how seriously the Indian government takes the insurgency.

At one of the several army checkpoints our bus was stopped and only we foreigners aboard were ordered off. I was more than a bit surprised at this, as in my mind, any Europeans on a full bus would seem the least likely to warrant the attention of the Indian military. After we disembarked the soldiers made us unload our backpacks from the luggage compartment and then proceeded to run metal detectors over them. As this happened, I remember glancing at one of the soldiers and smiling nervously at him. His expressionless face offered no response and his eyes were totally emotionless; he had a real aura of menace about him and frankly he scared the shit out of me. If that wasn't bad enough, I wasn't sure whether the search would next be extended to us personally, a potential problem because I had a quarter of a *tola* of *charas* inside a cigarette packet in my trouser pocket. After meeting the Australian chap Owen in Goa and following the nail-biting incident at the Maharaja Palace in Mysuru, I had been very cautious where *charas* was concerned, having bought this piece from a French guy at the hotel in Delhi.

If the army did intend to search us there was a good chance they'd find the *charas* and then who knew what might happen? I certainly wasn't keen to find out and decided to ditch the hash as surreptitiously as was possible at an army roadblock surrounded by soldiers. I pulled out the cigarette packet and, whilst taking a cigarette from it, discreetly removed the *charas* and secreted it in my other hand. After I lit the cigarette, I glanced around briefly to check I wasn't being watched before dropping the hash alongside my leg to the ground. This accomplished, I then slowly moved away from the immediate area and waited. I felt like one of those POWs in the film *The Great Escape*, trying not to look suspicious as they deposited soil from their escape tunnels underfoot by using sacks hidden under their trousers. Of course the main difference was that I was trying to avoid imprisonment not escape from it! With my heart pounding quickly as adrenalin coursed through my body, it occurred to me that on two occasions now I'd found myself facing khaki uniforms and potential imprisonment for the possession of *charas*. It seemed ridiculous that in India you could legally get off your face on *bhang* yet smoking a chillum or joint could get you locked up in some dreadful prison.

Anyhow despite my worrying the anticipated body search didn't materialise as the army were only interested in checking our bags with metal detectors. They were presumably looking for bombs and firearms rather than smuggled gold bullion. For sure, as we got back on the bus, one of the passengers then explained why we

Westerners had been singled out. Evidently, some Europeans with sympathy for the Kashmiri militants had previously been caught smuggling weapons into the Valley on their behalf. So, the upshot of this was all foreigners were now suspects in the dispute, this a situation far removed from the supposedly neutral status I'd been led to believe by the Delhi travel agent. Moreover, I was annoyed about dumping some good quality *charas* in a moment of panic, quite unnecessarily as it transpired. In light of this sacrifice, I felt somewhat irked that we were not frisked; after all, how did they know that one of us Westerners was not concealing a handgun under their clothing?

Chapter 13.

I hoped there'd be no further drama as we journeyed on towards Srinagar. Along the route I was continually taken by the breath-taking alpine scenery. The landscape is incredibly verdant and rice, the chief crop of Kashmir, is seen growing on terraces along the valleys. The climate and much of the terrain are also favourable for cultivating apple, cherry and pear orchards. It comes as little surprise therefore that agriculture is the mainstay of the Kashmiri economy and the population is a predominantly rural one. One notable product which originates from the countryside of eastern Kashmir is the ultra-fine goat's wool known as *pashmina* used to hand-weave shawls. This fine fibre is obtained from brushing the undercoat undercoats of *pashmina* goats whilst they're moulting. Once it's spun the yarn created is considered to be amongst the highest grades of cashmere wool, which itself takes its name from the Himalayan state.

Another prized fibre widely produced in Jammu and Kashmir is silk. Unlike some moths that eat fabric, the species *Bombyx mori* (silkworm moth) actually help to create one. Their name aside, the worms are in fact the moth's caterpillars, which as they enter the pupa stage, wrap themselves in a cocoon by secreting one long continuous filament of silk fibre. Then before the moths are able to hatch, which would damage the silk encasing them, cocoons are soaked in boiling water killing the insect inside. This also helps unravel the single silk strand which can be well over a kilometre in length, thread made from the silk is then weaved to manufacture the soft glossy textile.

The farming of silkworms to produce silk cloth, a practice called sericulture, had originated in neighbouring China during the 3rd century BCE, perhaps even earlier. Silk farming and weaving have long been an important sector of the state's agricultural economy, as it is elsewhere in the country. Only China produces more silk than India. Still, in recent years annual silk production in Jammu and Kashmir has fallen sharply by over two thirds. Attributable in part to the political unrest it is also a consequence of a decline in mulberry trees, the leaves of which provide the principal food of silkworms.

Even though I had pre-booked a houseboat in Srinagar through the travel agent, it turned out that my custom would be poached by others en route. In what was obviously some pre-arranged rendezvous, our prescient driver stopped off in Srinagar before we reached our final destination at the main bus station. Then, for the second time during this journey only we foreigners found ourselves being led off the vehicle, this time to a waiting taxi. By now tired and eager to get to my destination, I didn't care which houseboat I stayed on having paid no deposit.

We were promptly packed into an *Amby* cab in typical Indian sardine fashion and driven off to Dal Lake, the largest of Srinagar's lakes. Seeing how my fellow passengers had also arranged to stay on houseboats through ticket agents, intercepting the bus and whisking us away from competitors waiting at the station like this was certainly an audacious ploy. Indeed, that some houseboat owners were prepared to go to these lengths illustrated just how badly the unrest had impacted tourism.

Being met at the lakeside by those responsible for our *diversion*, the obligatory haggling over prices ensued. After agreeing a price, myself, James and two Dutch girls were paddled out on a small boat to one of the hundreds of houseboats. Unlike the *kettu vallum* houseboats I had seen on the Kerala backwaters, those in Srinagar are all permanently moored up and also connected to plumbing and electricity. The boats are constructed from a hardy, rot-resistant type of native cedar wood and our one, which had a decoratively carved front to it, was surprisingly spacious. I reckon it was easily over thirty metres long and four metres wide with en-suite bedrooms and a lounge and dining room, as meals were included in the cost.

The walnut décor of the boat's interior stemmed from British colonial times, this when Srinagar's houseboats had started. With its cooler climate, mountainous Kashmir had attracted the British during the long sweltering summer months; however the sale of land or property there to foreigners wasn't permitted. Desperate to escape the relentless heat of the Gangetic Plain further south, the British had the ingenious idea of building houseboats as a way round this ban. Now there are literally hundreds of houseboats in Srinagar, these all in fact quite old, as high timber costs eventually made the construction of any new ones unviable. I have to admit that in terms of accommodation, staying on the houseboat was a wholly charming and memorable experience.

Dal Lake adjoins south eastern Srinagar and covers an area of more than twenty square kilometres. Rather than an open body of water, the lake in fact consists of a collection of islands, clusters of houseboats, reed beds, floating gardens and causeways. Adding colour and beauty to the water are the aquatic blooms of lotuses and water lilies, the lotus being the national flower of India and considered sacred in all its indigenous religions. Around Dal Lake are the mountain peaks of the Zabarwan Range, which form a part of the Himalaya cutting through southwest Kashmir.

At an altitude of almost 1,600 metres, the lake and city beside it are comfortably cooler than Delhi and other parts of India I had visited. Such was the difference in night time temperature that a couple of times I even had to cover myself with a blanket whilst sleeping. It rained quite a lot in Srinagar during my stay, a notably colder rain than the monsoon downpours I'd experienced further south. I also recall a few thunderstorms breaking out, these being rather dramatic to watch from the lake at night time. Be that as it may, I soon learnt that the weather wasn't the only source of loud noises occasionally heard in the night sky.

One evening, the four of us guests decided to dine outside on the front decking of the houseboat and enjoy the sunset. Then, as darkness fell, cracking sounds echoing through the mountains suddenly began to punctuate the occasion. It's possible we were all subconsciously in denial about the source of these noises but I said they might be fireworks and my companions agreed. Maybe it was some Muslim festival being celebrated as are plenty of Hindu ones in this country. Still, as the sounds grew louder and clearer, they now took on an explosive quality and the four of us looked at each other in a real moment of panic. 'That sounds like gunfire' James stated, trying not to appear too alarmed. We all nodded. Let's just say it felt a little unsettling being outside as the invasive sound, of what we now knew to be sporadic gunfire filled the night air. 'If the shooting is getting louder,' rightly pointed out one of the women, 'does that not mean it's getting nearer?' 'You would think so wouldn't you,' I replied and at this we thought it wise to retreat indoors and rose to our feet. As we headed back inside the houseboat carrying our plates to finish eating, I actually heard a couple of rounds whistle overhead. Believe me it was scary stuff and the fighting must have been close by, although it was impossible to pinpoint exactly where the shots were coming from. I hoped that the boat would offer some security, although realistically a stray round could easily penetrate a wooden hull. Still, I think any kind of shelter instinctively feels psychologically safer when bullets are flying all around. Fortunately the shooting ended almost as soon as we went inside, not that we bothered going outdoors again. I suppose when it came to it; nothing puts the dampeners on el-fresco dining quite like hearing a nearby gun-battle raging!

In light of such exchanges between militants and Indian forces I was astonished that the houseboat's business cards offered to arrange 'trekking, fishing and *shooting*' trips for the guests. Well I don't know exactly what kind of shooting expeditions are possible in the middle of a war zone, but let's just say that I wasn't about to embark on any! It was safe to say that these business cards were fairly old and had been printed up in more peaceful times when foreigners were able to engage in such outdoor activities. Hunting ducks, pheasants and bigger creatures like the markhor, a common goat like animal with large impressive twisted horns, was indeed once an attraction for some visitors. Whereas killing the local wildlife had not been a tourist option for some time, being killed yourself on the other hand, by gunfire-or in some random bomb blast at a bus station-seemingly was a possibility!

Not all of Kashmir's woes had stemmed from warfare as natural disasters have brought destruction and misery just as easily as conflict. The worst in memory was a 2005 earthquake in Pakistan-controlled *Azad* Kashmir which had caused death and devastation over a wide region, including in Indian Kashmir. It's estimated that 70-80,000 people had perished and many more were injured. The destruction this caused had also displaced millions. Unfortunately for its inhabitants, in geological terms the entire region remains susceptible to seismic activity, this being a result of the continued movement of Eurasian and Indian tectonic plates which had first collided 50 million years ago to form the Himalayas.

Nature struck again, albeit this time on a less devastating scale in 2014, when a relentless deluge of rain fell in one month leading to flooding across both Indian and Pakistani Kashmir. Hundreds died and hundreds of thousands were left homeless and in need of rescue. During these natural catastrophes, the massive military presence in Kashmir was deployed in humanitarian rather than security operations for a change. Ultimately the ability of all those soldiers stationed on both sides of the border to respond quickly with rescue and relief missions, and to provide medical assistance, had doubtlessly averted even greater loss.

For getting around the lake or back and forth to the shore there are *shikaras*, small paddled boats which function as water taxis and seat up to six passengers. They are very comfortable, having shaded cushioned seating with backrests, and cheap: one thirty-minute boat ride I took around Dal Lake cost less than the price of a daily paper! Being paddled around quietly except for the gentle sound of water lapping against the boat was extremely relaxing. A *shikara* trip could also provide a good opportunity to spot eagles or even the odd kingfisher, although sadly I didn't get to see any *Kingfisher* beer in this overwhelmingly Muslim state as alcohol is banned. As much as I enjoyed being out on the water, a downside was the frequent approach of other *shikaras* ferrying bothersome hawkers, generally selling either papier-mâché items or saffron; neither of which I wanted.

Of all the spices grown in India, there are none more valuable than Kashmiri saffron, hence its sale on land and water. Derived from a lilac-coloured crocus flower which is well adapted for the state's wet, mountainous environment, it is a hardy plant capable of withstanding frost and snow. The actual spice is the dried, thin lightweight stigmas or threads from the flower of the plant. Each flower produces just three threads which measure only a couple of centimetres in length. It means therefore, up to a staggering 170,000 flowers are required to produce one kilo of saffron. No wonder it's the world's most expensive spice. Noted in cuisine for its subtle grass-like aroma and distinct, slightly bitter taste, saffron is further used to impart a rich yellow-orange colour to dishes and textiles. Kashmiri *Lacha* saffron is considered to be the best in the world amongst many, and is so highly sought after that decreased production due to drought and disease has in the past led to a ban on its export from the country.

Given its high commercial value, much of what purports to be Kashmiri *Lacha* saffron is adulterated. When sold as threads it can be mixed with other substances including things like strands of silk fibres simply dyed red to resemble the stigmas. In powdered form Lacha saffron is often blended with less costly lower-grade Iranian varieties of the spice. At times, even cheap spices like turmeric or paprika are used as diluting agents as they have similar colouring to saffron. If adulterating saffron is not bad enough some sellers pass off safflower as Lacha this an inferior cheap substitute which is sometimes referred to as 'bastard saffron'. Personally, I reckon that 'bastard's saffron' would more accurately describe the spice sold by such unscrupulous individuals!

Occasional thunder and gunfire aside, the general peacefulness of Dal Lake made it easy to forget that its shores lie next to the state's largest city, Srinagar, population 1.5 million. Even though a settlement likely existed on the site of modern Srinagar earlier, the city's foundation is widely attributed to the Hindu monarch Pravarasena II in the 6th century CE. During the centuries of Hindu and Buddhist control, Srinagar had prospered becoming the chief trading centre of the Kashmir Valley. The city eventually yielded to Muslim conquest and by the mid-14th century, Srinagar like the rest of Kashmir contained a Muslim majority population. Muslim governance of Srinagar continued under the Mughals and later Afghans; however its strategic and commercial importance had also led to Sikh and Hindu rule at different periods. Historically Srinagar had been the permanent capital of Kashmir until the Dogra *maharajas* began moving their administration south to the warmer climes of Jammu during the winter months. This practice continued until the state became a Union Territory in 2019.

Srinagar is built around the Jhelum, a major river of the region which is linked by a waterway to Dal Lake itself. During the 2014 floods, the Jhelum burst its banks when three times the normal volume of water gushed down its course. The consequent flooding had submerged much of the city leaving thousands destitute and causing untold damage. Spanning the river as it snakes through the city are nine bridges, the newest a wooden-arched structure oddly named 'Zero Bridge'. Flanking the banks of the Jhelum and the waterways around it are boats known as *doongas*. These are a more Spartan type of houseboat; ones traditionally home to those who had ferried people, goods and livestock around Srinagar. Today the river is no longer such a crucial means of transportation but a reasonably large community still live on these *doongas*.

Being very much a Muslim city Srinagar does have a noticeably different feel to it when compared to other Indian cities I visited. For one, there are none of the usual cows seen mingling amongst the traffic or scavenging for fodder in rubbish. Also, the men here generally wear the Islamic skullcap known as a *topi* and many of the women, when they were seen that is, are dressed in burqas. I wasn't surprised to see on a map that, from Srinagar, the Pakistani capital Islamabad is less than a third of the distance away than Delhi. Regardless of its obvious Islamic identity Srinagar and the surrounding Valley had once been home to a Hindu community known as Kashmiri *Bandits*. Regrettably, the basic sectarian nature of the insurgency meant that the majority of Kashmir's Bandits. had by now fled the region.

Around Zero Bridge and the area immediately west of it lie the tourist area of Srinagar. Here I found restaurants, banks, a tourist office and, for those who made it that far... the main bus station. Proving that not all visitors stayed on houseboats there are even a few hotels and a hostel hereabouts. Sadly, wherever one went in Srinagar, the large military presence made it impossible to forget about the unrest. Even out on Dal Lake I saw one small island with an army outpost on it. The odd sight of a protruding machine-gun barrel and a helmeted head peering out from behind sandbags on this island underlined that, for all its beauty, the lake was also a militarised zone. Moreover, the ever-present security forces had commandeered numerous public spaces in the city, amongst them local parks. For the very small number of visitors who did venture to Srinagar, many of its sights were off limits due to the troubles. These included the early 18th century Hazratbal Mosque, a sacred lakeside shrine said to house a hair from the prophet Muhammad and a place from where I often heard singing at night.

One day, in an effort to see more of the area, James and I took an auto-rickshaw to the Shankaracharya Hindu temple situated on a hill of the same name about a kilometre south of the lake. At the bottom of the hill we were stopped at an army checkpoint and our driver questioned at length which I assumed was routine security procedure. That said, whilst winding our way up the narrow road towards the summit we were then stopped a further *four* times by different soldiers. It was patently unnecessary and demonstrated that the troops were bored and simply harassing the driver. We felt genuinely sorry for him realising that this type of hassle from the military is something the locals suffer continually. I asked our driver how he felt about this, at which he acknowledged finding it intimidating and frustrating, before then adding with a tone of resignation that it was just a part of life he had to accept. Many people in India suffer on account of their caste, it seemed that here in Kashmir they frequently did so due to their ethnicity and religion too.

Our hilltop destination the Shankaracharya Temple, had taken its name from a famous Hindu philosopher who had supposedly visited the site in the 8th century CE. It's likely that a temple had stood on the hill as far back as the 4th century BCE, although the present structure dates from around the 9th century. Dedicated to Shiva, the temple is a reminder of a pre-Islamic Kashmir when most of the population were Hindu rather than Muslim. Kashmir remains significant in Hinduism as it is believed a cave there had been the abode of Shiva and his consort Parvati. For sure, the cave at Amarnath is considered one of the holiest sites in Hinduism and frequently attracts over half a million devotees during an annual pilgrimage.

In all truthfulness the Shankaracharya Temple wasn't the most impressive I saw in India, although it was one of the oldest and definitely the most heavily guarded. For me, far more spectacular than the actual temple were the views that the complex affords of the surrounding scenery. In spite of the weather being overcast, there were still some great vistas of Srinagar and Dal Lake on one side of the hill and the Jhelum River on the other side. Adding to this picturesque landscape, I could just about make out in the far distance, the soaring snow-capped peaks of the Pir Panjal range to the west. These mountains are in fact home to India's best skiing, an activity impossible to imagine in the heat that envelops most of the country. Seeing such varied topography alone really made the trip remarkable.

Seeing how the use of local public transport had attracted the unwanted attention of the army, on another occasion James and I hired bikes. Together we cycled around 10 km along the shoreline road to the Shalimar Garden on the north eastern side of Dal Lake. Created in 1619 by the Mughal potentate Jahangir, father of Shah Jahan, it's the first of two gardens or *baghs* built by the Mughals around the lake. Covering nearly 12.5 hectares, it is spread over three well-tended terraces, these containing manicured lawns and shrubs, a colourful fusion of flowerbeds and lines of *chinar* trees, a common type of plane growing in Kashmir. There are a number of marble pavilions too, whilst a central water channel runs for over half a kilometre through the middle of these garden feeding pools and waterfalls.

I was particularly taken by the way the neatness and symmetry of the well maintained garden contrasts with the natural backdrop of the lake and rugged mountains. When it came to producing stunning gardens, as with their stunning buildings I'd seen in Old Delhi, the Mughals were masters. That said, I suspect the Shalimar Bagh may have been even more spectacular had some of the hundreds of fountains been working; but with so few tourists due to the unrest unfortunately they were all turned off. Still on the plus side, the dearth of visitors did mean we literally had the whole place to ourselves. Not even the grey skies or the light drizzle which began falling could detract from the remarkable beauty of the gardens and the landscape around it. It was easy to understand why the Mughal Emperors of India had fallen in love with this part of Kashmir, as had the British after them. What's more, without the multitudes of Old Delhi, this Mughal creation enjoyed a wonderful serenity about it. I could quite easily picture a Mughal emperor strolling through the *bagh*, enjoying the subtle scents of flowers and appreciating its splendour and calm, much as I now did. In fact the Mughals created their gardens as earthly representations of paradise based upon Quranic descriptions, and this peaceful, beautiful place was certainly heavenly, the best part of my time in Kashmir in fact.

Alas the tranquillity and enjoyment of the moment was shortly broken by the approaching clatter of engines. Before we knew it, a convoy of army trucks had pulled up and dozens of soldiers began spewing out the back of them. Running about excitedly, they then began to position themselves around us as though battle ready to engage some immediate enemy. With all these assault rifles and machine guns now poised to open fire, for me it was one of those gigantic Ganesha statues on the road moments which beggared belief! Worried we were perhaps about to become caught up in some exchange, I expressed this concern to James. 'Surely they'd tell us if there was any danger?' he said. 'I'd bloody well hope so' was all I could answer. In truth they appeared indifferent to our presence, so seeing how it's unlikely any militants were hiding in the bushes or *chinar* trees, we presumed that this was merely an exercise.

Within a few short minutes the scene had transformed from a delightful idyll into what now resembled an imminent battlefield. What's more I had yet to take any pictures and photographing the military is strictly forbidden. Therefore, to avoid getting any shots from the soldiers; I had to seek permission from them to get shots of the gardens! The sight of all these armed troops positioned around Shalimar Bagh seemed incongruous to say the least. It appeared that wherever we visited there was just no escaping the military presence here in Kashmir. 'Sod this for a game of soldiers' we then both aptly agreed and decided to leave. At least being on bikes we could do so quickly, had we come by taxi instead, doubtless the army would have spent thirty minutes giving the driver the third degree before we could get going!

Such experiences only highlighted further the ongoing troubles which for India meant hostilities with a neighbouring state as well as with internal militants. The bottom line was that the situation in Kashmir had deteriorated into a vicious conflict, one in which ruthless Indian security forces could with impunity harass, torture, imprison, rape and murder civilians and even massacre protesters. India is a democracy but evidently not one that cares much for human rights. However, none of this is to suggest that separatist rebels in Kashmir were actually any better in light of their record of perpetrating atrocities, in particular against the Hindu minority population of the Valley. Further instances of religious violence directed against civilians during this bloody dispute have included militant attacks on Hindu pilgrims visiting the Amarnath Cave.

In addition to this background of carnage and amidst strikes and heightened tensions, a curfew was also imposed in Srinagar over a couple of days. As much as I enjoyed staying on the houseboat, being unable to leave made me feel like a captive in a gilded cage. Frankly I hadn't travelled over 3,500 kilometres from the beaches of Kovalam – even the shit-speckled ones-to be stuck indoors all day. If the restrictions on our movement weren't bad enough the dreaded *shikara*-borne vendors started boarding the houseboat to try and sell their wares. Equally disconcerting were the continued noises of gunfire exchanges that intensified at night. What's more this was now interspersed with heavier thuds of what sounded like artillery fire.

When the curfew ended James and I took a *shikara* to the shore intending to go into Srinagar and buy a few things. We'd walked only a hundred metres from the lake before meeting a Swiss guy returning to his houseboat. He immediately warned us not to go into the city explaining how he'd just witnessed an attack there. It happened when a couple of militants riding on a scooter threw a hand grenade at an army checkpoint a short distance ahead in the direction he'd been walking. If this explosion itself was terrifying, worse followed when panicked soldiers responded by opening fire indiscriminately upon anyone in the vicinity. In complete shock and fearing for his life, the poor guy had instinctively run from the scene at full speed.

It happened close to the market and the area had been busy he explained, so injuries or death were highly likely. Chillingly he then commented with a shaky voice that if it had happened just one minute later, he'd have been caught up directly in the middle of the shooting. We'd experienced on the houseboat ourselves the frightening sound of bullets whizzing about in the dark, so we could well imagine his horror seeing all this first hand in daylight. Unsurprisingly this was enough to convince us to turn around and return to the lake with him. Listening to his scary testimony was hardly consistent with the Delhi travel agent's assertion that we tourists were safe from the violence afflicting Kashmir. It is hard to believe that the louche travel agent had shamelessly promoted a war zone, but then again I suppose many things are quite hard to believe in India. Although there could be no denying the natural beauty of Kashmir, there could be no denying the bloodshed there either. In light of this reality and the miasma it had created over me, I decided with James to board a bus back down to Jammu the following day.

Chapter 14.

From Jammu I bought a bus ticket to the Punjabi city of Amritsar, saying goodbye to James who continued on towards Delhi. Having a couple of hours to wait before my bus left, I went for something to eat with a woman from London I'd met at the station. Besides being hungry, in light of the recent bombing at Jammu bus station, the less time I spent hanging about there the better. We found a nearby restaurant that gauging from its rather plush carpeting, flock wallpaper and white cotton tablecloths was slightly more upmarket. Before long we were both seated at a table enjoying delicious food and two other things very much appreciated on a hot afternoon: air conditioning and cold beer. In particular, after the abstinence of Srinagar a chilled beer with my lunch was really welcome. It seemed all in all, the restaurant was an ideal choice.

Unbelievably that conclusion was then abruptly revoked by the appearance a rat on the floor right in front of our table! It was massive, almost the size of a small dog, and filthy looking, its grey-black hair stuck down with dirt and Vishnu knows what else. As we both looked on in total disbelief at this unsanitary and rather unexpected sight, it took a moment or two for the initial shock to subside. When it did, I could have sworn that the thing caught my gaze with its beady black eyes and stared me out provocatively, as if to say, 'I live here so what are you gonna do about it?' Then the creature started sniffing around the table leg, seeming quite at home and unperturbed by the presence of a dozen other people, none of whom seemed to notice this uninvited guest. Or maybe they had and they just didn't care, such was the ubiquity of rats round here. Certainly the rodent was unlikely to be the only one scavenging around the place for morsels suggesting an infestation.

I had seen rats as big before in India, although not indoors and definitely not whilst dining in a restaurant. I panicked. If a waiter's thumb inserted in my dhal sounded unhygienic, what if this rat had contaminated our meals whilst it snooped around in the kitchen? The presence of these vermin is hardly conducive to safe food preparation; back in Britain rats carry things such as Weil's disease, salmonella and listeria, so I dreaded to think what sort of bacterial nastiness rats in India harbour. Then of course it's even possible to catch *the* plague from rats, a disease which sounds medieval to Westerners but has yet to be eradicated in India. In light of the health risks, it was naturally deeply unpleasant seeing this rodent brazenly wandering around the restaurant. When it moved away from our table, I decided to take action and swiftly grabbed the salt cellar and threw it at the rat. I just missed but did cause the thing to scurry off with its thick, whip-like tail waving cheekily at me.

Having a meal interrupted by the rat-a tat of gunfire in Kashmir was bad enough, but having one interrupted by an actual rat in a restaurant was too much. In disgust I summoned a waiter over and told him angrily what I'd just seen. Mistaking my protestation for a mere observation, his response was priceless as he declared 'Yes sir, big rats, small rats, there are many, many rats here sir!' Probably thinking that I'd just stated the bloody obvious, he then walked off, doubtless satisfied that his customer service skills had been diligently exercised. Even if his reply proved that restaurants round here weren't too bothered about horrendous breaches of hygiene safety, at this point my companion and I just burst into uncontrollable laughter. Such absurdities were quite difficult to take seriously at times and it was indeed hard to argue with the waiters' logic. I suppose on this occasion the elephant in the room happened to be a rat!

Rodent welcoming restaurants aside, I continued my journey on the standard 'video coach' which rattled and honked its way into neighbouring Punjab and on towards Amritsar. At one stop along the way, some children carrying chilled soft drinks in buckets of ice approached the open windows of the bus. After the requisite negotiation, I agreed to buy a bottle of Limca off one of them. As the youngster was about to open the bottle and luckily before I'd handed over any rupees, I noticed that the cap he was removing had the logo of the Indian cola Thums Up on it. It's most likely the bottle contained a squash concentrate diluted with tap water, this of course something I'd been studiously trying to avoid drinking for health reasons. I promptly told the young vendor to get lost, doubtless saving myself a considerable amount of toilet paper in the process!

The flat terrain along much of the route towards Amritsar was dull in comparison to either the mountains of Kashmir or the lush tropical landscapes of the south. Nonetheless what the Punjab lacked in scenic value it made up for in fertility, it being a region of the Gangetic Plain irrigated by five key tributaries of the Indus River, including the Jhelum. These waterways give the Punjab its name meaning 'land of five rivers'. Their plentiful supply of water, together with the rich soil it irrigates, had made farming the focus of the Punjabi economy for centuries. Be that so, large tracts of the Western Punjab beyond the flow of these rivers and their tributaries, had once been semi-arid dusty terrain unsuitable for cultivation. I say 'had once been' because an extraordinary canal irrigation scheme, one started by the British in the 1880s had created around 14 million acres of agricultural land by the time of independence. Over a number of decades this ambitious agrarian project developed nine so called canal colonies, these planned to relieve the growing pressure that population growth was placing on food production elsewhere in the Punjab. Transforming all this barren land required more than just water and the canal colonies had also been an experiment in social engineering as 100,000s of people were settled on the newly formed farmland.

Some land in these colonies was sold but the majority had been granted to mostly peasants who became tenants of the colonial administration. Other grants provided eventual ownership of the land, either for those existing landowners willing to invest in its agricultural development, or for those who had served the British in some capacity, pensioned ex-servicemen and civil servants for example. Amongst the new farming communities established in the canal colonies the authorities promoted better hygiene and sanitation. These settlements had soon come to be regarded as a model for rural life. Opening up all of this farm land had naturally brought about a commensurate increase in the agricultural output and affluence of the Punjab. The canal colonies were largely given over to crop cultivation, although livestock was also introduced as the authorities had stipulated that some land be used for horse-breeding in order to supply the army with horses and mules.

The canal colonies weren't an entirely altruistic undertaking as the higher living standards of those working the land, provided a lot more tax revenue for the colonial government. In addition, the British felt that the general improvement in conditions enjoyed by those settling the colonies, would eventually cement their loyalty to the Empire. Whatever the real motives behind them were, the development of these canal colonies by the British had been a momentous achievement that had both vastly increased food production and raised many peasants out of poverty. With the partition of the Punjab in 1947, Pakistan had become the principal beneficiary of these colonial endeavours when it inherited this impressive irrigation network. Much like the construction of New Delhi, the building of the canal colonies in the Punjab and similar projects elsewhere left a physical imprint on the sub-continent worthy of admiration, even if ultimately such grand schemes did symbolize British colonial power.

It wasn't only the British who'd brought significant agricultural change to the Punjab countryside. Following independence, the so-called Green Revolution of the 1960s had also transformed the state's rural economy. Vitally, this ushered in the introduction of higher-yielding crop strains and improved irrigation technology, these massively boosting its agricultural productivity. Since these advances in agriculture, land farmed in the Punjab for pasture and cultivation now supplies much of the country's dairy products and wheat. The Punjab's role being the proverbial 'bread basket of the nation' had brought prosperity to many in rural Punjab, making them better off than countless subsistence farmers and peasants toiling elsewhere across the Indian countryside. In 2020, the BJP attempted to reform farming, bringing in laws which encouraged farmers to sell their produce privately. It sparked huge opposition from farmers in the Punjab and other states, who demanded the continuation of government markets which guarantee a minimum price for their produce. Such was the scale of protest; Modi had been forced to repeal these farming laws in late 2021.

Due to mountainous terrain to the north and desert to its south, the Punjab had provided a natural route into North India for those historically invading from the west. From around the 8th century CE onwards these were the armies of various Muslim dynasties, including those of the Delhi Sultanates and the Mughals. During this period Islam was able to establish itself as a major religion in the Western Punjab which would eventually form a major part of Pakistan.

In religious terms the Punjab is notably home to the Sikhs, one of India's best-known minorities. In 1469 the founder of the Sikh religion Guru Nanak had been born in a part of the Punjab now found in Pakistan. Becoming established by the first half of the 16th century, Sikhism had sought a bridge between Hinduism and Islam and was a reaction too against the rigid caste system. After the death of Guru Nanak Sikhism evolved under the guidance of a further nine Gurus, attracting both Hindu and Muslim converts. Even though their numbers are small when compared to Hindus and Muslims there's still over twenty million Sikhs in India. Most live in the Punjab where they account for almost 58 percent of the total population, but Sikhs can be found throughout the country, often working in transport or serving in the country's military. Instantly distinguished by their turbans and beards, orthodox Sikh men are those initiated into the Khalsa, the religious codes and practices introduced in 1699 by the tenth and final Sikh guru, Gobind Singh. The image of bearded men in turbans is perhaps the one most readily identified with Sikhism whereas in reality the majority of Sikhs tend to be non-orthodox.

With the decline of Mughal power, the Sikhs rose to become the dominant political and military force in the Punjab during the first half of the 19th century. Under the leadership of *Maharaja* Ranjit Singh who'd governed from Lahore, now in Pakistan, a Sikh empire extending beyond the Punjab was carved out. Conquests by a formidable Khalsa army brought the whole of neighbouring Jammu and Kashmir plus strategic parts of Afghanistan under Sikh control.

This rise of Sikh hegemony in north India happened to coincide with the expansion of the British East India Company across the sub-continent. Conflict between them broke out in 1845, which after some fierce battles concluded with a British victory and the seizure of large parts of the Sikh Empire. In the wake of defeat the Sikhs had still remained defiant and in 1848 tensions triggered a second Anglo-Sikh War. This ended within a year and once again the Sikhs lost, this time marking the end of their empire as the British took control of all Sikh territories, including their historical homeland the Punjab itself.

The military prowess displayed by their adversaries during the two Anglo-Sikh Wars had impressed the British. So much so that thereafter the British had eagerly recruited Sikhs into the ranks of their Indian army, a preference strengthened by the loyalty of Sikh soldiers during the mutiny and revolt of 1857. Consequently the Punjab continued to provide large numbers of men for the British military even right up until the time of independence. During both world wars, hundreds of thousands of Sikh troops served in India and overseas. In the 21st century, this Sikh martial tradition is still reflected by their disproportionate numbers in the Indian armed forces. You only have to consider that whilst they constitute less than two percent of the country's total population, Sikhs make up twenty percent of the Indian military.

Partition was undoubtedly the darkest chapter in the history of the Punjab. As with Bengal in the northeast of India, the province was truncated, with its eastern part being ceded to India whilst its larger western territory was given to Pakistan. Owing to various historical religious tensions, the massive exchange of populations between its two parts that partition had entailed erupted into a maelstrom of horrific, unparalleled communal violence. Millions of Punjabis on both sides of the border were affected by killings, torture, rape, abductions, looting and mass forced expulsions. The monumental scale of violence witnessed during partition, fuelled the animosity between India and Pakistan still being played out today in neighbouring Kashmir.

After independence, the Indian state of Punjab had been much larger in area than it actually is today, its boundaries changing in 1966 when the state of Haryana was created from its southern part. During the same time other areas of the Punjab were being incorporated into the state of Himachal Pradesh further reducing its overall size. With Haryana containing almost an entirely Hindi speaking Hindu population, the new smaller Punjab became as the Sikhs themselves wanted, a Punjabi speaking Sikh majority state. Be that so, in the holiest Sikh city of Amritsar where I was now heading, surprisingly around half of its inhabitants were Hindus.

Arriving in Amritsar, I immediately made for the Golden Temple rather than seek the usual cheap place to stay. I did so as hostels for Sikh pilgrims inside the temple complex also allow foreign visitors to stay for up to three nights. This accommodation called a *niwas* was basic but then again it was *free*, although I donated the equivalent amount of a room elsewhere. For me it was wholly about the experience not economising. No other religious site I'd visited had offered the opportunity of staying within it, so I saw it as an opportunity to get a proper feel for the place.

The centrepiece of the vast complex is the stunning three-storey white marble temple, or *gurdwara,* called the Harmandar Sahib, meaning 'Temple of God'. This is the building better known to non-Sikhs as the Golden Temple, a popular appellation down to the gold-plated copper sheeting adorning its upper two thirds. The gilded walls of the temple are embossed mainly with floral patterns, but it is the ornate small domes, *chhatris* and majestic large dome of the roof which give this edifice its exquisiteness A temple had existed on the site since 1601 during the time of the fifth guru but, like so many historical buildings, it was destroyed and rebuilt over time. The present structure dates from the 1760s with the vast majority of its adornments being added during the decades following construction. For example, the gold for which the temple is famed was donated by *Maharaja* Ranjit Singh.

Enhancing its overall splendour, the Harmandar Sahib stands at the centre of a large rectangular pool or *sarovar* and is reached via a 60 metre-long marble causeway. This body of water surrounding the temple is referred to as the 'Pool of Nectar' or *Amrit Sarovar* in Punjabi giving the city its very name. With this water considered sacred in Sikhism, pilgrims bathe in the *sarovar* for its spiritual and physical benefits. Although the 150 square metre pool had been built, it is fed by a natural spring and is home to some quite large koi carp.

This *sarovar* and the wide marble walkway around it are both enclosed by wonderfully carved high white marble buildings, all with colonnaded arches and verandas. Besides providing offices and homes for temple staff, these buildings house a number of shrines, another *gurdwara* and a museum. Entrances to the large temple courtyard are at the four cardinal points, the identical south and north ones certainly the most eye-catching as both are decoratively topped with *chhatris* and a domed clock tower. The gateway I used most though is a great open archway located at the

141

eastern end, as this leads to the rest of the site including the *niwas* buildings and other *gurdwaras.*

It was wonderful staying so near to the temple as it allowed me ample opportunity to saunter around this extraordinary place and soak in its atmosphere. Although lively with pilgrims and tourists alike during daytime, the complex still retained a certain reverent ambience. At night time when the crowds disappeared, I found it especially relaxing. Following the gloom, tension and oppressive security of Kashmir, the temple was an altogether safer, happier environment to spend time in. As a Westerner, I felt privileged being welcomed into the spiritual centre of a religion I had first encountered in Britain many thousands of kilometres away. The spirituality of the site seemed to have a calming effect and even as a non-Sikh I felt a sense of contentment and happiness there. Certainly aiding this positive experience was the absence inside the complex of the everyday beggars, hawkers and hustlers found elsewhere in India. Even the issue of petty theft was addressed by putting up posters in the *niwas* and other places of those caught stealing inside the place. I'd seen first-hand in Kerala during the bus ticket overcharging incident, how dishonest people receive beatings. Those pictured here definitely looked as though they'd been roughed up, a stark warning to any would be thieves of their possible fate. It struck me as being a good visual deterrent and reinforced the sense that this was a hallowed site; somewhere people could be free from the material concerns of the outside world. Importantly the Golden Temple complex provides an oasis of spiritual peace amongst the usual hustle and bustle of Indian life, a respite from the madness beyond as it were.

Without a doubt, the highlight of my stay was following in the footsteps of endless pilgrims and entering the actual Harmandar Sahib. Access to the causeway which links the temple is via an intricately carved marble archway located on the west side of the complex. With its gilded ceiling the doored gateway is surrounded by an ornate building topped with beautiful minarets and *chhatris.* Beyond it is the balustraded causeway lined with gilded lamps on columns which runs straight to the temple in the centre of the *sarovar.* Upon entering it, the Harmandar Sahib interior was every bit as lavish as its exterior, boasting as it does an impressive mix of:

paintings, marble inlay, ivory mosaics, silver and yet even more gold.

Within the temple building, worshippers continuously recite the Sikh holy book, this titled the *Guru Grant Sahib*. The focus of Sikh religious devotion, the scripture was completed in 1708 by Guru Gobind Singh and taken from the teachings of the gurus and other holy men. Moreover, the title *guru* bestowed on the sacred text signifies its acceptance as the final word on Sikhism. During the hours of daylight, a special copy of the *Guru Granth Sahib* is used for recital and is placed on a throne under a jewelled canopy at the heart of the temple's main floor. Inside the inner sanctum, I found myself mesmerised by the intonations from the holy *Granth* amidst devotional singing and music.

Elsewhere, the *mandirs* I'd visited had forbidden those of other religions from entering into the inner sanctuaries. But here and at all other Sikh *gurdwaras* all are welcome to do so. The Harmandar Sahib had even been built with its four doors facing the cardinal points so that people of different castes and faiths could enter the building from any direction. Like staying at the complex itself, being able to see the inside of Sikhism's holiest shrine made this trip to Amritsar especially worthwhile.

Not all inscriptions inside the temple complex are of a religious nature. For example one is a quotation from the 1958 work *East to West: A Journey Round the World* by the English historian Arnold Toynbee. It read in both English and Punjabi 'They (the Sikhs) are the burliest men on the face of the planet tough and capable and slightly grim. If human life survives the present chapter of men's history, the Sikhs, for sure, will still be on the map.' Personally I did not find the Sikhs 'grim', not even slightly; still the remainder of Toynbee's statement is, I suspect, an accurate appraisal.

Across a concourse from the causeway's entrance and built at a slight angle to it stands the Akal Takhat, the second holiest site in Sikhism after the Harmandar Sahib. This is a wonderful five-storey white edifice crowned with a gilded dome. When it's not in use the *Granth Sahib* from the inner sanctum of the Harmandar Sahib is kept in the Akal Takhat, with the holy book being carried back and forth each day with great ceremony.

Not that you could tell due to the restoration work, but back in 1984 the Akal Takhat had been extensively damaged and many of its artefacts destroyed when it was shelled by Indian army tanks! At the time, the Akal Takhat, Harmandar Sahib and other parts of the complex had been taken over and fortified by armed militants demanding Khalistan, a separate Sikh state. The military operation to remove them succeeded but at a cost of hundreds of lives and injuries, many of whom were innocent pilgrims caught up in the crossfire. Whereas the physical damage to the Akal Takhat and Golden Temple has long since been repaired, the deadly attack was still commemorated in the temple museum. Displayed inside this museum were gruesome pictures of those killed during the clash, disturbing to look at, though to be expected I suppose in a country where even newspapers contained graphic images on their front pages.

The 1984 Indian army assault on Sikhism's two holiest sites had achieved its military objective, but at a high price beyond just the immediate casualties. The operation, codenamed Blue Star was to have serious ramifications by triggering at first bloody rioting by enraged Sikhs in the surrounding city, and in other parts of the Punjab. Soon too thousands of Sikh soldiers mutinied across India. Within months Mrs Gandhi, the Prime Minister responsible for ordering the attack, had paid for the decision with her own life when killed by her personal Sikh bodyguards. This assassination in turn tragically led to a further upsurge in violence during which thousands of Sikhs were killed by Hindu mobs in Delhi and other cities. Figures for casualties are uncertain; nonetheless an army clampdown across the Punjab during the following years resulted in the further deaths of thousands of Sikhs.

Regardless of all this bloodshed within four years of the 1984 siege, trouble returned to Amritsar after separatists once again took over the temple courtyard and its buildings. Learning from its mistakes last time, the Indian military adopted a more restrained approach using attrition and sniper fire to flush out those inside. After ten days of being pinned down and with around forty of their number dead, the remaining militants had surrendered thus sparing the site any major damage this time. These bloody events all go to prove exactly how disparate and divided India can be on

144

occasion, how this cultural melting pot can boil over and burn at any time. They also demonstrated that, whether from Sikhs in the Punjab or from Muslims in Kashmir, violent demands for secession would be ruthlessly put down with military force. However, unlike in neighbouring Kashmir, at least in the Punjab peace has pretty much returned to the state.

In recent years there have been a handful of incidents involving Sikh separatists and the Indian authorities have seized weapons in the Punjab. Moreover, Pakistani military intelligence has a track record of encouraging and arming Sikh militants with the aim of destabilising India. Even so, today, there is no mass support for a Khalistan in the Punjab and the majority of Sikhs are concerned more with socio-economic issues than independence. Demands for a Khalistan homeland remain strongest amongst the diaspora. In 2012, Sikhs tried to kill a retired Indian army general who'd been involved in Operation Blue Star, as he holidayed in London. The knife attack had failed when the victim fought back and his assailants were soon arrested and subsequently receiving heavy prison sentences. This assassination attempt went to show the depth of anger, even after three decades, amongst sections of the Sikh diaspora.

Along with their welcoming attitude towards other religions at the temple, another admirable Sikh practice is the offering of food at *gurdwaras* to anyone, irrespective of religion, race or vitally in India, caste. This, I thought, demonstrates a very compassionate and open-minded attitude to all strangers. A communal canteen known as a *langar* in the Harmandar Sahib complex feeds around 10,000 people daily, typically with a meal of *dal* and *chapatti*. This shared experience where diners are seated on the floor reflects the key Sikh principle of equality. In *gurdwaras* across India all, including male and female, dine together in this manner. Those who are able to provide a donation towards the costs do so, but obviously not all can. Providing meals for such large numbers in a country where hunger is commonplace is no small achievement. Without question, such charitable provision for the benefit of all was refreshing in a country with no state welfare.

I only dined once in the communal *langer* and, whilst this was a humbling experience, it goes without saying that a greater choice of food is available in the city. Okay, in the bazaars of the old town around the temple this was fairly limited to *chana dal* made from chickpea and the fried flatbread *puris*. However, a short way north in the newer part of the city were plenty of restaurants serving my favourite type of Indian food, *tandoori*. By chance this well-known style of Indian cooking comes from the Punjab making Amritsar an optimum place to eat it, especially when washed down with the oddly named but enjoyable *Godfather* lager. Equally appreciated in light of a recent dining experience, was the fact that restaurants I frequented in Amritsar appeared to be rodent-free!

For me *tandoori* food with its delicious meats, accompanied by flatbreads like *naan* and *kulcha,* is the pinnacle of Indian cuisine. The meats are first marinated in yoghurt and spices and then cooked, as are very briefly the breads, at high temperatures in a deep, cylindrical clay oven known as a *tandoor*, hence the name. The *tandoor* is fired by charcoal or wood which smokes any meat being cooked, imparting it with a taste similar to barbecued food. Together with Punjabi dishes such as *tandoori chicken* and *chicken tikka,* the ovens themselves have become popular across India and far beyond. Arguably nowhere was tandoori food savoured more than in Britain, making a *tandoor* an essential part of the kitchen in most UK Indian restaurants. I was naturally pleased to pay my respects, as it were, to the Punjab's indispensable contribution to Indian food, one that enriches the palates of innumerable diners in both the sub-continent and Britain.

The newer area of Amritsar where I enjoyed this *tandoori* food was built by the British, and not for the first time in India, this past was easy to figure out simply from some of the road names seen, amongst them: Queens, Albert, Court, Links, Taylor and Mall. The British may have brought the railways to the city and extended its boundaries, but Amritsar had of course existed long before their arrival in the wake of the second Anglo-Sikh War. Amritsar had been founded in 1577 by the fourth Sikh Guru besides the 'Pool of Nectar' whose waters were reputed to have curative properties. With the construction of a temple at the site by his successor, so began the expansion of the settlement into both a place of Sikh pilgrimage and a thriving town.

Amritsar continued to prosper eventually becoming a city, albeit one overshadowed historically by Lahore which had been the pre-partition capital of the Punjab. With the loss of Lahore to Pakistan in 1947, Amritsar thus became the commercial centre and largest city of the Indian Punjab. Still, for all of the changes and upheavals throughout its long history, Amritsar had nonetheless remained at heart exactly what it was founded to be: a Sikh holy site.

By the 1700s, the old town had been contained by the wide, unimaginatively named Circular Road which encircles it. The old town being a confusing warren of narrow thoroughfares means that cars are few and far between here, with any motorised traffic consisting chiefly of scooters and the ever present auto-rickshaws rickshaws. Most of the traffic was bikes and cycle rickshaws, the former being the only mode of private transport affordable to many Indians. The Punjab happens to be home to India's most popular make of bicycle, the Hero, which is manufactured in the central city of Ludhiana. Over 10,000 Heroes are produced a day, making the Hero brand one of the world's best-selling bikes.

Amritsar contains a few public parks or *baghs* with one named Jallianwala being located very close to the Harmandar Sahib site. Infamously Jallianwala is remembered for a 1919 massacre there of civilians by British troops. In the run-up to this mass murder, the British had passed ever more repressive legislation to counter political unrest, a move which had provoked strikes and rioting in Amritsar. In defiance of a British ban on any protests, thousands of demonstrators gathered at Jallianwala, which back in 1919 had been a piece of waste ground rather than a formal garden. Later in the day, a contingent of British troops had arrived and, without any warning, began firing on the peaceful, unarmed crowd, killing hundreds and wounding more than a thousand. As the site was walled-in by several buildings with only a couple of narrow exit points, many of those who were not shot during the ten minutes of continuous firing were crushed to death as they attempted to flee. Amidst the bloodshed, others jumped into a well from which 120 corpses were later recovered.

Far from quelling dissent towards British domination in India, the massacre had the opposite effect of hardening the resolve of Gandhi and other nationalists. Having previously pushed only for autonomy, Congress now shifted its position and demanded total independence. The following year witnessed Gandhi launching his non-cooperation movement, thereby starting a campaign of civil disobedience which, as history revealed, delivered independence within three decades.

The Jallianwala site later became a public *bagh* as a memorial to this pivotal event in the independence struggle. The well where many sought shelter and died has been preserved and has a small pavilion built around it. The centrepiece of the Jallianwala bagh is a ten metre-high, four-sided tapering monument titled the Flame of Liberty. This red stone monument set in a small pool, together with other structures including a gallery; serve to commemorate the slaughter. None though, do so as powerfully as the sections of wall still bearing discernible bullet holes in them. Exact casualty figures resulting from the massacre which had included women and children have never been fully verified. The British claimed that 379 died, while locals put the toll a lot higher and it's possible that up to a thousand people were killed that day. As I walked around Jallianwala *bagh*, I reflected sombrely on how this atrocity had exposed the brutal nature of Britain's oppressive governance in colonial India.

However many had been killed during the Amritsar Massacre, it could never be comparable to the vast numbers slain during the bloodshed of 1947. With Amritsar a mere 30km east of the border with Pakistan and 50km away from the city of Lahore, it along with Lahore had been at the very epicentre of communal violence during partition. Of the in excess of 180,000 Muslims who had formerly lived in the city, no one knows exactly how many had died during that bloody period. Conversely, whilst the Muslims were being driven from Amritsar, massive numbers of Sikhs and Hindus fleeing Lahore and other parts of Western Punjab sought refuge here. As a result of these tumultuous upheavals, Amritsar differs in its demographics from the other Indian cities I'd visited by not having a Muslim population.

It was time to move on from the Punjab and I purchased a train ticket for the city of Agra, this a good twelve hours journey to the southeast. At Amritsar station, I got chatting with an Australian bloke who was going as far as Delhi. As we waited together on a platform bench, I naturally agreed to keep an eye on his backpack whilst he went to the toilet. Whist awaiting his return I started to hear a dripping noise and looked up to see a couple of workmen painting the roof supports. At the same time they were dripping liberal amounts of blue paint everywhere, including all over the Aussies' bag on the opposite end of the bench.

Jumping up and grabbing both our bags, I moved away before these slovenly workers could deposit any further paint in my direction. As I watched these Jackson Pollack wannabes proceed, I noticed a policeman standing nearby was at risk of receiving a blue speckled addition to his uniform. 'You might want to move,' I told him, pointing up to the painters. In so doing I most likely spared them both from a beating with the policeman's *lath*, the bamboo cane weapon he carried. Understandably, the Aussie was none too pleased when he returned from the toilets to discover blue paint was splattered all over his newish looking backpack. By contrast, I found the incident amusing and fairly typical of India. It seemed crazy that without even sectioning off the area to the public, workmen climbing amongst the rafters could haphazardly slap paint about above waiting passengers. When it came to carrying out maintenance work, apparently there were no health and safety regulations here and clearly not much consideration for the general public either.

Chapter 15.

My next destination is a city that receives millions of visitors each year, both Indian and foreign. Attracting all these tourists to Agra is none other than the famous Taj Mahal, as I went from visiting one beautiful building to yet another. Located in the west of Uttar Pradesh state, Agra, like Delhi, is built around the River Yamuna. While vagueness surrounds the ancient origins of this city, an established settlement on its site was first chronicled in the 11th century CE during an Afghan invasion. It was in 1504 that Agra grew to prominence after the Delhi Sultanate moved its capital there, technically rendering it the Agra Sultanate, I guess.

Following his 1526 victory over the Sultanate, Babur made Agra the imperial capital of the Mughal Empire. As home to the Mughal royal court, the city burgeoned enjoying a golden age as a centre of arts and learning. With the eventual decline of Mughal power in India, Agra subsequently fell to both the Hindu Jats and Marathas, and finally to the British. Like so many other Indian cities, Agra is a palimpsest of successive cultural influences. Under the British the city had initially served as a provincial seat of government, but after heavy fighting there during the 1847 uprising, this was later moved. Agra was never to regain its position as a centre of power; nonetheless as home to one of the world's best-known buildings, its popularity as a tourist attraction is at least eternally assured.

Even though tourism is important to its economy, the modern Agra also happens to be a sprawling, industrialised city of factories and foundries. Here heavy industries operate alongside traditional ones like leather-making, as the smoke spewing from chimneys combines with the traffic fumes to create a somewhat less than healthy environment. For visitors like me, this poor air quality was a temporary unpleasantness, for residents though it constitutes a long-term health risk.

At least by taking a cycle rickshaw from the railway station to a cheap hotel in the Taj Ganj area, I didn't contribute further to this appalling pollution. The hotel I found was, as always, budget and basic although conveniently very near to the city's number one sight, this close proximity being quaintly expressed as 'More & More Taj' on the hotel's business cards. So it was that not for the first time here in India, I found myself staying only a short walking distance from a famous city landmark.

Like the Red Fort and Jami Masjid I had seen in Delhi, the Taj Mahal dated from the reign of Emperor Shah Jahan. Famously, the grief-stricken emperor had it built as a mausoleum for his wife and the Taj Mahal is praised by many, as the definitive monument to love. Clad in white marble and delicately inlaid with semiprecious stones which create Quranic calligraphy and floral motifs, the Taj Mahal's a showcase of various architectural styles. Considered the epitome of Mughal architectural achievement, the structure took a huge workforce of 20,000 more than 20 years to complete. The grounds include a Mughal Garden, with the fountains thankfully working in this one.

Surmounting the Taj Mahal is its renowned onion-shaped dome that rises on its drum around 38 meters skywards and is crowned with a finial depicting a Mughal emblem. Also adorning the roof are decorative spires known as guldastas that extend upwards from the edge of the walls to accentuate the building's height. The central big dome is complimented by four *chhatris* spaced evenly around it, these being a distinctively Indian addition to the design of the the mausoleum. Indian influence on the architecture is also evident in the lotus petal design carved on the tops of the main dome and surrounding *chhatris* and *guldastas.* The lotus of course is a symbolic flower in all indigenous Indian religions; indeed I'd seen the lotus pattern only recently on the dome of the Golden Temple. Its inclusion on what is essentially an Islamic edifice is a perfect example of the way that the Mughals integrated Indian features into their own architectural designs.

Thankfully in light of the heat, I was at least able to enter the Taj Mahal wearing a T shirt, which was more than could be said for its hotel namesake in Mumbai. I discovered the inside of the famous structure to be every bit as spectacular as its exterior. Inside are a number of halls, these richly decorated with some amazing inlaid marble, stucco work and sculptured panels. In the middle of a central octagonal chamber lie the marble tombs of Shah Jahan and his wife. Surrounding the tombs is a delicately carved eight-panel marble screen adorned with gemstones. Both cenotaphs are beautifully inlaid with not only semi-precious stones, but valuable jewels such as emeralds, rubies and sapphires. 99 names praising Allah further inscribe the tomb of the emperor's wife, whilst that of Shah Jahan has a small sculpture of a pen box on its top, the traditional mark of a Mughal ruler. Though it may not seem like an obvious sign of imperial power, signing documents from decrees to death warrants would have been a large part of any emperor's duties. Surprisingly, for all their elaborate decoration, these two tombs aren't in fact their final resting places. As Islamic tradition proscribes lavish adornment of a grave, their actual sepulchres are in a modest crypt directly below the main chamber. Thus, Shah Jahan and his wife, not only have the most glorious mausoleum in the world; they each have *two* tombs within it.

While the Taj Mahal had been created as Shah Jahan's grand declaration of love for his adored wife, it hadn't all been adulation and devotion in the Shah's family. As has occurred throughout history, dynastic siblings often murdered, battled or banished one another over succession, and the Mughals were no different. After Shah Jahan fell ill in 1658, his third son had raised an army and defeated a force commanded by his eldest brother, the heir, who he later had executed. Despite Shah Jahan making a full recovery from his illness he was deposed and imprisoned until his death in 1666 by the younger son, who then became Emperor Aurangzeb. In one final slight against his father, Aurangzeb then denied Shah Jahan a state funeral, instead having him interred next to his wife in the Taj with the minimum of ceremony. Responsible for the construction of some truly magnificent edifices in Agra, Delhi and Lahore, no other Mughal emperor managed to leave behind such an incredible architectural heritage as Shah Jahan. In light of this tremendous contribution to the sub-continent, not least towards its tourist industry, it was a sad thought that his life, unlike his creations had been far from perfect.

Staying nearby, I was easily able to visit the Taj Mahal several times. When viewed at different times of the day, the play of light changes the subtle hues of this grand marble structure. Having said that, I woke early next morning in order to see the Taj at sunrise only to find they were charging an extortionate *ten* times more than usuall to enter at that time of morning. I thought this particularly excessive even in a land where rip-offs are rife. As far as I'm aware sunrises and sunsets are free of charge, so I didn't bother going in. Not that this really mattered, as the incredible beauty of the Taj Mahal can be appreciated whatever time one went there. It is no overstatement to say that in its totality, its design, decoration and size, the place is truly astounding.

Of course, with India's most iconic structure constantly drawing crowds, regardless of when I visited, it was nigh on impossible to enjoy its splendour in any kind of peace and quiet. Still on a more positive note, this particular Mughal site was at least overrun by regular tourists and not battle-ready soldiers!

The sight of cows is a familiar one around Agra, unsurprising as Uttar Pradesh is part of the so called 'cow belt'. I frequently saw other animals too in Agra and elsewhere, including dogs, water buffaloes and monkeys. Being quite human-like, I found monkeys particularly intriguing to observe usually as they foraged. India has several species, although I saw only bonnet macaques and more usually rhesus macaques on my trip. In fact, apart from humans, rhesus macaques are the most widely distributed of any primates, being found across large tracts of southern Asia.

Whilst relaxing on the hotel roof terrace in Agra, I watched one rhesus macaque approach my clothes as they dried on a line. The phrase 'cheeky monkey' seemed particularly apt when it suddenly jumped up and grabbed my boxer shorts from the line. I looked in surprise at its mischievous pink face as the monkey then sat on a parapet about three metres away from me. Its eyes immediately caught mine and the thing stared at me defiantly. Like the rat in Jammu, this creature almost seemed to be taunting me, knowing full well that its agility and speed outmatched mine. Even the macaque's mouth seemed upturned in a smirk as it awaited my response and the tension between us mounted. With my gaze fixed on its alert brown eyes I slowly rose to my feet and began inching forward, hoping as I did so, that the monkey might drop and abandon my underwear. Next with a quite strange mixture of annoyance and laughter, I watched the pilfering primate scarper across the roof tops, needless to say with my boxer shorts still in hand. Aware of their reputation as opportunists, foolishly I hadn't realised until then that this includes grabbing items of clothing as well as foodstuffs.

As I knew from visiting temples, monkeys along with numerous other animals are afforded a sacred status in India. Be that as it may, that some monkeys were basically thieving bastards made them undeserving of religious respect in my opinion. Then again, I couldn't discount the possibility that someone had trained this monkey to nick laundry from washing lines, either to sell or maybe simply to wear themselves. Training monkeys to steal is evidently something of an industry in India, and items worth more than my shorts are often purloined. In 2016, a macaque managed to open the door of a jewellery store in eastern India, open the till and make off with more than £100. Theft is always a concern when travelling, although to be fair, I would normally expect it to be committed by humans rather than these earthly representations of Hanuman.

Though they could be a nuisance in this way, monkeys are rarely deadly, which is more than can be said for another sacred species I encountered the following day in Agra. On some street, a snake charmer was playing his *pungi* pipe and apparently mesmerising an Indian cobra which slowly rose from an uncovered basket. In point of fact, a snake is incapable of hearing the music and moves in this cautious way because it feels threatened by the charmer and the movement of his *pungi*. Despite the perceived risk of the charmer being bitten, these snakes are defanged, thereby rendering them harmless. In Hinduism snakes are associated with happiness and fertility, and India certainly has no shortage of highly venomous ones. Statistically there is nowhere else in the world where more people suffer from snake bites or, for that matter, die as a result of them. The World Health Organisation has estimated that globally 100,000 people die annually from snakebites, with about half of these fatalities occurring in India. Of India's numerous venomous snakes, the biggest killers are saw-scaled vipers, Russell's vipers, the Indian krait and the Indian cobra. The cobra is probably the country's best-known serpent and the only type I actually saw, albeit courtesy of a snake charmer. Noted for their hood which becomes extended when the snake feels threatened, an Indian cobra grows up to a metre and a half in length and can deliver a fatal dose of poison to humans. Also native to India and larger still is the king cobra, which easily reaching four metres or more in size is the world's longest venomous snake.

Whilst fortunately I didn't come across any wild snakes in India, another animal whose bite also kills many Indians each year is fairly ubiquitous. These are the stray dogs, plenty of which carry rabies. Consequently the country suffers the highest incidence of both rabies and deaths ensuing from it in the world. One World Health Organisation article in 2014 estimated that up to 20,000 Indians a year die from rabies infections, these primarily resulting from dog bites. Whereas humans are instinctively wary of wildlife, evidently in India less caution is taken with domesticated animals. Frankly this is a startling number of people killed by an animal that few Indians even regard as being dangerous.

From Agra I booked an eleven-hour train ride to the southeast of UP and the city of Varanasi. While awaiting my train at Agra station, I noticed a white line painted on the floor beyond which it was forbidden to sit and wait. People did so nevertheless and I watched with incredulity as, from time to time, they were moved back over the line 'encouraged' to do so by a few swift strikes from a policeman's *lath*. This quite robust enforcement of waiting regulations appeared to be accepted with a note of resignation by those being herded like cattle back across the line. It is possible some being struck by the *lath* were illiterate and unable to read about any restrictions, nevertheless like petulant children being admonished for a wrongdoing, there was no remonstration. It was incidents like this that really underlined the immense cultural differences between India and the UK. I mean could you imagine the public outcry if the British Transport Police routinely deployed their truncheons to beat people back from the platform edge?

On the way to Varanasi, I witnessed something which brought a smile to my face: namely the large number of people to be seen performing their ablutions in the passing fields. These squatting individuals were not in the slightest bit embarrassed about being observed by a train full of people. Quite the contrary in fact, as they would often smile and happily wave at the passing train, at which I could not help but wave back at them with a bemused grin. It highlights how many in rural India have no access to toilets, or even a daily tide to flush their waste away. As a reality check, sights like this and my experience on a Kerala beach, humorous as they were, did make me recognize that, even in the modern age, basic facilities like lavatories are sadly not available for much of the world's population.

Chapter 16.

The ancient city of Varanasi is one of the holiest sites in Hinduism and a place of pilgrimage for millions of Indians. Varanasi derives its status as a centre of devotion on account of its location on that most spiritual of all Indian rivers, the Ganges. To Hindus, the river they call Ganga meaning 'Great Mother' is indeed a living goddess providing a connection to their ancestors. Hindus also believe that the Ganges flows from the hair of Lord Shiva and that the deity had founded Varanasi itself.

Archaeological evidence is imprecise, but Varanasi, likely existed as a settlement about 3,000 years ago. It is certainly India's oldest city and was part of the Hindu Kingdom of Kosala during its early history. By the 6th century CE, Varanasi had established itself as a key centre for Hindu mysticism, culture and philosophy. From the 11th century onwards, Muslim invaders attacked Varanasi with both the Afghans and later the Mughals sacking the city. Still, even during the long periods of Muslim rule in India, Varanasi was able to flourish as a site of Hindu pilgrimage and learning. From the 18th century up until the time of independence, Benares as the city had by then been named, was the capital of a Hindu princely state bearing the same name.

Where the Ganges flows through Varanasi, a long succession of terraces and buildings, many of them temples, line its west bank. Also flanking the riverbank are *ghats*, flights of stone steps leading down to the water's edge where thousands come every day to ritually bathe in the murky waters of this sacred river. A couple of sections though serve a more morbid purpose as burning *ghats*, these cremation sites from where ashes can be easily scattered into the Ganges. In Hinduism to die and be cremated in the holy city of Varanasi is regarded as a way of guaranteeing *moksha* and thereby freedom from the cycle of reincarnation. It explains why never-ending devotees arrive there to end out their days. What makes the place totally absorbing for foreigners like me is the fact that, in Varanasi, death itself is very much a part of everyday life.

In the old city south of the railway station, I booked into a hotel like no other I'd ever seen. It was situated alongside both one of the burning ghats and a rather grim-looking crematorium building.

'Agreeable views overlooking the local crematorium' was never going to be a big selling point for the majority of hotels, however this guesthouse was positively proud of their location. As such its business cards advertised the hotel's close proximity to Varanasi's 'oldest burning ghat and only electric ceramotory' (sic). There can be no denying that it was a perfect spot to watch with morbid fascination the funeral pyres burning, although I never actually saw the electric crematorium being used whilst staying there.

The only funerals I have attended were solemn, sad occasions, so I found it odd that in India, those carrying the deceased to their place of cremation did so whilst chanting and singing. Seeing such spectacles highlighted the sharp disparity in attitudes about death which Hindus view as a cause for public celebration rather than mourning. Reflecting this, the hotel owner had a cheerful outlook on the subject, once even jokingly commenting 'Varanasi is a very holy place where Hindus are coming to learn and burn!'

The corpses arriving at the burning *ghat* are wrapped in simple shrouds and tied to basic wooden stretchers. Once a body has been covered in wood and ignited, the cremation process takes the best part of two hours. Taking pictures of these funeral pyres is officially taboo, although this being India unsurprisingly a small payment of *baksheesh* to the priest presiding over the ceremony is a way around this. One thing was for sure, watching all these cremations certainly caused me to cogitate on life and its ultimate finality. For somewhere which really drove home the final reality of human mortality, the burning *ghat* has a very surreal quality about it. One thing that is assuredly real on the other hand, is the often malodorous air generated by decomposing bodies. At times this could be quite overpowering.

The cremations take place fairly constantly throughout the day and well into the night. At night time, the flames would project an eerie flickering glow onto the darkness of the adjacent river. The frequency of the cremations soon had me almost blasé about the omnipresence of death and the regular stream of bodies being delivered for burning. The word 'delivered' indeed seems fitting as I didn't see any proper hearses being used to transport the dead. Remarkably, I observed one corpse arriving at the *ghat* tied to the roof rack of a taxi, whilst others would turn up in the back of auto-rickshaws! I guess these kinds of taxi passengers never tipped the driver.

At least in the modern age, those being cremated tended to be dead first which had not always been the case here in India. In the past, some Hindu communities had observed the custom of *sati,* when a recently widowed woman would be expected to commit suicide on their husband's funeral pyre. A related ritual had been *jauhar,* whereby when faced with inevitable capture by foreign invaders Hindu women would burn themselves alive en masse. *Sati* was more prevalent, though, and went back to at least the 6th century CE and was still happening during the early decades of the 19th century in colonial India. Ostensibly, a voluntary sacrifice performed as an act of religious devotion, in reality the woman in question was often coerced into the act. The British banned it in 1829, this one of their more progressive achievements during three centuries of colonial involvement in India.

As late as 1987, the Indian government had to pass legislation prohibiting *sati* following a notorious case in Rajasthan, one which received nationwide coverage. It involved an 18 year old widow named Roop Kanwar, who'd committed *sati* whilst watched by hundreds of cheering villagers. After the event thousands visited the site of the pyre believing it to be a holy place and Kanwar's house became a museum. In fact, commemorating the *sati* had even brought economic benefits to the village due to the influx of pilgrims. Such veneration wasn't unusual either as Rajasthan has temples and festivals which glorify sati. Not everyone was in awe of this *sati* though and women's groups in the state demanded prosecutions against those involved. They had also opposed the proposed building of a temple on the site as a shrine. As a result of these activists, the state government were forced into taking action and dozens of arrests were made, amongst them family members. They all claimed that the *sati* had been a voluntary act and furthermore that any attempt to stop it would have incurred a curse (*sati shraap*). All of those charged over the matter were nevertheless subsequently acquitted. The case did however force the government to introduce legislation which made participating in any *sati* processions or even watching *sati* illegal. The incident raised many questions about the treatment of women in India. It was shocking to think such appalling things still happened in the late 20th century.

A prime attraction along the riverbank in Varanasi is the *aarti* ceremony that takes place at dusk every day. During it, a row of priests elevated on a stage perform a synchronised rite in which they wave incense sticks around in patterns and move burning lamps in a clockwise circular motion. The light from these lamps is offered as *puja* to the river goddess Ganga and it's believed their flames receive her power during the ceremony. *Aarti* is a noisy affair to watch amidst the sound of *pujaris* singing and chanting mantras, bells ringing, cymbals clanging and conch shells being blown. It all combines to create quite an atmosphere, even if the spirituality of the occasion is questionable, appearing to me more like some choreographed show than an actual ancient religious ceremony. The collecting of money from the audience at the end of the ritual only reinforced this impression, although to be fair their performance was highly enjoyable to watch. Entertainment value aside, it also made a refreshing change to see flames that weren't in the process of consuming corpses.

Away from the *ghats* a lot of the old city seems to be a maze of alleys, some too narrow for traffic. Where there is traffic, as per usual in India it was extremely congested, chaotic, noisy and polluted. Beside its religious status, Varanasi is a city noted for its silk production. It is such a big business that everywhere I went rickshaw wallahs and touts, all doubtless on a commission, were eager to lead me to some silk factory. I read how the silk weavers received a pittance for their work whilst the slick salesmen made all the profit, this precisely the type of exploitation which appears to be a hallmark of so much global commerce.

Following a hot sticky day in the heat and traffic of Varanasi, the breeze from the river made the hotel's rooftop terrace a good place to unwind and eat. When night fell it was quite atmospheric up there with the amber glow and crackling sound of burning wood coming from the funeral pyres below. One such evening, a group of us travellers were sitting around a table dining, drinking and chatting. The latter as usual mostly revolving around mutual experiences and observations. At some point during our repast, a strong gust of wind suddenly engulfed our table in a thick acrid cloud of smoke which stung the eyes. Everyone jumped up and moved away from the table, this being accompanied by much coughing and swinging of arms before the smoke gradually began to dissipate.

When we eventually sat back down and were about to resume eating, one observant soul at our table pointed out that the ash deposited everywhere by the smoke, including all over our food, had emanated from the cremations taking place next to the hotel. At the disgusting thought of our *dal* and rice now being sprinkled with charred particles of human remains, unsurprisingly we all instantly lost our appetites. I for one was normally quite partial to smoked food, needless to say on this occasion I decided to give it a miss. It then occurred to me that dining outside in India was not without its occasional problems caused by people, either living ones trying to kill each other with guns, or indeed by those who were already deceased and being cremated!

Around dawn is considered the most auspicious time for Hindus to perform their ritual bathing in the sacred Ganges. So, I rented a boat in order to witness this spectacle of hundreds of men and women praying and performing various rites, whilst they washed themselves in the brown muddy waters of the Ganges. The river, which is easily 400 metres wide, looked deceptively calm but the water level was high and the current perilously fast. This naturally made heading downstream effortless unlike going against the strong current, when all six of the crew had to row furiously. It was a far cry from any gentle *shikara* ride and not since my canoe trip off the Kerala coast had I felt quite so ill at ease about being on water.

As we slowly made our way upstream, at one point I spotted something indistinct floating in the water ahead. As it speedily neared the boat carried by the current, I then suddenly realised in horror that it was the bloated body of a dead child. Apparently, in Hindu tradition when young children die, rather than cremating them they're either buried or, as in this case, placed directly into a holy river. The decomposing child's corpse only narrowly avoided colliding with our boat and the macabre sight was truly stomach-turning. A moment of panic came over me as I had a scary vision of the boat capsizing. It went through my mind that, if this were to happen, I'd either drown in the raging current, or if by chance pulled out from the water, die later from some fatal water-borne disease. Not a happy choice! I managed to compose myself and signalled my desire to head back to the *ghats*, feeling relieved once we reached the safety of terra firma.

Later on in the day I read some tourist brochure which waxed lyrical about the river at Varanasi having, 'offerings of saffron-coloured garlands and twinkling oil lamps bobbing lazily in the currents'. It conveyed a delightful image and one which I am sure at times is true, however, what I had seen bobbing in the currents that morning was obviously far less appealing. The reality is that by the time the Ganges reaches the city, it is heavily polluted, having flowed hundreds of kilometres from its Himalayan source through one of the world's most densely populated regions. Along its course, industrial waste, agricultural run-off and masses of raw untreated sewerage feed into its waters. Added to this is further pollution resulting from: general rubbish, cremation ashes, animal carcasses, and, as I'd just seen, even human bodies.

In a nutshell, the impact of millions of people has contaminated India's holiest waterway, turning it into a toxic river whose waters you wouldn't wish to imbibe. It seemed astonishing therefore that devout Hindus would gladly immerse themselves in the Ganges given its risk to health. From my understanding, cholera, typhoid and hepatitis amongst other water-borne diseases were rife on the Gangetic plain. With high levels of disease-causing bacteria in the water, it was inevitable that many of those who bathed in it would contract some form of illness. And to think that, back in Britain, I used to be worried at swimming pools about picking up a verruca!

Of all my destinations in India, I'd say Varanasi was by far the most profound and fascinating. This was a sentiment echoed by scores of other foreigners I met, many of whom had travelled in India far more extensively than me. This incredibly spiritual place of funeral pyres and piety built on a stretch of Hinduism's holiest waterway is really unlike anywhere else I ever visited. Its popular sobriquet for obvious reasons is the "City of Temples" but in truth Varanasi could equally be described as the city of death, a place where death is dealt with in a very public way which is absorbing to observe, if also a little macabre at the same time. I would have stayed longer but there was somewhere a lot further north of the city that I really wanted to visit, this being not only a different town or city but a different country, namely Nepal. Kashmir had whetted my appetite for the mountains and with the Nepalese capital Kathmandu by now a lot closer than Delhi, I took a coach to the border town of Sunauli.

Chapter 17.

As the bus journeyed northward through the countryside of Uttar Pradesh, we passed endless fields of sugarcane, this being a native crop which had been crystallised into sugar in India since the early centuries CE. The ancient Greeks, who reached North India under Alexander the Great, had been the first Europeans to encounter sugarcane, naming it quite descriptively as the 'reeds that produce honey without bees.' It would be another 1800 years, however, before Portuguese traders introduced cane sugar from India to the European table. Like pepper it was initially a luxury item that in the fullness of time would become a standard kitchen necessity across much of the world. Even so, it is worth remembering that for all the sweetness it afforded, sugarcane introduced from India and cultivated in the Americas and elsewhere in the world caused untold misery and suffering through slavery and colonisation.

In contemporary India, sugarcane is of course indispensable for sweetening all that *chai* drunk, not to mention its use in distilling 'whisky' and other spirits. The juice extracted from sugarcane is a popular beverage, often drunk when mixed with different spices. Commonly the juice is also processed into *jaggery,* a concentrated type of crude cane sugar used in cooking both sweet and savoury dishes. In line with most agricultural production in India, wastage is minimised with crushed sugarcane stalks used as cattle feed and fuel or in the manufacture of pulp and fibreboard.

On the bus with me and similarly making for Nepal was Bendik a Norwegian chap who I'd befriended at the hotel in Varanasi. The journey took us the best part of a day, but for once the vehicle wasn't packed, enabling me to sprawl across the back seats and sleep for some of the journey. After obtaining a visa at the border we crossed into Nepal and exchanged some money. By now the evening was drawing in, so instead of pushing on, we got ongoing bus tickets for the following morning and took a room in Sunauli for the night.

Sunauli, a town which straddles both sides of the border, is an unexceptional place people generally travel through rather than stay in. Such lack of tourism meant that our accommodation was ridiculously cheap even by the standards of South Asian, with a twin room costing us each less than a bar of chocolate would back in Europe... and there was room service to boot. With little to see or do in Sunauli, after dining we decided to get shitfaced in the room on some *bhang* I'd bought in Varanasi. This, washed down with a few cans of Tuborg beers courtesy of the room service, did the trick and ensured a sound night's sleep.

Having agreed to meet up with Bendik in Kathmandu later, I left alone early next morning to visit Chitwan National Park where my intention was to go on an elephant safari. Sat on the minibus I felt decidedly rough and deservedly so from the excesses of the night before. Still, I sought comfort in the prospect of soon riding on an elephant, this something I was really looking forward to doing. By the time the minibus was roughly two kilometres from Sunauli, I had a sudden realisation that left me mortified. I had only left my money belt under the pillow back in the hotel room. In it was not only a considerable amount of Nepalese cash, but my bank cards, passport and airline ticket home; basically everything I could not afford to lose.

As the shock fully registered, I instinctively stood up and yelled out for the bus to stop. Then, rushing to the front of the vehicle, I insisted that the driver pulled over, which he promptly did. I spent the next few minutes trying to persuade him to turn around and return to Sunauli. His command of English was limited and mine of Nepali plainly non-existent, but I got the impression that he was unwilling to go back due to the schedule. I implored him to do so, offering him payment once I had retrieved my money belt, but my supplications were in vain and he wouldn't oblige.

At this juncture it was fair to say that my stress was reaching coronary-inducing levels and I started shouting at the somewhat bewildered driver. Just at the moment I was beginning to accept that my protestations were in vain, a ray of hope appeared on the otherwise deserted road in the form of a cycle rickshaw heading towards us. Then with my backpack in hand, I leaped down from the minibus and thanked the driver for nothing. I think in light of my invective, it was probably just as well that his grasp of English had been limited.

Flagging down the approaching cycle-rickshaw I dispensed with the customary haggling and immediately boarded. Telling him the name of the hotel, I instructed the cycle-wallah to 'Ride as fast as you can to Sunauli'. Throughout the tense journey, I sat nervously on the edge of the seat, fretting over the consequences of losing my money belt and being effectively stranded here in Nepal, with nothing but my backpack and its contents. Understandably it was a scenario which filled me with a sense of foreboding.

When at last we arrived back at the hotel, the poor wallah was sweating profusely. Leaping from the rickshaw, I literally ran into the building and up the stairs straight to the room, surprising a woman who was cleaning it. I approached the bed and lifted the pillow to see with utter relief that my money belt was still there. With my anxiety instantly dissipated I felt elated. Had the cleaner, or anyone else for that matter, found my belt before me, there's a good chance I wouldn't have seen it again.

Returning outside, I immediately gave my cycle wallah a big hug and a day's wages. He was delighted but, trust me, nowhere near as much as I was. In hindsight, my loss of temper on the minibus earlier was regrettable even if the stakes were very high. Quite what the driver and other passengers must have thought about the demented foreigner aboard, God alone knew. Still, one thing I did know for sure was my days of getting wasted on *bhang* were well and truly over.

By chance sat there on the minibus I caught next was Bendik, who understandably seemed a bit surprised to see me boarding. I proceeded to tell him all about my hair-raising episode earlier that morning. If this testing start to my day had not been bad enough, within about an hour of this fresh attempt to get to Chitwan I began to feel unwell and had a high temperature. My illness was likely caused by something I had eaten at the station earlier and became so bad, at one point I thought I was actually going to pass out. When we stopped for a short break en route, unable to find any lavatories, a sudden bout of diarrhoea forced me to go to the toilet behind a tree. Feeling utterly dreadful, I somehow managed to endure the remainder of the journey.

After bidding Bendik goodbye for a second time that day, I got off at a bus stop near a village called Sauraha. Waiting there were some people from one of the lodges inside Chitwan National Park. By now I was so desperate to get to a bed and lie down, so after haggling and being assured that the lodge was not very far away, we headed off in their jeep. Well distance is of course relative and when compared to Kathmandu it wasn't that far, but it did take over an hour to get there.

The first part of the journey seated in the back of the jeep was comfortable. However this ended after only five minutes when we came to a river, which we then crossed by canoe. On the other side I found myself transferred to a bullock cart of all things. Not only was this tediously slow but it lacked any effective suspension meaning I got bounced around, this only exacerbating my delicate state. Throughout this bullock cart ride, in between my bouts of nausea I groaned and cursed whilst asking repeatedly like some restless child passenger, 'Are we there yet?'

Reaching the lodge, I found out that what had been described to me as a 'bungalow' at the bus stop, was in reality a rudimentary hut without electricity. Accommodation does not get more basic than that, though it did have one vital thing I needed in my febrile condition: a bed. Between then and the following day when at last I felt better, I spent my time intermittently sleeping and also doing a lot of something else beginning with the letter 's'. I' d wager that whoever claimed that, 'to travel hopefully is a better thing than to arrive' had likely never been bounced around the back of a bullock cart whilst feeling like crap!

Famously synonymous with mountains, Nepal boasts five of the world's ten highest peaks within its borders. What I hadn't known however was that a large part of southern Nepal known as the Terai consists of a mixture of sub-tropical jungle, swampland and fertile alluvial plain. For a long time the Terai had been extremely malarial until the eradication of the disease opened the territory up to settlement and farming. Concerns over the impact of human encroachment on the natural environment of the Terai prompted the establishment of Chitwan National Park and other reserves, set up to protect the region's wildlife.

Founded back in the early 1970s, Chitwan was Nepal's very first national park and covers 900 sq. kilometres. An area of wetlands, savannah and forests with dense undergrowth, the park lies in a lowland valley between two small mountain ranges and is drained by two major rivers. The woodlands in Chitwan consist mainly of chir pine and sal trees, both species widely used in construction in Nepal. The landscape here in the Terai was not how I'd imagined Nepal to be, reminding me more of South India than mountainous Kashmir.

The humid, jungle habitat of Chitwan National Park supports a large variety of flora and fauna. For all this diversity, my own first encounter with the local wildlife was not any more exciting than ants crawling all over the hut. There were plenty of ants around but disappointingly no other guests were staying at the lodge. This wasn't good news for a gregarious chap like me, so asking staff where the nearest bar was, I sought company there that evening.

It took a good fifteen minutes of walking along the main paths running through the reserve to find the bar. The place was quiet but I did end up talking to a girl from Birmingham for most of the night, enjoying a drink and a laugh with her. Later, as I was leaving the owner casually said to me, 'Mind out for any rhinos on your way back.' 'Yes very funny indeed' I laughed. He then added, 'No seriously, there are rhinos about and they're active at night'. The sternness of his tone made me realise he wasn't kidding!

Quite honestly, 'Mind out for any rhinos' is the last thing you want to hear as you're about to make your way drunkenly home from a bar at night time. At this warning I nervously headed back to my lodge, hoping all the while that I didn't come across any rhinos in the darkness. That it was pitch black didn't offer much comfort either as rhinos; which are partly nocturnal, have poor eyesight, relying instead on both their excellent sense of smell and acute hearing. Worse still, rhinos have a fearsome reputation for charging at anything they consider a threat.

With the risk posed by rhinos, I suddenly began to wish that I was walking through some city rather than a jungle. At least in the urban environment, the only animals I need worry about are rabid dogs and maybe the occasional thieving monkeys, not two-tonnes of beast hurtling towards me! I was all in favour of seeing wildlife on my trip, but preferably minus the fear of injury or worse in the process. Maybe my sudden paranoia about encountering a rhino was heightened by the alcohol, but then again, the proprietor had felt the need to mention the matter. For all I knew, previously customers have been gored or trampled by rhinos after leaving his bar, necessitating such a word of caution. Whatever the reason, now being aware of the potential danger lurking in the darkness, only made the walk back feel like an eternity. Given my state of fright, it was just as well that the bar owner hadn't brought my attention to all the tigers, leopards and sloth bears also roaming the park. Between them these animals managed to kill and injure hundreds of people throughout the sub-continent every year. Fortunately I did not see any rhinos that night although an even larger animal managed to scare the life out of me. This happened when I got back to the lodge and in total darkness nearly walked straight into one of the elephants from the lodge's own stable.

After almost bumping into an elephant that night, the following morning it was time to see some more of these beasts, only in a more relaxed manner. I hired a bike and cycled out to a breeding centre. It was worth the effort just to see the baby calves, which besides being pretty cute were of course the whole purpose of their breeding programme. A guide explained all about the centre and its elephants, remarkable creatures which can weigh up to five tonnes. Their vast bulk means elephants can easily consume up to five percent of their own body weight in fodder every day. This whopping appetite is why they roam free grazing in the jungle for much of day. Nonetheless, whenever they are stabled at the centre the elephants are chained up.

During the tour, our guide pointed out one stud bull chained to a large tree well away from the other elephants. He went on to tell us that the animal was in a state of *musth*, this being when its testosterone levels were unusually high. As this condition makes male elephants become exceptionally aggressive, even those bred in captivity become unmanageable and dangerous to humans and other elephants. Bulls don't actually need to be in this heightened sexual state in order to breed so any that were had to be kept isolated and chained up for safety reasons. To shorten the period of musth, the elephant's food and water supply is stopped, which I can only imagine would antagonise them further. Looking at this particular pachyderm and its fearsome looking tusks, the thought of it rampaging through the place was frightening and the chains restraining it therefore reassuring.

The centre itself was established 1989 as a conservation project in response to Nepal's dwindling wild elephant numbers, a sad consequence of past overhunting. Some of the animals bred and then trained at the centre supply Chitwan's numerous lodges, all of which kept elephants for safaris. Other elephants born there are used for religious ceremonies, warden patrols and agricultural work, whilst a number are retained for breeding. It was wonderful that tame elephants were being bred in captivity, but it was also pleasing to hear that some wild herds still exist in the park. The centrality of elephants in Chitwan became apparent from visiting the centre. This is a place where even polo is played on elephants and Chitwan hosts an annual world championship in the sport. It's an interesting take on the game and when it comes to minority sports, elephant polo is definitely one of them!

Early next morning, there were yet more elephants when at last I was able to embark on a safari on the back of one. By now others had booked into the lodge and so four of us climbed upon the seated elephant, each sitting with a post between our legs in the corners of the square frame *howdah* strapped to the animal. Then with our *mahout* (driver) seated upon the creature's shoulders it stood up and off we went in search of wildlife. The landscape of dense jungle, streams and swamps, was no obstacle to the beast as it lumbered effortlessly through the soft dawn light. At the same time, I was surprised at the amount of damage the elephant caused to its own natural habitat by stomping on vegetation and small shrubs as it went along.

To spot *any* kind of large wildlife on a safari would be gratifying but my dearest hope was to see a Royal Bengal tiger. Amongst the biggest tigers in the world, there are an estimated 120 of these powerful predators within the park. At the top of the jungle food chain, these magnificent creatures' prey on the abundance of deer hogs and even water buffalo here in Chitwan. The *only* real threat to tigers in the animal kingdom comes from humans who, through hunting, had almost wiped them out. Even though hunting was banned and tiger numbers are slowly rising, sadly poaching is still a problem.

Such poaching is driven by overseas demand for tiger skins and for the application of their bones in traditional Chinese medicines, in spite of there being a ban on their use in China for many years. The scale of this problem is revealed by the fact that poachers in neighbouring India kill an estimated hundred tigers a year. That said, killings aren't always one way when it comes to tiger-human interaction. Historically tigers have quite a frightening track record in this respect. In the latter 19th and early 20th century one tiger alone is credited with killing over 400 people in India and Nepal. During that period, on average more than 900 people a year were killed by these stripped predators in British India. Today with a much-reduced wild tiger population such attacks are much less numerous, although dozens of fatalities do still happen each year across the subcontinent. Another big cat prowling the forests and grasslands of Chitwan is the spotted leopard, which are more numerous than tigers. Unfortunately, on my safari, both of these elusive beasts proved to be...well *elusive*. Ultimately the closest I came to seeing either animal was those depicted upon Nepalese bank notes.

Rhinos, by comparison, luckily turned out to be altogether less retiring and we spotted several, some with their calves. After I had been so anxious to avoid them coming back from the bar the other night, I now felt exhilarated to see these one-horned Indian Rhinos from the safety of an elephant's back. Then at one point, amazingly our elephant got within about five metres of one rhino and her calf wallowing in a pool. It was fantastic how closely we were able to observe these formidable armoured creatures from our elevated position. There was something entirely natural about the moment involving as it did three animal species in such close proximity, two of them the largest found on the sub-continent, the third being the most dangerous!

After quietly watching the rhino and her offspring for several minutes, we suddenly and dramatically charged forwards chasing them both off into the jungle. It was pretty exciting stuff as we hung on tight whilst our elephant stormed its way through the undergrowth. When I queried our *mahout* as to why he had done this, he explained that it was a pre-emptive move just in case the mother rhino thought us a threat and decided to charge first. Well frankly, if rhinos are potentially prepared to attack an elephant, then I was doubly relieved to have avoided any on my recent night -time return from the bar.

Mirroring the plight of tigers, rhinos had almost become extinct at one stage due to extensive hunting for so-called sport. In the modern age they are killed solely for their horns and nothing else, this further decimating Nepal's remaining rhino population. Just like tiger bones, rhinoceros horns are valued in Chinese medicine even though the horns are composed of little more than keratin, exactly the same protein which forms human finger nails and hair. The establishment of sanctuaries like the one in Chitwan, which is under the protection of the army, has at least succeeded in bringing poaching under control and as a direct result there are now several hundred rhinos in the reserve. Regrettably however these conservation efforts started to be undermined back in 2018, when China ended a 25 year old ban on the medicinal use of tiger bones and rhino horns. The Chinese authorities claim that this trade will be tightly regulated and only parts from animals bred in captivity permitted. Critics though fear it will only fuel poaching and result in global tiger and rhino numbers dwindling.

Chapter 18.

The elephant safari achieved, I departed from Chitwan National Park later that day for the capital Kathmandu, a city located in a valley of the same name. I would have preferred to take a train but, unlike India, Nepal seems to lack a railway network; in fact the country had not even possessed any major roads up until the 1950s. Kathmandu lies around 150 km north east of Chitwan, this not a huge distance away, but poor roads and increasingly hilly terrain beyond the Terai, made for a slow journey of almost seven hours. Still, it was an ideal opportunity to ponder this landlocked country of around thirty million people, one which is sandwiched between the two massive populations of India and China. While small by comparison, the population of Nepal is still actually quite ethnically and linguistically diverse, being of Mongoloid and Indo-Aryan descent. The major culture in Nepal is that of the Newars, the original inhabitants of the Kathmandu Valley, the very place to where I was now travelling. In spite of being a minority nationally, the culture of the Newars manages to dominate Nepal, it having been spread by Newari merchants who had established bazaars across the country.

About a third of the population of Nepal are Janajaati, a tribal people who inhabit the hilly Pahad region extending across the middle of Nepal. A community of Tibetan heritage known as the Bhotiya are found in the high alpine Himal belt stretching across the north of this country. They include the Sherpas, probably the best known of all Nepalis abroad and famed for their hardiness and mountaineering skills. I must confess that, prior to coming to the country, I hadn't realised that Sherpas are actually an ethnic group erroneously believing that the word refers to porters who assist on Himalayan climbing expeditions.

A Chinese invasion of Tibet in 1950 had caused a great number of Tibetans to flee to both Nepal and India. Amongst them had been the Tibetan spiritual leader, the Dalai Lama, who had lived along with many of his followers in the north of India since 1959. Following its annexation, Tibet had become a de facto province of China which had ruthlessly suppressed any internal demands for independence. In reaction, Tibetans settled in India and Nepal and their descendants, have been quite vociferous in highlighting the plight of their homeland. On an international level, lobbying by the Free Tibet Campaign founded in Britain has attracted support, although realistically Chinese control over Tibet is unlikely to end any time soon, if ever at all.

In terms of its religious composition, Nepal has a predominantly Hindu population, which makes it the world's only Hindu majority country besides India and Mauritius. Compared to its southern neighbour, Nepal has a relatively small number of Muslims and Christians. Whilst Hinduism has existed in Nepal for a long time, it only became the mainstream religion there following a massive influx of Hindus fleeing the Muslim conquests of North India. For centuries previously, Buddhism had been pre-eminent, and in spite of its eventual decline is still followed by roughly ten percent of Nepalis today.

It so happens that the actual founder of Buddhism, Siddhartha Gautama, had been born not very far from the border town of Sunauli where I had just stayed. The exact date of his birth is not known and disputed, although many claim it was around 623 BCE. Buddha's teachings were discernibly rooted in the traditions of Hinduism sharing as they do such concepts as *ahimsa*, karma and reincarnation; although significantly Buddha hadn't accepted the caste system which Hinduism advocates. At the core of Buddhist philosophy is the acceptance that all life is suffering derived from human desires. By living our lives in the right way according to the cause and effect of karma, it becomes possible to eliminate desire and other unwanted negative qualities such as hatred, greed and delusion. If an individual achieves this, then they are deemed to have reached the ultimate goal of *nirvana* and thus freedom from the cycle of life and death.

Buddhism was first established in North India, where Siddhartha Gautama had gained enlightenment and first began preaching his message, his first sermon was in fact delivered near Varanasi. Although Buddhism reached a few areas of Nepal earlier, during the 8th century Guru Rimpoche spread the faith across the whole country. Essentially a monastic faith at heart, Buddhism split into different branches over time, the two major ones being Theravada and Mahayana. It was the latter tradition that gained popularity in

Nepal where it soon became intertwined with both the Hindu cult of *tantrism* and local shamanist beliefs. Together with the original Buddha, a further five known as the *panchabuddha* form part of Nepalese Buddhism, each one representing a different aspect of the religion's founder. Indeed images of these meditating Buddhas can frequently be seen on statues, pictures and carvings in Nepal.

With the mass-arrival of those fleeing Islamic conquest in India, in time the Hinduism they brought with them had more or less subsumed Nepalese Buddhism. Vajrayana Buddhism introduced by refugees escaping the Chinese seizure of Tibet, has become the commonest form of the religion followed today in Nepal. With an emphasis on mysticism, Vajrayana, which is also sometimes called tantric Buddhism, is strongly identified with neighbouring Tibet. In Nepal the general syncretism of Hinduism and Buddhism makes it virtually impossible to completely separate the two; with temples, deities, rituals and customs all usually being shared by both faiths.

From at least the first millennium, the territory which became Nepal had been settled by different migrant groups arriving from Tibet to the north and India to the south. In the past, many of the powers which came to prominence in Nepal had their origins in India. The first recorded was the Licchavi dynasty that emerged in the Kathmandu Valley sometime around the 2nd century CE. By the 5th century, wealth from trade between India and Tibet had made the Licchavi monarchs powerful and their kingdom lasted up until the 9th century. Another kingdom thought to have had Indian roots was that of the Khasas, who by the 12th century had become a major regional power in the west of modern-day Nepal. Although their domain had fragmented by the 15th century, the Khasa had left one important legacy in their Indo-Aryan language which survives today as the national language Nepali.

Another noteworthy monarchy to have ruled in Nepal had been the Hindu *Mallas* who were based in the Kathmandu Valley. Their name means 'wrestler' in Sanskrit, and this title was adopted in the 12th century by the king of a city named Bhaktapur. A united Malla kingdom ruled the west of modern Nepal until the death of Yaksha Malla in 1482. It was then divided between his three sons creating three new realms, these centred on the valley cities of Bhaktapur, Kathmandu and Patan. As these three Malla kingdoms prospered in the Kathmandu Valley, elsewhere across the region dozens of small states and kingdoms also existed, amongst them the territory of Gorkha less than 80km northwest of the valley. Gorkha would later be the birthplace of modern Nepal when, in the mid-18th century, its king, Prithvi Narayan Shah, launched a military campaign that would eventually unify the whole country. By 1769, he had conquered the three kingdoms of the Kathmandu Valley, thereby putting an end to over five centuries of Malla reign there. After these victories, Prithvi Narayan, himself a descendent of Hindus who'd fled North India, moved the capital of his new kingdom from his native Gorkha to Kathmandu. Subject to much infighting and fluctuations in their political fortunes, nonetheless the Shah dynasty he had founded would manage to reign in Nepal until the early 21st century.

The continuing expansion of the Shah empire had in due course been curtailed by conflict, at first in the north with neighbouring Tibet and then against the British East India Company in the Terai. By the time the British had defeated the Nepali army in 1816, the boundaries of modern Nepal had been pretty much been finalised by its Shah monarchs. For all their achievements in unifying the country, the squabbling Shahs had lost their grip on power in 1846 after a palace coup had relegated them to mere figureheads. This takeover was orchestrated by Jung Bahadur Rana and the dynasty he founded in his name, wielded power in Nepal for more than a hundred years. Nonetheless, the Ranas singularly failed to develop the country's infrastructure and effectively shut Nepal off from the wider world. Opposition to Rana governance eventually led to the formation of a Nepali Congress Party based upon the Indian model. In 1951, pressure from a newly independent India ended the Rana regime and restored the power of the Shah Monarchy.

The country took its first tentative steps towards democracy with a general election in 1959 and the formation of a Congress Party government. The progress was short lived because in 1960, the reigning King Mahendra, seized control of the government, imprisoned opponents and banned all political parties. This re-emergence of Nepal's Shah's as absolute monarchs saw a national assembly introduced without political parties, its members being merely royal appointees. Three decades of the Shah dictatorship led to some economic growth, but this wasn't sufficient to offset the effects of a population explosion. Tourism had increased in this period too bringing economic benefits, but Nepal by then had grown massively over-dependent on foreign aid.

By 1990, economic failure and political repression, coupled with the usual corruption found in all governments, had provoked large -scale protests. In the wake of bloodshed, riots, curfews, strikes, mass arrests and international pressure, the king was forced to step down and agree to become a constitutional monarch. After a gap of more than thirty years, democracy had returned to Nepal in May 1991 with elections to a multi-party parliament which the Congress Party won. Various communist parties also did well in these elections. Even so, in 1996 one of them, a Maoist party, had broken away from the democratic process and began conducting a 'people's war'. The rebels were able to gain a foothold over much of rural Nepal as civil war gripped the country for a decade.

Against this background of internal conflict, political instability further dogged the country as the monarchy retook power. This followed a palace massacre in 2001 when the heir to the throne shot dead nine members of his own family including his parents, the king and queen, before fatally shooting himself. Fuelled by a mix of alcohol and drugs, the crown prince had apparently been motivated by anger at family disapproval of his plans to marry his girlfriend. Soon the slain monarch's younger brother, Gyanendra, was crowned and wasted no time in asserting his authority.

In early 2005, Gyanendra assumed direct rule over the country just as his father King Mahendra had done a quarter of a century before; subsequent repression led to thousands being imprisoned and civil liberties suspended. However far from quelling dissent, these repressive measures only united Nepal's political parties in their opposition to the king's rule, and decisively they formed an alliance with the Maoists rebels to resist his dictatorship. With the masses mobilised in what now seemed like a rerun of the events of 1990, large-scale strikes and demonstrations amidst martial law and curfews led to bloodshed. By April of the following year in the face of resolute opposition and continuing unrest, King Gyanendra had little choice but to relinquish power and reinstate parliament. In a further positive development, a peace agreement finally put an end to the Maoist rebellion, thereby bringing them back into the democratic fold. Within two years the Maoists were elected to power in a new Nepalese Constituent Assembly and after forming a coalition government declared the country a republic, and in so doing, ended the Shah's reign of almost 240 years.

With peace and democracy restored, regardless, political crisis, systemic corruption and deadlock continued to characterise the country's governments with a constitution not agreed upon until 2015. Even then, it was claimed the constitution lacked safeguards when it came to the representation of minority ethnic groups. Resistance to it from ethnic Indians in the Terai, a group who had previously made violent demands for independence, prompted the Indian government to impose a blockade on exporting goods to Nepal. The resulting shortages hit hard and, after four months the Nepalese government were forced to alter the constitution to ensure adequate representation for the country's minorities.

The embargo also forced the Nepalese government to reassess its relationship with India, which viewing Nepal as a client state exerted influence over the country's polity for a long time. Since this reappraisal, the government in Nepal has moved increasingly closer to China as an economic partner, resulting in huge Chinese investment in Nepal's infrastructure. Naturally the Maoists and other allied communists who govern Nepal are broadly speaking ideologically compatible with China's own government. Whereas religion has gained greater importance in Indian politics during the early 21st century, in Nepal communist ideology appears to have done the same. Together with Chinese economic assistance, this development has clearly facilitated the shift in Nepalese regional alignment away from India towards China. Unlike China, though, Nepal is a democracy...well at least for the time being.

Ultimately, the civil war and political chaos which have affected Nepal are the results of human failure, but equally disastrous have been the forces of nature. Avalanches, floods and landslides are frequent hazards, although none have been as devastating as the earthquake which struck the centre of Nepal in April 2015. It was the country's biggest earthquake since 1934, and killed around 9000 people and injured more than 20,000. Hundreds more had died subsequently in avalanches and aftershocks triggered by the earthquake. Although these catastrophes are mercifully rare, the major one in 2015 was a reminder that they could happen at any time. It also showed how the landscape which imbued Nepal with some striking scenery, also has the capacity to be as destructive as it is beautiful.

Chapter 19.

My bus arrived on schedule in the Nepalese capital, a city which spreads out across the north-west of the Kathmandu Valley and is built around the River Bagmati and its tributaries. After my stay in rural Chitwan, the grubby, noisy, polluted, cramped and traffic-ridden streets of Nepal's biggest city was an unpleasant contrast. Amongst the endless traffic were plenty of the familiar Bajaj auto-rickshaw taxis, so I caught one to the tourist district of Thamel. I'd arranged to meet Bendik there in a recommended hostel, but the driver seemed unable to locate the place. I found another guest house instead, taking a room with some decent views – weather permitting – of the distant mountains north of the city. Unlike my last accommodation, this one also benefited from a little luxury called electricity...well at least until the daily load-shedding kicked in.

My hotel proved accommodating in a way I had not expected, for the woman who ran it came to my room unprompted to ask if I wanted to buy any hash. Well the answer was obvious and she returned shortly with a large slab of resin from which she cut a substantial piece. The unconventional but much appreciated room service explained their business card advertising proudly, if a little grammatically incorrectly, 'Welcome to our place to have your stay a happy one'. All I can say is that being stoned most of the time certainly helped my own stay there to be a very happy one.

Even though hashish had once been perfectly legal to buy in Nepal and notwithstanding its somewhat easy availability in my hotel, a poignant reminder of the risks in possessing hash were the notices seen posted in the bars and restaurants frequented by travellers. These were placed on behalf of foreigners doing prison sentences, the majority seemingly for drug offences. Providing the inmates details plus the length of their gaol sentence, these were requests for people to visit and bring listed items with them, a range of things from toiletries to clothing. I knew from meeting Owen, the Aussie bloke in Goa, that many foreigners like his best friend served time in Indian gaols; clearly they did so here in Nepal too.

I met one American couple in a bar who'd visited a countryman serving five years for possession of a small amount of hash. To my surprise they told me how the visit took place in the street outside the prison, with a guard in attendance but no handcuffs on the American prisoner. Was he tempted to make a run for it?' I asked. 'With no money and no passport, *where* exactly could he run to?' the boyfriend pointed out, which was a fair enough answer.

The American offender's incarceration in a distant foreign land understandably made his visits few and far between. As such the visiting pair enquired about the possibility of him perhaps getting transferred to serve out his sentence in the States. I was intrigued to hear that the prisoner actually preferred to remain where he was, stating that while conditions in a Nepalese gaol were bad, at least he didn't face violence and rape. In light of the apparently crowded, rat-infested squalor of his incarceration in Kathmandu, his response spoke volumes about the brutality of the US penal system!

During my stay in Kathmandu, I got sick again and spent most of my time either in bed or on the toilet. Gratefully, as the city is at an altitude of 1,400 metres, the temperature was a lot cooler than down on the Terai which at least made my illness a bit more sufferable. Another consolation was the relative ease of obtaining medicines in countries such as Nepal and India where the only prescriptions required are called rupees. For me self-medicating with antibiotics and the occasional joint were the best remedies for my condition. In the evenings, despite feeling tired I'd still drag myself out during the load-shedding to a bar with a generator, as the thought of being alone in a dark room was far too depressing.

After recovering from this latest bout of sickness I spent more time looking around Thamel. I have to say the area is a lot more commercialised than I'd envisaged. Abounding with eateries and Western-style bars, there's no shortage of places there to scoff and quaff. Dining in Thamel was cheap enough albeit mostly a substandard attempt at Western fare catering for the tourists. The local food I tried was similar to what I'd eaten in India with *dal bhat,* lentil soup and rice the national dish. *Dal bhat* is generally accompanied by curried vegetables and pickles. One very popular Nepalese food which I'd not come across in India is *momos,* small steamed dumplings containing meat or vegetables. Served with a spicy chilli sauce, they're a cheap and tasty snack I often enjoyed in Nepal. Meat dishes seem popular and typically contain chicken, goat and in particular water buffalo. As with India, tea, or *chiya* in Nepali, is the most commonly consumed beverage, here too drank white and sweet or with *masala*. I was pleased there was slightly more choice of beer here in Nepal and, besides the local brands Everest and Gorkha, there are European lagers like San Miguel, Tuborg and Carlsberg. Still, on the downside, despite these beers being brewed under licence in Nepal rather than imported from abroad, they are a bit pricey in comparison to the Kingfisher and Godfather I'd drank in India.

The shops and bazaars around Thamel sell a lot more imported goods than any I had seen in India and the whole area is patently geared up for foreigners. This made sense given that most visitors to the city end up staying in Thamel at some point. Even those intending to trek or mountaineer elsewhere in Nepal normally had to obtain the required permits in Kathmandu first. With the vast majority of foreign travellers gravitating towards Thamel, it wasn't hugely surprising to one day bump into Bendik there. As always, it was good to see a familiar face and next day he moved into my guesthouse, where he was more than a little impressed with its room service.

During the 9th and 10th centuries CE, Kathmandu was known as Kantipur. Its location on a major trade route between India and Tibet ensured that the town expanded steadily. By the time of the Malla monarchy Kathmandu was flourishing, initially so, as an independent city-state and later under a unified Malla kingdom, although it was never their capital. When the Malla kingdom was divided in 1482 Kathmandu again prospered as a city state, this time whilst competing with Patan and Bhaktapur for dominance of the Kathmandu Valley. Later on of course, the city fell to Prithvi Narayan, the founding monarch of modern Nepal. After 1768 the king moved his capital from Gorkha to Kathmandu thereby making it the centre of power in the newly unified country.

With around 1.4 million people, Kathmandu's population is not huge by South Asian standards but sadly, just like the Indian cities I had visited, the Nepalese capital suffers from appalling levels of poverty and homelessness. This deprivation is largely a result of political corruption and economic underdevelopment and is, alas like India, widespread across the country. Here too, there is no state welfare and scant provision of basic healthcare for millions. Worse still, Nepal is amongst the poorest countries in the world ranking below India, Pakistan and Bangladesh. Furthermore, its economy has for some time remained heavily reliant on foreign aid. With endemic poverty comes all the attendant evils, amongst them child labour, bonded labour (a euphemism for slavery) and the sale of girls as sex workers in India. As with India there is free elementary education available in Nepal although it's by no means compulsory. With children of poor families often needed to work, schooling is a low priority and dropout rates high.

Whatever its material woes, judging by the many temples I saw in Nepal, at least spiritual life is well catered for. It occurred to me that thus far on my travels, I had visited places of worship from a number of religions but no Buddhist ones. To rectify this I went to the Kathesimbhu Stupa tucked away in a courtyard a short walk south of Thamel. In Buddhism a stupa is a mound like religious structure which can have numerous designs, but is normally built upon a square plinth and topped with an ornate spire. The one at Kathesimbhu takes the form of a large white dome at the bottom supporting a tiered beehive-shaped spire which sits atop a cube base. The top of the gilded spire is itself crowned with a parasol shaped decoration and above this an upper finial. Depicted on the four faces of the spire's cube base are the eyes and eyebrows of the Buddha, whilst squiggled underneath as though his nose is the Nepali symbol for the number one, this supposedly standing for unity.

The circular base of the dome is ringed with prayer wheels spun as worshippers make a clockwise circumambulation of the stupa, this practice of *kora* forming an important part of Buddhist ritual. Arranged in the square surrounding the actual stupa are scores of Buddha shrines and rows of stone monuments known as *chaitya*, some of these sculptures dating as far back as the Licchavi period. The stupa itself is a 17th century construct, and in fact a smaller version of the impressive Swayambhu Stupa located just a couple of kilometres to the west. As such, I was curious to visit this larger stupa at Swayambhu, so that's exactly what I did later that day with Bendik.

Positioned dramatically a top a wooded hill, the Swayambhu Stupa is accessed via a straight line of hundreds of well-worn steps lined with occasional statues and plenty of rhesus macaques. It would appear that monkeys are as welcome in Buddhist shrines as they are in Hindu ones; there are such a large troop of them at Swayambhu Stupa that it's earned the soubriquet 'the Monkey Temple'. Be that so, it could equally be coined 'the Pigeon Temple' for, much like the Kathesimbhu Stupa, there is an abundance of these birds at this site too.

Once we got to the top of the steps the solid white dome at the bottom of the stupa came into full view, it is vast and easily has an impressive diameter of over twenty metres. Set at the cardinal points around its circular base are statues of the *panchabuddha*, each occupying a decorative gilded niche with the one on the east side containing two statues. Acting as a balance to these male Buddha images, similar niches at the sub-cardinal points around the base contain shrines to their female counterparts. Positioned in between each of the ornate niches is a line of copper prayer wheels for pilgrims to spin, each one inscribed with the Buddhist mantra translating as 'Hail to the jewel in the lotus'. The 'jewel lotus' being petitioned in prayer is a holy figure or bodhisattva associated with compassion, he is known as Chenrezig amongst other names.

Towering over the whitewashed dome and rising up more than 23 metres is the stupa's elaborate gold-plated spire. Mirroring the spire at Kathesimbhu, each side on its square base, known as the *harmika*, is painted with the nose symbol plus the all-seeing eyes of the Buddha, these also facing the four cardinal points. It was difficult to appreciate with the naked eye the intricate repoussé patterns and other images on the upper part of the gilded copper *harmika*, although fortunately they were depicted on postcards I bought. Given my appreciation for detail on structures I found it frustrating that such artistic endeavours were so high up on the stupa. I am sure those who had crafted these adornments would have felt annoyed that their creative efforts would forever remain unnoticed by most visitors...well until the invention of postcards at any rate.

Surmounting the *harmika* and forming the beehive-shaped bulk of the spire are 13-tiered discs of diminishing sizes. Each of these discs represents a step towards enlightenment, with the ultimate Buddhist goal itself being symbolised by an even less discernible decorative parasol and finial which complete the spire. From the apex of the stupa rope lines all bedecked in colourful prayer flags stream down to the ground, such flags a common sight across the Himalaya.

Traditionally, Swayambhu has been central in Newari Buddhism, and legend links it to the creation of the valley by the bodhisattva of wisdom, Manjushri. The earliest surviving chronicle mentioning the stupa dates from 1370, although it's possible Swayambhu had been a Buddhist holy site or *caitya* since the 5th century CE. For certain any stupas on this site, the current one included, would have been rebuilt several times over the centuries. The present structure had proved to be sturdy enough to withstand the 2015 earthquake, only sustaining minor damage. Over time, the stupa and complex around it has become sacred to Tibetan refugees and their descendants, attested to by a Tibetan monastery sited there. Swayambhu may well have been Buddhist in origin, but this being Nepal, it is unsurprisingly equally holy to Hindus who had added various shrines and temples to the complex. Of these the most conspicuous are the tall, white, Malla-era *shikhara* towers of two Hindu temples in front of the stupa on either side of the steps leading up to the site.

Amongst the myriad shrines is a vast gold-coloured statue of a seated Buddha on an ornate pedestal. The stone structure is easily twenty metres in height and an extraordinary sight as are the two similarly large sculptures of Guru Rinpoche and the bodhisattva Chenrezig either side of it. I thought Swayambhu was an amazing site and one of the most entrancing places I visited in Nepal. Like other religious locations I'd seen on this journey, as a bonus it had some panoramic views of the surrounding area. Dare I say that in my time I'd been in a few *stupors*... but none quite like those I experienced in Kathmandu!

Chapter 20.

A short way south of Thamel is found Kathmandu's major tourist attraction, this its mostly medieval Durbar Square. Even though Bendik had already been there it was the type of place well worth visiting more than once so he was happy to join me. The square and its vicinity make up the historical heart of the old city. Here a palace and courtyards are found, as are an assortment of temples, monuments and statues. This area had suffered extensive damage during the 2015 earthquake, although it's testament to skilled restoration that little evidence of the devastation remains. With such an abundance of historical structures around Durbar Square and its locale, this place is as often proclaimed one big open-air museum. That said, with all the hawkers flogging souvenirs and other goods to the crowds drawn there, in places, it resembles more a market.

Much of the architecture in the area is distinctly Newari being constructed from red brick and distinguished by intricately carved wooden doors, windows and balconies. Even so, quite a number of the buildings looked to me decidedly Chinese in appearance on account of their classic pagoda-style tiered, roofing. Even though it's generally thought of as being a quintessentially Chinese form of building, the pagoda is actually believed to have been a Nepali invention and introduced to China during the 13th century CE. Whatever the origins of these distinctive-looking edifices, if what I saw was anything to go by, Nepal seems to have no shortage of them.

Pagodas in Nepal are in general built on stepped plinths and can have up to five roofs which are traditionally covered in red tiles but occasionally gilded in metal. The struts supporting the roofs of these pagodas are often decoratively carved, this lovely detail unfortunately often hard to appreciate on account of their height. However this isn't the case with the lower roof supports of the Jagannath temple in Durbar Square, which just happens to include erotic images! These somewhat explicit sexual depictions, which are coincidently over 400 years old, would be unimaginable on an average religious building in any other country. Nudity might have appeared in European Renaissance art but nothing quite as bawdy as these carvings created during the same period. They portray couples, and sometimes three or four people, engaged in various sexual positions, not quite what I expected to see at a place of worship! They aren't unique either being found on other temples here in the capital and across the Kathmandu Valley. In India too there are many Hindu sites containing graphic sexual carvings. In fact the ones I saw at the Jagannath Temple are relatively modest compared to others which are decidedly hard-porn. These display any number of people involved in all manner of sexual activity, including: masturbation, oral and anal intercourse and bestiality! Hindu imagery at its most vivid and enough to make any imam, priest or rabbi blush. Nowadays, Nepal much like India is a deeply conservative society which makes these erotic carving on a public temple even more remarkable.

It is uncertain why the Jagannath temple and others have such sexually candid carvings. One possible explanation is that, as the goddess of lighting is considered a chaste virgin, she would never strike a temple containing such lewd images. Another belief is that such sex sculptures were intended to be educational, a visual aid to encourage procreation. Regardless of its reason, I thought this pious pornography quite incredible, the kind of thing which speaks volumes about cultural uniqueness. Whilst leaving little to the imagination, these carnal representations for the most part acknowledge an important aspect of human life. Moreover, they certainly exhibit a very liberal and open outlook towards sexual activity, a topic most religions remain reticent about. They also show how cultures change in their attitudes towards subjects like sex, as pornography is currently banned in Nepal...well apart from these kinds of historical exceptions that is. We generally think of societies today, being more open about sexual matters than they were in the past, not the other way around. The change towards a more conservative society in Nepal can be traced to the Shah's, whose dynasty was more puritanical in nature than those of earlier rulers.

The largest of the temples around the square is the 40-metre high Taleju Mandir, its great size making it stand out even in an area strewn with temples. Constructed in 1564 during the reign of King Mahendra Malla, this three-roofed structure had been the city's tallest building up until the mid-20th century. It was built in honour of the goddess Taleju Bhawani who according to legend had turned up at the temple's dedication ceremony in the form of a bee. Amongst the various interesting manifestations of Hindu deities I'd read about, frankly a striped insect seems a little dull.

Taleju Bhawani is in fact South Indian in origin having been the patron goddess of the Malla kings who'd introduced her to Nepal in the 1300s. With the seemingly inscrutable world of Hindu gods, I was not surprised to learn that she was considered yet another form of the mother goddess Durga. As had happened with other Hindu deities here, in time Taleju Bhawani became incorporated into the fold of Nepalese Buddhism, she in the shape of the tantric goddess Taras. Anyhow, her large temple in the Nepalese capital can only be viewed from the outside as it is rarely open to the public. Even when it is, non-Hindus are not allowed in.

Dominating the eastern side of Durbar Square are the different buildings which make up the Hanuman Royal Palace. We entered this through the Hanuman *Dhoka* or Gate which, like the palace beyond is named from the Shiva monkey god Hanuman. The name aside, there was a conspicuous absence of our simian relatives performing their usual monkey business by liberating food and belongings, including laundry from lines. The oldest parts of the Hanuman Royal Palace date from the mid-16th century, but it is likely that a palace stood on the site before that time. Further buildings were added in subsequent centuries, including lookout towers from the reign of Prithvi Narayan. The later Rana-era had contributed a glaring white neoclassical section to the royal palace which frankly looked more than a little out of place. For all its grandeur, Nepal's former rulers had vacated the palace in the last decades of the 1800s. Nowadays, partially open to the public, the Old Royal Palace is a major attraction for visitors to the square.

Located at the southern end of the square is the Kumari Bahal, a three-storey structure built in 1757 by the Malla potentates and arguably one of Kathmandu's most intriguing buildings. Its interior courtyard or *chowk* boasts plenty of superbly elaborate carved wooden windows, doorways, pillars and balconies. Still it isn't the building itself that stimulated my interest but rather its resident, a young girl who astonishingly is considered to be a reincarnation of the goddess Taleju Bhawani. Conferred with the title Kumari, this Hindu child deity is actually picked from a Buddhist clan and, following a thorough selection process, the chosen girl lives in the Kumari Bahal until she reaches puberty. Once this happens it is believed that the living goddess will revert back to a human form, thereby triggering a search for the next Kumari. At the end of her term, the former Kumari then departs the Bahal with a modest pension presumably free to live out her by then ordinary mortal life as she pleases.

A living goddess sounds unique and yet there are several other Kumari throughout Nepal. Be that so, the ones residing here are regarded as the foremost even being worshipped by Nepal's kings in the past. Throughout her divine tenure, a Kumari sees very little of her family instead being cared for and guided on performing duties by aides. Kumari only ever leave the building for occasional religious ceremonies, carried on a throne whenever this happens as her feet are never allowed to touch the ground when outside. For anyone not around during these rare events, the only other opportunity to catch a glimpse of her is at a certain window where she makes irregular appearances.

Alas, there was no sign of her when we visited, but there was a crowd of expectant devotees waiting there patiently in the *chowk* below. Not that we personally contributed anything, but I'd read how financial offerings could help encourage a sighting of the Kumari at the window. If true, then it basically went to show how much more mercenary these living deities were when compared to the more usual sorts!

Worshipping a living person as a deity is upon examination no less rational than revering a dead one, or indeed some idol. It was at least a benign practice unlike some other aspects of religious devotion in Nepal. By this I refer specifically to the distinctly gory animal sacrifices regularly carried out in temples. Here pigeons along with chickens, ducks, goats, sheep, pigs and even water buffaloes were all routinely butchered on the sacrificial altar, but ironically not *lambs*.

These offerings are made to the mother goddess Kali, who in this part of the Hindu world is worshipped in this bloodthirsty manner. By all accounts, these sacrifices are public events and it is possible for tourists to watch them, with some temples reportedly awash with blood and entrails from slaughtered animals. It was all a bit too gruesome for my liking and I couldn't help thinking a little contradictory for a country, where like India, killing a cow could get you locked up in some grimy prison.

T-shirts declaring 'Free Tibet' are commonly seen being sold in the tourist hotspots and many travellers liked to wear them as a way of demonstrating their solidarity with the cause. Whilst dining in a Thamel restaurant one evening, I got into conversation with a German chap wearing one. He complained bitterly at length about hanging around the Chinese embassy for the whole afternoon trying to obtain a Tibetan visa, only for his application to then be refused. Looking at his blazon 'Free Tibet' T-shirt, I assumed he hadn't been wearing it whilst visiting the embassy, but decided to ask anyway. To my astonishment he admitted that he had!

I felt compelled to point out the distinct possibility that this might just have prejudiced their decision in some small way. He unbelievably claimed not to have given the matter any thought. Let's be brutally honest, anyone going to a Chinese embassy with this less than anodyne political slogan clearly visible on their clothing must be pretty stupid. Whatever next for this clueless individual? Was he planning a trip to Israel, where he would attempt to enter the country while sporting the legend: 'End the Zionist Occupation of Palestine on his T-shirt!

If people wearing inappropriate apparel could be amusing then so too could those wearing unusual shoes. None more so than a Dutch chap named Ernie who we bumped into around Durbar Square. Even before speaking to him, we guessed Ernie might be from the Netherlands, with the giveaway being the pair of bright yellow wooden clogs he was wearing. It was certainly a novelty to see someone walking around in clogs, a sight I'd never seen when in the Dutch capital never mind the Nepalese one. Ernie explained that, whilst travelling, he liked to wear the clogs whenever it was practical, because as he proudly liked to remind others they were part of his country's national dress. Very audible whenever he walked and conspicuously colourful, Ernie's clogs seemed to be a source of both bewilderment and amusement to Nepalis. His bright yellow footwear was undeniably comical even for someone like me who understood the association between clogs and the Dutch. Not that Ernie really cared about the locals' mockery, pointing out that as far as he was concerned, they were no more ridiculous than the Hindu custom of having a red dot on the forehead. Ernie was a real character and funny not least because of his bright yellow clogs which undeniably brought a smile to people's faces.

Chapter 21.

My next excursion was a day trip to Bhaktapur which I took alone as Bendik had already visited this historical city. The bus journey there of around 15 kilometres cost next to nothing, unbelievably only about a third of the price of a first-class UK postage stamp. Its precise origins are something of a mystery; but Bhaktapur evolved on account of its location on an early main trade route between India and Tibet. Bhaktapur was of course the birthplace of the Malla dynasty in the 12th century and capital of their kingdom. The considerable wealth that commerce created for the Malla kings allowed Bhaktapur to become a centre of religious worship, containing at its peak over 170 temples and monasteries. Fittingly, its name means 'City of Devotees' in the Newari language.

After the death of Yaksha Malla in 1482 and the division of his realm between his three sons, Bhaktapur continued to enjoy a golden age as one of the three prosperous rival city-states in the Kathmandu valley. The most easterly of the three Malla kingdoms, it had been the final one to fall to the army of Prithvi Narayan. Thereafter, the emergence of Kathmandu as the new capital of Nepal had resulted in the power of this former Malla capital being permanently eclipsed. In the fullness of history this had at least saved Bhaktapur from some of the worst excesses of urbanisation. The city and its treasure of historic buildings sustained damage during an earthquake in 1934 and again in 2015. Sadly some of the Malla structures that withstood the earlier quake were then destroyed in 2015. Wherever possible, skilful reconstruction had erased evidence of this recent, literally seismic catastrophe and the city remains a popular tourist destination.

As in Kathmandu, a large concentration of Bhaktapur's historic architecture lies in and around the city's Durbar Square. Gracing an entrance into the former Malla Royal Palace is a masterpiece of Newari artistic metalwork known as the Sun Dhoka, or Golden Gate. Crafted from gilded copper and illustrating numerous Hindu deities, this superb detailed repoussé work was added to the palace during the mid-18th century. Beyond this showpiece gate is the equally fabulous eastern section of the royal complex known as the Palace of 55 Windows. Bearing images of- what else -but figures from the Hindu pantheon, the palace's spectacular carved wooden windows and upper frieze rivalled any that I had seen in Kathmandu.

Just a minute's walk from the Durbar Square lays Taumadhi Tol, another large bustling square, with this one boasting the country's tallest temple, the Nyatapola. Built on five large receding plinths and reaching a height of 30 metres, this imposing pagoda with its five-tiered roofing, towers above the skyline. The steps I climbed up to its entrance are lined with a series of large stone statues of various mythical and religious creatures and figures. Alas, at the top of the steps it is not possible to enter inside. Completed in 1702, the Nyatapola, whose name aptly translates as *five-stepped roof,* apparently contains a total of 180 finely carved roof struts. Dedicated to some obscure incarnation of Durga, this lofty temple escaped both the 1934 and 2015 earthquakes with little damage; testimony to its exceptionally sturdy construction.

I headed next to Bhaktapur's Potter's Square, located a short way south. The square was filled with neat rows of clay pots, jugs, piggybanks and other pottery being dried out prior to firing, this making for some good photos. Strolling around the square, I spent a while watching with interest some of the potters busy at their wheels moulding their wares from clay. I tend to view pottery in Britain as more of an arts and crafts thing, whereas, here it seems to be a thriving mainstream business and a traditional one at that. I have to admit that, in an age of synthetic materials, it felt rather satisfying to see a more natural substance like clay being used in commercial manufacturing, even if many of the finished products were tatty tourist souvenirs.

Returning to Taumadhi Tol, I took the main road running north-easterly to the oldest parts of Bhaktapur around Tachapal Tol. As such, this square contains one of the oldest temples in the city the Dattatreya Mandir, this having been built in 1428 during the reign of Yaksha Malla. As with all temples, practically, this one needs priests who in turn require accommodation, hence next to the Dattatreya Mandir, a rather sumptuous building stands to house them. Known as a *Math*, it dates from the 1700s and its lattice wooden-window carvings equal any found in the former royal palaces.

One in particular is the acclaimed Peacock Window, which as described is carved in the image of this striking bird displaying its famous tail feathers. Regarded as the finest in the whole valley, this outstandingly beautiful window is a paragon of Newari wood carving skill. Justifiably, a museum dedicated to their woodwork and exhibiting some exquisite examples of it, is based inside the *Math*. The Newaris can proudly claim a rich artistic heritage that is brilliantly showcased in the historical architecture of places like Bhaktapur and Kathmandu.

When compared to Kathmandu's Durbar Square and historical centre, I thought that the old city in Bhaktapur was a more relaxed and rewarding place to explore. For one thing, the architectural attractions are very similar and whilst busy it is far less hectic than the capital. Secondly and perhaps more importantly, a lot of the streets around the tourist sites are pedestrianised. Apart from anything else, the resulting absence of traffic together with all its accompanying noise and fumes helps the 'City of Devotees' retain more of its historical character.

Before returning to Kathmandu, I made for a small place named Nagarkot located about an hour away to the northeast of the city. The minibus I caught there was typically packed which required me to stand for the duration of the journey. It was just another forgettable bus trip until we reached one stop when I suddenly felt something nudge my legs from behind. It made me jump and looking down I saw the head of a goat emerge between my thighs. A local... I deduced he most likely was not a tourist, had boarded accompanied by a couple of goats, one of which was now treating my lower limbs as some type of improvised collar.

This caprine caper might have been amusing were it not for the animal's considerable horns, which were now poised to connect with my genitals should it decide to move backwards. In order to avert this potentially tearful scenario, it was necessary for me to tightly grip the creature's horns whilst also attempting to balance on the moving bus. So it was, that wedged in amongst other standing passengers and whilst holding a goat's horns between my legs, I remained in this apprehensive position for the best part of twenty minutes.

Not being a goat herder, it is unsurprising this was the longest period I'd ever spent in the company of a goat. During this time it entered my thoughts that the Rolling Stones had once released an album titled 'Goats Head Soup'. Although I have never heard the album its somewhat strange name had stuck in my memory. The creature I now found myself in such close proximity to, was itself most probably off to be slaughtered. I wondered would its head then be rendered down into some Nepalese broth, ensuring that no part of its carcass got wasted. Indeed had Mick Jagger sampled such a potage thereby inspiring the title of the album? On the other hand perhaps this goat was to be sacrificed at some temple or festival. I'd read about the Gadhimai festival held every five years in the Terai. Millions attend this event which involves the en-masse ritual sacrifice of hundreds of thousands of animals. It's definitely not the sort of festival the Rolling Stones would play at that is for sure. These were bizarre thoughts, but let's face it my situation of standing on a crowded bus gripping the horns of a goat between my legs, was hardly normal. Along with a rat and a thieving monkey, I could now add a goat to my list of unexpected animal encounters on my trip. As with restaurants, buses are not somewhere I expect to come across animals, well apart from the occasional guide dog, not in Britain at any rate.

Each time the bus made a stop, understandably I hoped that the goats would be taken off. When the owner eventually reached his destination, I had to push the goat's head down as it backed away, relieved that the threat to my crown jewels was finally removed. To me as a foreigner, it seemed pretty strange that transporting livestock by public transport was a perfectly accepted practice, especially given the potential hazard of genital injury goat horns pose to any standing male passengers. After all, this was the kind of thing likely to get someone's goat...in this instance mine! Still, taking something positive from the annoying experience, the next time a lack of vacant seats forced me to stand on a bus I'd just be grateful if no goats were aboard.

The now goat-free minibus soon reached the village of Nagarkot which sits at an elevation of 2,000 metres on the eastern fringe of the Kathmandu Valley. Its vantage points offer the possibility of seeing the country's most famous sight. For whilst India has the Taj

Mahal, Nepal possesses a more natural wonder called Mount Everest. Nagarkot is known for its vistas of the mighty Himalaya, including the world's highest peak. This mass of rock approaching almost nine kilometres in height is reportedly only a dot on the horizon given that it's about 140 kilometres away. But even such a distant sighting was still setting eyes on this famous mountain. Alas, the heavy cloud cover meant that I could only catch partial fleeting glimpses of some Himalayan peaks but not Mount Everest itself. At the mercy of the weather, I thus had to content myself with buying a postcard image of the world's best-known mountain which in fairness, I could have bought back in Thamel. There were no direct buses running to the capital from Nagarkot so I managed to conveniently hitch a lift back to Bhaktapur in a truck. Seated comfortably in the cab and minus the fear of some goat's horns impaling my balls at any moment, thankfully on my return journey I could relax and enjoy the scenery.

Chapter 22.

The following day I said farewell to Bendik and left Kathmandu for Pokhara, a city located in the centre of Nepal roughly 200 km west of the capital. On the bus journey there I had the company of Shiri and Shelley, a couple of Israeli girls I had befriended at the hash-dealing Thamel hotel. Our bus travelled along the Prithvi Highway which connects the two cities and had been named in honour of the nation's founder. It is certainly a dramatic road which, after climbing out of the Kathmandu Valley, descends to follow river valleys for much of its route. Seen along the way there are some stunning views of verdant rice terraces on steep hillsides, sugar plantations, small woods, gorges and the occasional village.

As it traverses this rugged terrain, the Prithvi Highway isn't only prone to traffic accidents but faces the added dangers of flooding and landslides. Landslides regularly block it and, on more than one occasion during the trip, the traffic inched cautiously past as the military cleared the debris of a recent landslide using bulldozers, diggers and trucks. Seeing the aftermath of landslides up close like this emphasises how risky it really is travelling on these precarious mountain roads. It took a good nine hours to reach Pokhara due to these delays, which, at an average speed of little over 22km an hour, demonstrates just how easily nature can slow up travel in Nepal.

Sited in a valley of the same name, Pokhara fortunately escaped the devastation wreaked elsewhere in Nepal by the earthquake of 2015. It is a relatively flat city which spreads out from the eastern shores of Phewa Lake and is the country's largest metropolitan area in size. Most foreign visitors to Pokhara, ourselves being no exception, stay in the Baidam area extending alongside the lake, a location which accounts for its popular English name of Lakeside. Unlike Dal Lake in Kashmir, Phewa is a more usual open expanse of water without any houseboats. It is Nepal's second largest lake and covered a small area of 4.5 square kilometres at the time. I say at the time as, unfortunately since 1967 and the construction of a dam on the main river draining the lake, a build-up of silt from an inflowing river has substantially reduced its size. It went to show that the benefits of irrigation and electricity brought by damming rivers can often come at a high environmental cost. In the case of Phewa, at some point in the future the lake itself could all but disappear.

For the time being at least, the diminishing Phewa Lake is ideal for boating and even swimming, given that its waters are clean. Whatever its merits are, the city's lakeside location is not the chief attraction as what actually draws people are, weather permitting, the commanding views of the snow-capped Himalaya seen to the north. These include the world's seventh, eighth and tenth highest peaks, all of them over 8,000 metres in altitude. These mountains visible from the city are mostly part of the Annapurna range, the base of the nearest being only 25 kilometres away.

During the first few days of my stay in Pokhara, clouds obscured these mountains until finally clearing to reveal a mind-blowing panoramic vista. The peaks rise so dramatically that their sheer magnitude is quite awesome to behold. Such is their epic size that seeing them for the first time I was completely awestruck; I felt as though I could literally reach out and touch them. No mountains I've ever seen, including those northwest of here in Kashmir, have left such a deep impression on me as this majestic massif. This was the kind of truly inspiring scenery Nepal is famed for and it is easy to understand why.

The city which overlooks these incredible mountains has the country's second largest population after Kathmandu, with over 400.000 inhabitants. Pokhara existed for centuries as a market town and, as seems to be the case with virtually every other place in Nepal, sat on some trade route to Tibet. A great deal of the old town, located a few kilometres northeast of Lakeside, burnt down in 1949 and nowadays very little remains of its original buildings. Further ruination of another sort had occurred in the early 1960s when the Chinese occupation of Tibet pretty much ended the caravan routes there, this severing the vital trade link that had underpinned Pokhara's traditional economy.

Whilst being responsible for this decline in Pokhara's fortunes, ironically China had also helped to rebuild the local economy by funding the construction of the Prithvi Highway during the late 1960s and early 70s. Since its completion, this highway linking the capital city has been bringing ever greater numbers of tourists and trekkers alike to Pokhara. With Pokhara's growth in popularity as both a lakeside resort and a gateway to the nearby Annapurna, its population swelled, expanding the town into the city of today.

Being on average 600 metres lower in altitude than Kathmandu, the temperature in Pokhara was noticeably warmer when I was there. Like the Terai, the flora of the city and the valley around it is markedly sub-tropical, with citrus and banana trees growing alongside rice paddies and fields of mustard. Even if Pokhara does lack the historical importance of Kathmandu, I personally thought it a far nicer city than the capital. Despite being commercialised it has a more relaxed pace of life and feels less congested. What's more, when it's not shrouded in clouds the surrounding landscape provides some stupendous scenery. It also went without saying that unlike another lakeside city surrounded by mountains I had recently visited, an absence of any ongoing conflict and curfews in this one was a veritable bonus!

In order to get a better look at the mountains, very early one morning I rode a hired motorbike up Sarangkot, a viewpoint found a couple of kilometres north of Phewa Lake. Getting there proved to be a real test of my riding skills as I ascended steep inclines on the rough road snaking up to the ridge. In the dawn light, even in first gear I struggled to cope with the gradient of what became just a trail nearer the summit. This type of terrain is more suited to a scrambler than a road bike so I parked up and walked the last bit. At the top I joined others in time to marvel at the mountain views unfolding with the sunrise. With Sarangkot elevated about 800 metres higher than Lakeside, from here, the searing peaks felt even more tangible. It was vistas like this that made the entire trip worthwhile as I was filled with a real sense of amazement; indeed observing these colossal chunks of rock in the soft hues of dawn really put the 'awe' into awesome.

The closest and by far most prominent mountain viewable from Sarangkot is the impressive Machhapuchhare. Its name translates as 'Fish Tailed' due to its twin peaks, although only one of these is visible from Sarangkot. Still, the sharp triangular summit that I could see was certainly very distinctive and, whilst not the highest mountain in the Annapurna range, Machhapuchhare is considered sacred by the Nepalese. Reflecting its holy status, it remains the only unclimbed peak in the country.

I just about had time to admire the views of Lake Phewa and the Pokhara Valley to the south of Sarangkot before clouds appeared, signalling an end to the visual wonder for the time being. As I had learnt by now, the great views in Nepal are weather dependent and often ephemeral, so I was really grateful for the earlier clear conditions. Before descending I went for breakfast in a teahouse situated close to the top where I watched with curiosity a delivery arriving by mule. The use of pack animals appeared to be a viable way of transporting heavy loads up Sarangkot, though 10 minutes later another delivery arrived this one being carried in a basket on some chap's back. I'd seen people laden with huge loads going up and down mountain paths plenty of times in Nepal. Such labours illustrated the toughness of the Nepalese people and it is hard not to admire their stoicism.

For all the harshness of their environment; and for the majority the harshness of their poverty ridden lives as well, those Nepalis I encountered were always welcoming and friendly. When dealing and bartering with them they tend to be far less pushy than their Indian neighbours. Possibly this may have something to do with the stronger Buddhist influence on Nepali society. But one aspect of everyday Indian life that does permeate Nepali society is the caste system, which had been imposed by the Mallas in the 14th century and is still rigorously observed throughout the country.

It caught my attention on a map of Pokhara that the city's home to a British army Gurkha camp. It is strange to think that long after the British had left the Indian sub-continent, a training base for their military still operates in Nepal. The Gurkha soldiers take their name from the ancestral home of the Shah monarchy Gorkha, whose armies had unified Nepal. Gorkha troops who fought the British East India Company between 1814 and 1816 showed such bravery and martial prowess, that the British were soon recruiting Nepalis into their own army. Sure enough, exactly the same thing would happen later with the Sikhs in the Punjab. As with the Sikhs, the loyalty of Gurkhas to the British during the 1847 uprising in India consolidated their trustworthiness as dependable soldiers. So, ironically an example of multiculturalism existed even within the military of a colonial power that dismissed and denigrated the indigenous cultures of the sub-continent.

Ever since that period the tradition of Gurkha regiments serving in the British Army has continued and the camp at Pokhara is still training them. Deployed by Britain across the world in numerous wars and military campaigns, Gurkhas have earned themselves a legendary reputation for courage. They'd even won an impressive ten percent of the Victoria Crosses awarded in the Second World War. With their blunt motto, 'Better to die than be a coward', you wouldn't wish to be on the receiving end of a Gurkha *kukris*, the fearsome looking large curved knife commonly sold as souvenirs in Nepal.

Gurkha troops may be strongly associated with the British Army but over ten times as many actually serve in the Indian military. When Britain departed India in 1947, six of the then ten Gurkha regiments were incorporated into the newly created Indian army. The Indian army has continued to recruit heavily from Nepal and their Gurkha soldiers have seen action during the conflicts with neighbouring China and Pakistan. Gurkha ranks are drawn from a number of ethnic groups across Nepal and being one carries great status here, providing an important source of income for families through salaries and pensions.

Nepal's harsh environment of jungle and mountains with their extremes of heat and cold, probably endow Gurkha troops with a resourcefulness and toughness desirable in any military force. So respected are the Gurkhas for their indomitable spirit, that as well as Britain and India they also serve in the security forces of Brunei, Malaya and Singapore. If truth be told with all this foreign military recruitment going on, it was a wonder that Nepal has managed to raise an army of its own.

On my last day in Pokhara, I hired a boat with Shiri and Shelley and we whiled away a few relaxing hours rowing around Phew Lake. The afternoon sun was so intense we decided to cool off with a swim in the calm, inviting water. After enjoying a refreshing dip, I pulled myself back onto the boat and sitting down glanced downwards only to notice that a black leech was attached to my shin. These blood-sucking worms are widespread in Nepal. When feeding, leeches secrete an anti-coagulant to ensure that the blood keeps flowing and, seeing the thing gorging on mine, was a repulsive sight. I had heard somewhere that a biting leech should not be pulled off the skin as this might leave part of its mouth behind and potentially infect the bite. Before this particular leech had the opportunity to ingest any more of my blood, I lit up a cigarette and burnt the thing causing it to drop off. I read later that this wasn't recommended either as it can cause the leech to puke up into the wound, which might also lead to infection. In spite of this risk of infection from vomiting, parasitic worms, thankfully my bite healed without any problems.

Unlike those other insidious little bloodsuckers, mosquitoes, the parasites found in leeches are not harmful to humans. In fairness, leeches have of course long been used in medicine. Still, there is a risk that wild leeches could act as vectors for transmitting disease and parasites from previous blood 'donors'. Let's face it, catching a disease is terrible enough but contracting one from one of these predatory little bastards would be really unfortunate. Mosquitoes had been the greatest bane of my travels thus far; even so I have to admit that they are nowhere near as gross as these vile blood-sucking creatures.

As we rowed our way back to shore, a motor boat full of tourists disturbed the tranquillity of the occasion as it chugged closely past us. Those aboard were oriental in appearance and we instantly became the focus of their phones, I-pads and cameras as they all happily snapped away. It was hard to comprehend why exactly these tourists would travel thousands of kilometres to another country in order to photograph other foreign tourists in a rowing boat. Who knows, maybe they were exhausted and confused from the frenetic pace of some gruelling itinerary of the sub-continent. Then again, I joked with Shiri and Shelley, there was always the distinct possibility that, notwithstanding our non-Nepali features; all foreigners looked the same to this tour group!

Chapter 23.

Having said goodbye to the girls who had been great company, the following morning I began my return to the Gangetic plain and Delhi, from where I'd a flight booked back to the UK. The ten-hour bus journey which took me back to the border town of Sunauli proved to be extremely uncomfortable. There was little leg room and the Nepali guy seated next to me kept taking up all the space. Then, after crossing back into India with the minimal fuss, it was a further four-hour bus trip to the Uttar Pradesh city of Gorakhpur from where I was able to catch a train.

Being on the railways I now expected my progress to hasten but this wasn't to be the case. Annoyingly, within twenty minutes, the train came to a halt somewhere between stations only to remain there for the next *nine hours*. It turned out that a section of the track had broken and needed to be replaced before we could continue. Besides sweating profusely, there was little else to do but read and doze whilst sat in the carriage waiting to resume my journey. Tedious as this was, in defence of Indian railways such a delay could happen anywhere including the UK. A key difference here though was the absence of irritating announcements being repeated ad infinitum over speakers, which to be honest actually made the lengthy hold-up infinitely more tolerable.

By the time the train eventually got into Lucknow station predictably I had missed my connection to Delhi. Despite having a few hours to spare before the next one, I made no effort to look around this capital city of Uttar Pradesh, India's most populous state. Frustratingly, I realised that by now a coach from Gorakhpur would have probably already got me into Delhi.

Not having seen another foreigner since the border, I welcomed the company of two English guys who arrived at the station. The pair were making for the capital too where they hoped to obtain Tibetan visas before travelling on to Nepal. They had been led to believe that the Chinese embassy in Delhi was far more likely to issue these visas than the one in Kathmandu. In light of their plans I naturally told them all about the idiot German bloke I had met in Kathmandu who had worn his *'Free Tibet'* T-shirt to the Chinese embassy there, something that they both unsurprisingly thought hilarious.

When our Delhi-bound train arrived it was already so rammed full that I did wonder if we would even be able to get on it. The three of us walked a good distance along the platform looking for any room aboard before finding one carriage with vacant seats. Upon boarding, we noticed that a large number of the passengers occupying the carriage were soldiers, although unlike in Kashmir these ones weren't armed or even on duty. As the train jerked and pulled away from Lucknow station, I felt glad to be finally moving again as we settled in for the journey ahead.

That said no sooner had we departed when some of the soldiers began slapping and striking other passengers with belts, forcing them to flee the carriage. Being taken aback by these unprovoked assaults and, not wishing to be on the receiving end of the same treatment ourselves, the three of us stood up in order to move elsewhere. At this one of the soldiers approached and insisted in broken English that we remain. 'You are gentlemen and welcome,' he said. 'But *they* are thieves.' It sounded plausible; after all, I had seen how dishonest individuals can find themselves being beaten in India during the bus ticket rip-off episode in Alappuzha. Besides they were the army and therefore presumably knew more about these matters than we did, so we sat back down.

As the journey unfolded, we could see that a small group of seven or eight of these soldiers were drinking rum and getting quite inebriated. Their raucous manner was hard to ignore as like many people the more alcohol they consumed the louder they became. I'd never seen soldiers drinking in Kashmir so it seemed slightly odd watching this bunch get drunk. Unfortunately things turned nasty again as they then started to arbitrarily beat any unsuspecting individuals who took a seat in our carriage. It just proved that their earlier purge of supposed undesirables was in reality directed against innocent passengers. We may associate the military with order and discipline but this rabble displayed neither. Later, a few of these troops approached and offered to share their rum with us which we politely declined. Friendly as they were towards us foreigners, given their casual use of violence against their countrymen we were rightly wary of their attention.

One of the main instigators of their alcohol-fuelled assaults, an imperious sergeant, was clearly relishing events and even boasted about his strength in a pathetic macho fashion. Although bullying and belittling people is part of a sergeants' remit, he seemed to me, an obnoxious sadistic coward. This was confirmed at one point when he approached a burly Sikh chap and began shouting and gesturing at him. Plainly not intimidated by his belligerence; the Sikh responded with nothing more than a disdainful look. Here was someone likely to hit back if struck by some drunken lout, even if his assailant was a soldier and part of a group. There was of course a reasonable chance that the Sikh guy was ex-military himself. Realising this, the sergeant stepped back and smiled as if to suggest he'd only been joking with the Sikh, before walking away. To me, this demonstrated what a spineless individual he really was.

Throughout the night the violence dished out by these drunken soldiers continued intermittently. Screaming and shouting from people could be heard coming from adjoining carriages too, as periodically they'd search out victims elsewhere on the train. In one sickening display of cruelty, we watched the soldiers beat a blind beggar who'd boarded at one station. After doubting his disability by waving their hands in front of his eyes, they began to slap him hard around the head and face whilst taunting him. The blind man cried and pleaded for them to desist. We were relieved for the poor chap when, after several minutes of this abuse, his tormentors finally threw him out of the carriage.

Witnessing this wanton behaviour all three of us felt disgusted but also powerless to intervene. The reality was, if these soldiers were challenged, then their earlier amicableness could easily turn to aggression if they thought that we were interfering in matters, which as foreigners, didn't concern us. Informing the police was not an option either. How did we know this? Well, at one of the stations a policeman boarded our carriage and, far from trying to help any of their victims, he instead lent the sadistic sergeant his *lath* which was then used to beat the crap out of anyone he could corner. Shockingly, when I went to use the toilets at one point during this hellish journey, I was totally appalled to see an elderly man cowering inside, he having presumably been on the receiving end of the ongoing brutality.

The word that sprang to my mind was 'thugs', ironic given that the noun *thug* is of Indian origin. For many centuries, thugs were bandits who preyed on those travelling through this very region of India. Being worshippers of the goddess Kali, thugs strangled their victims as a sacrifice to their bloodthirsty deity prior to robbing them. Operating in gangs they would join individuals or caravans on the trunk roads posing as fellow wayfarers. Having gained the trust of these unsuspecting travellers, the thugs would then await the opportunity to throttle and kill their targets before stealing their possessions and disposing of the bodies.

As their killings were intended as sacrifices to the goddess Kali, the thugs were regarded as a sect, albeit a particularly nefarious one. During the 1830s the British launched a campaign to get rid of the thugs, arresting about 4000 of their members over the next two decades. Of those detained, some 400 had themselves been appropriately strangled, only on the end of a gallows noose. This crackdown had effectively put an end to this murderous cult.

When speaking earlier to some of these latter-day thugs aboard our train, I ascertained that they were returning from deployment in the eastern state of Assam. As with Kashmir, Assam has been a persistent trouble spot for the Indian government, one where for decades the military had been confronting separatist and ethnic violence. If this was the way the army treated its own citizens on public transport, then just imagine the beatings meted out to any suspected enemies of the state in these conflict zones? I suspect these soldiers were so brutalised by their routine use of torture whilst on duty that they had forgotten how to behave humanely, even when on leave. In reality, the use of violence in interrogation is standard in military operations anywhere, but to see it directed towards innocent people simply for amusement was appalling! Understandably, the three of us were massively relieved when we finally reached Delhi and this unpleasant episode came to an end. As I bid farewell to the other two, I knew one thing for sure; even if we wanted to...this was one train journey that none of us would forget in a hurry!

Chapter 24.

From New Delhi station I walked down the adjacent Main Bazaar Road towards Paharganj and booked into a cheap hotel. My return from Nepal had been quite a quest and exhausted I slept for much of the remainder of my time in the capital. Late the next day I took a taxi to Indira Gandhi International Airport located southwest of the centre. On this occasion there were no giant Ganesha images being hauled across the road to marvel at. There was however an opportunity to muse on my time here in the sub-continent as it came to an end.

Without question the worst thing about the place had been the staggering scale of grinding poverty which exists. Its enormity is genuinely saddening to contemplate and reinforces exactly how fortunate *and* complacent we in the developed world really are. Healthcare, welfare, housing and sanitation to name but a few, are things denied to millions in countries like India and Nepal, and yet they are simultaneously taken for granted by millions of people elsewhere in the world. Witnessing first-hand, the sad destitution endured by countless people, certainly gave one cause to ruminate about the reality of life for millions of less fortunate humans in this world.

The causes of this poverty are numerous. Even with consistent economic growth in recent years, overpopulation has meant that unemployment and underemployment continue amongst a large unskilled workforce. A lack of any investment and infrastructure in poor areas also contributes to huge poverty in India and Nepal, as indeed does political corruption. Then there is the *varnas* system operating in both countries, one that inhibits social and economic mobility. In short, poor education, low incomes, low savings and debt compounded by a lack of affordable credit, all feed into the problem too. Insufficient government intervention is yet another cause of poverty. In rural areas, issues of unequal land distribution and low agricultural productivity often due to weather do not help the situation either. The magnitude of poverty in India and Nepal observably worsened the impact of Covid there. Mortality rates aside, the economic impact of Covid lockdown measures not only caused further suffering for the poor masses, they also brought considerable hardship to the middle classes.

Some blame India's colonial past for its modern social woes and there can be no denying the exploitative nature of British rule. Far from advancing economic conditions on the Indian sub-continent, during British intervention India had saw its share of the global economy drop by around eighty-eight percent. Colonial policies stifled India's industrialization and even ended its textile industry in order to enable Britain's own Industrial Revolution. The truth of the matter is, the wealth and resources plundered over centuries of colonialism seriously weakened India's ability to tackle poverty after independence.

Even so, in assessing the impact of the colonial state on modern India, it's worth bearing in mind that Nepal wasn't colonised and yet is poorer than any part of the former British India. This tells us that whilst colonialism had quite undeniable negative economic consequences for the sub-continent, enduring mass poverty at the end of the day is a direct result of a combination of all the above demographic, economic, societal, political and climatic factors.

For all their privation, I was amazed just how many of the poor people I met appeared to be pretty happy. Such spirited geniality certainly provides a lesson in humility, but the very fact that I am surprised by this reflects a Western materialism and consumerism that conflates pleasure with happiness. When all is said and done, happiness is a state of mind and not something that is necessarily determined by the physical world around us. I may equate poverty with misery, but it is my Eurocentric perception of the nature of poverty informing that judgement. Amongst the poor of India and Nepal there could at least be a sense of being the majority, the norm, the ordinary citizen in an impoverished nation. Ultimately, if a person's hardship is no different to that of millions of others, then what is special or unique about that individual that should make them unhappy? The truth of the matter is contentment in life is not mutually exclusive to the affluent of any society, Maybe the paradigm of the less people have, then the happier they are, holds some credence. This is not to say that poverty is therefore an acceptable facet of life only to point out the resilience of the human condition in the face of it.

Thankfully, there were less depressing aspects of my travels in India and Nepal. The food had generally been an immense part of the enjoyment. Whether dining in a rat-infested restaurant or just snacking at a street stall I had enjoyed some delicious grub. Even more so when a meal was not contaminated by cremated human remains! Being a foodie with a fondness for South Asian cuisine, I had especially appreciated the variety of dishes, from *momos* to *masala dosa,* which were all new to me. When it came to more familiar fare, the curries too are as varied as are the cultures in both India and Nepal. Humble dal served with rice or roti was the staple diet of millions, meaning that between Kerala and Kashmir, endless different recipes exist for the masala used in its making. For all the variety of flavoursome spicy food, the culinary highlight of my trip though had to be the tandoori delights of the Punjab.

From a purely financial perspective the relative cheapness of my trip was another real bonus. Was it then a case of 'cheap holidays in other people's misery', as the Sex Pistols sang? Or, to be more accurate when it came to Kashmir, a question of; cheap holidays in other people's war zones! Alongside other issues, tourism as an industry undeniably raises questions about the exploitation of locals involved in it. Still without it, how much more impoverished would many Indians and Nepalis be? For me it is a bit like the use of cycle-rickshaws, as I always feel slightly uncomfortable about some poor emaciated chap cycling me around in the sweltering heat. The difficulty is if I allow this guilt to stop me from taking cycle-rickshaws, then I am denying their wallahs the custom they so depend upon to make a living. Whatever the downsides of tourism maybe, the reality is, it's Nepal's main industry and brings in desperately needed revenue to both countries.

Along with the low cost of living I had also delighted at some incredible scenery in India and Nepal. From the coconut palms and beaches of the south to the *chinar* trees and mountains of the north, I got to see some diverse and stunning landscapes. Besides nature I had also admired some superb imaginative architecture since arriving here, a large number of these memorable structures being places of worship. It's true that imposing religious buildings are not unique to this part of the world, but what struck me were the differing types I'd managed to visit. All told I had been to see

Hindu, Jain and Buddhist temples, churches, mosques a *gurdwara* and even a synagogue in Kochi.

Whether people believed in one God or a multitude of deities, the religious practices of the masses in India and Nepal had been a real source of fascination for me. It was intriguing learning about different faiths and undoubtedly religion, whether it is indigenous or introduced, is a significant part of people's everyday life. When it came to Hinduism the holy city of Varanasi had been particularly remarkable, a totally unbelievable place of devotion and of course death. Few I suspect could explore the Ganges at Varanasi and not be impacted to some extent by its spiritual and religious intensity, amazingly one where both life and death are equally embraced.

Such is the role of religion in both countries that even regional identities which revolve around language and ethnicity, tend to be underpinned by equally strong religious associations. It was a far cry from the ever-growing secularism of the UK and whether a religion is devoutly followed or not; and on the whole it is, for the population in general it forms a fundamental part of their cultural identity. What is more this is something which applies to every religion from the Hindu majority of India and Nepal right down to the tiny Zoroastrian community of Mumbai.

I'd seen how different faiths overlap, for example how Hinduism had influenced Islam in India and virtually subsumed Buddhism in Nepal, in turn both Hinduism and Islam had clearly impacted the development of Sikhism in the Punjab. A more obvious example of syncretism is the way Hinduism's *varnas* system also operates in other religions, including non-indigenous ones like Christianity and Judaism. Other less discriminatory religious blendings, highlight a number of commonalities in the nature of human life. These are shared values and beliefs in relation to existence, ritual, love, life and finally death, a truly innate spiritual quest in humankind that binds us all. Even as a foreigner in a foreign land, they are themes I could totally relate to on a personal level.

Unfortunately the key problem with religion in India has been its politicization. It's an issue which predates independence; one only has to think of the 1906 foundation of the Muslim League in Bengal, this a political party formed to further Muslim interests in British India. Hindu nationalist organisations also existed during the British Raj, notably the RSS (Rashtriya Swayamsevak Sangh) or National Volunteer Organisation, established in 1925 and still very much active in India today. Considered by many to be essentially paramilitary in nature, the right-wing RSS has spawned a myriad of other like-minded Hindu nationalist groups under the umbrella Sangh Parivar movement. What's more, this, the world's largest voluntary movement with millions of members is closely affiliated with the governing BJP.

For me, the ongoing expansion of Hindu nationalism in the 21st century is as worrying as the prospect of continuing mass poverty in India. Back in 1947, the country's founders had acknowledged the heterogeneous nature of this vast nation and they'd sought to accommodate it. By contrast the current BJP government seeks to create some homogenized Hindu version of society, this in a land whose cultures are in reality as rich and varied as its curries.

Centuries of history show how India has absorbed and adapted external influences, indeed much in the same way that Chicken Tikka Masala illustrates the same thing in contemporary Britain. Whatever the long-term consequences of BJP ambitions might be can only be a matter of conjecture. Still, as the historical and more recent communal clashes clearly lay bare, the mixing of politics and religion is never a recipe for social cohesion.

Nepal had made an interesting comparison to India not least of all because religion there largely remains outside of the political sphere. There is an active Hindu nationalist party in Nepal, but the Rashtriya Prajatantra Party doesn't engage in anti-Muslim rhetoric nor does it actually perform very well in elections. Also Hinduism had been the official state religion until 2007 when Nepal declared itself a secular country.

Politics by itself, uncomplicated by any religious dimension, has brought sufficient woes to Nepal. As I'd learnt, political instability like seismic instability has unfortunately created huge problems for the country. Its multicultural population is now recognized in a federal political system; even so there are disparities in poverty levels between different social groups and regions. If UN concerns about corruption and civil engagement in Nepal's governance are addressed, and if foreign investment can be attracted, Nepal has got potential for economic growth. Providing the development is sustainable and properly regulated, it remains Nepal's best hope for reducing poverty, although as with India, sadly it is unlikely to ever eradicate it completely.

By now my arrival in Mumbai felt like an awfully long time ago. My travels since that night had left me plenty of memories, not all of them entirely enjoyable but happily most were. In between the moments of hedonism and moments of hell, I'd enjoyed learning all about the history, politics, geography and culture of different places. For me this made visiting them infinitely more rewarding. As often cited travel is itself an education, an extraordinary one at that achieved by experiencing countries like India and Nepal.

I would stress that my travels had also been greatly enriched by meeting other people, be they locals or fellow wayfarers. Ignoring the frequent scams and incessant attempts to overcharge, those Indians and Nepalis I'd met had for the most part been amicable and helpful. Then there were the fellow foreigners I'd befriended and it was wonderful sharing experiences with them or hearing all about their own adventures. As you would expect a lot had their own amusing anecdotes about their travels and laughing with, and sometimes *at* other travellers, had offered a welcome distraction from the often less palatable realities of the trip.

If humans formed a central part of the travel equation, then on occasion so too did the wildlife, whether encountering a rat in a restaurant or hoping *not* to encounter a rhino when in the night time jungle. Of course I'd also come across a pilfering primate and seen first-hand how goats being transported on public transport could present a risk of genital injury. Well rats, rhinos, goats and thieving monkeys all indubitably added to the adventure. When it came to animals, I had learnt that in India and Nepal the urban environment wasn't limited to the usual domesticated creatures, for alongside the cats and often rabid dogs there were typically some cows, goats and water buffaloes mingling freely with all the traffic and people on the streets. Frankly, the animals which really amazed me were the elephants, both the ones I saw in Kerala and in Chitwan. The sight of these beasts in a city makes for a slightly surreal, but nevertheless wonderful image. Equally the elephant sanctuary and safari in Chitwan National Park had been an utterly unforgettable experience and one of the highlights of my trip.

So on a valedictory note when all things were weighed up, I'd journeyed in not only a different continent but in a sense a totally different *world*. No matter if the things I had witnessed there had been sublime, bizarre, tragic or humorous, or anything in-between for that matter, to me as an outside observer they were invariably intriguing. Ultimately my trip turned out to be a totally absorbing, intense experience in a weird and wonderful place, one which was in equal measures both amazing and appalling but most certainly never boring. Indeed just like that first heavenly taste of curry in the Sharma's shop as a teenager, it had been a truly memorable experience.

.

Bibliography.

A Shikari, The bullet and the ballot box: The story of Nepal's Maoist Revolution, Versco, 2014.

K B Ahmed, Kashmir: Exposing the myth behind the narrative, Sage Publications India. 2017.

S Baru, India's Power Elite, Penguin Books, 2021.

T Bell, Kathmandu, Haus Publishing, 2016.

Berlitz, India pocket guide, Berlitz Travel, 2017.

D Coffey & D Spears, Where India goes: Abandoned toilets, stunted development and the cost of caste, Harper-Collins India, 2017.

R Dalal, The religions of India: A concise guide to nine major faiths, Penguin Global, 2011.

W Dalrymple, The Anarchy: The Relentless Rise of the East India Company, Bloomsbury Publishing, 2019.

J S Deepak, India that is Bharat: Coloniality, Civilisation, Constitution, Bloomsbury India, 2021.

R Ferguson, Nepal: Footprint handbook, Footprint Travel Guides, 2017.

R Gandhi, Modern South India: A history from the 17th Century to our times, Rupa & Co, 2018.

House of snow: An anthology of the greatest writing about Nepal, Head of Zeus, reprint 2017.

M Husain, Geography of India, McGraw Hill Educational, 2017.

M Hutt, Nepal: A guide to the art and architecture of the Kathmandu Valley, Adroit Publishers, 2010.

C Jaffrelot, A Kohli, K Murali (Editors), Business and politics in India, Oxford University press, 2018.

P Jha, Battles of the new republic: A contemporary history of Nepal, C Hurst & Co Publishers Ltd, 2014.

S Khan, History of Indian architecture: Buddhist, Jain and Hindu period, CBS Publishers & Distributors, 2014.

Y Khan, The Great Partition: The making of India and Pakistan, Yale University Press, 2007.

S Khilnani, Incarnations: A history of India in fifty lives, Farrar, Straus & Giroux, 2017.

A K Kole, R Roy, D C Kole, Human rabies in India: a problem needing more attention, Bulletin of the World Health Organisation, 2014:92:230.

P Lal, Indica: A deep natural history of the sub-continent, Penguin Books India, 2016.

T R Metcalf, An imperial vision: Indian architecture and Britain's raj, OUP India, 2002.

A R Mulmi, All Roads lead North: China, Nepal and the Contest for the Himalayas, Hurst Publishers, 2021.

A G Noorani, The RSS: A Menace to India, Leftword Books, 2018.

R Rae, Kathmandu Dilemma: Resetting India-Nepal Ties, Penguin Vintage, 2021.

K S Rathore, Ambedkar's Preamble: A secret History of the Constitution of India, Vintage Books, 2020.

215

V Schofield, Kashmir in Conflict: India, Pakistan, and the Unending War, I B Taurus, London 2000.

A Sen, The Argumentative Indian: Writings on Indian history, culture and identity, Picador, 2006.

C T Sen, Food culture in India, Greenwood Publishing Group, 2004.

R Shah & R M Mitchell, Wildlife in Nepal, Nirala, 2001.

S Shakya, Unleashing Nepal: Past, present and future of the economy, Penguin Books India, 2009.

S Sharma, The Nepal Nexus: An Inside account of the Maoists, the Durbar and New Delhi, Penguin, 2019.

V P Shrestha, A concise geography of Nepal, Mandala Publications, 2007.

K Singh, A History of the Sikhs, Vol 2:1839-2004, OUP India, 2004.

A Subramanian, Of counsel: The challenges of the Modi-Jaitley economy, Penguin Viking, 2018.

B Thapar, Introduction to Indian architecture: Arts of Asia, Tuttle Publishing, 2005.

S Tharoor, Inglorious Empire: What the British did to India, Penguin, 2018.

S Tharoor, S Saran, The New World Disorder and the Indian Imperative, Adelph Books, 2020.

M E Tritch, Wildlife of India, Harper-Collins, 2006.

C Tumbe, India moving: A history of migration, Penguin Viking, 2018.

P K Varma, The Great Hindu Civilisation: Achievement, Neglect, Bias and the Way Forward, Westland Non-fiction, 2021.

G Wahab, Born A Muslim: Some Truths About Islam in India, Aleph Books, 2021.

J Whelpton, A history of Nepal, Cambridge University Press, 2005.

S Yengde, Caste Matters, Penguin Books, 2019.

Websites.

Government of Kerala, https://www.kerala.gov.in/ 2021.

Government of Maharashtra, https://www.maharashtra.gov.in/ 2021.

National portal of India, https://www.india.govt.in/ 2021.

Government of Punjab, https://www.punjab.gov.in/, 2016.

The official portal of Government of Nepal, https://www.nepal.gov.np/, 2017.

Government of Uttar Pradesh, https://www.up.gov.in/, 2004.

Government of India, Ministry of Road Transport & Highways, Road Accidents in India-2017, Annexure P49, statistics of persons killed and injured: 1970-2017.http://www.indiaenvironmentportal.org.in/files/file/road [accessed March 13 2022]

R Bedi, Sacred cow ambulance service launched in India for ill, injured or abandoned cattle, https://www.telegraph.co.uk/news/2017/05/02/indian-state-launches-ambulance-service-sacred-cows. [accessed 24 January 2022].

D K Dash, The Times of India, March 12 2019.
https://timesofindia.indiatimes.com/india/in-2018-india-had-fewer-road-accidents-but-more-fatal-ones/articleshow, [accessed January10 2022]

R A Ferdman, Scientist have figured out what makes Indian food so delicious,https://www.washingtonpost.com/news/wonk/wp/2015/03/03/a-scientific-explanation-of-what-makes-indian-food-so-delicious. [accessed 30 Dec 2021].

S Saaliq, India's train mishaps in the last 10 years, 28 August 2017, https://www.news18.com/news/immersive/indias-train-mishaps.html [accessed March 3 2021]

https://en.wikipedia.org/wiki/List_of_railway_accidents_and_incidents_in_India, edited 25 April 2019 [accessed 4 June 2021].

Open Government Data India, Persons killed and injured in railway related accidents 2002-2015, https://data.gov.in/catalog/number-persons-killed-and-injured-railway-related-accidents, [accessed January 16 2022]

https://www.who.int/snakebites/epidemiology/en/, 2022.

http://data.un.org/Search.aspx?q=india, 2020.

https://www.who.int/countries/ind/en/, 2021.

https://en.wikipedia.org/wiki/Demographics_of_India, 2019.

https://data.worldbank.org/country/india, 2022.

http://uis.unesco.org/country/IN, 2021.

http://data.un.org/Search.aspx?q=nepal, 2020.

https://www.un.org/development/desa/dpad/least-developed-country-category-nepal.html, 2018.

https://www.who.int/countries/npl/en/, 2021.

https://data.worldbank.org/country/nepal, 2022.

https://en.wikipedia.org/wiki/Demographics_of_Nepal, 2021.

https://cbs.gov.np/, 2021.

https://www.adb.org/sites/default/files/institutional-document/454881/nepal-macroeconomic-update-201809.pdf, 2021.

https://en.wikipedia.org/wiki/Nepal, 2020.

http://www.kathmandu.gov.np/en, 2022.

https://www.welcomenepal.com/, 2021.

https://data.gov.in/, 2021.

http://www.pmindia.gov.in/en/, 2021.

https://en.wikipedia.org/wiki/India, 2021.

https://www.cia.gov/library/publications/the-world-factbook/geos/in.html, 2021.

https://www.indiatoday.in/india, 2022.

https://www.amnesty.org/en/countries/asia-and-the-pacific/nepal/, 2021.

https://asiafoundation.org/where-we-work/nepal/, 2022.

https://www.amnesty.org/en/countries/asia-and-the-pacific/india/report-india/, 2021.

https://www.indiatoday.in/india/story/40-deaths-in-75-accidents. [accessed 12 May 2020].

Richa Jain, https://theculturetrip.com/asia/india/articles/the-dark-history-behind-sati-a-banned-funeral-custom-in-india May 2018 [accessed Jan 12 2022].

Mishra B, Chakraborty S, Sandhya MC, Viswanath S, https://www.researchgate.net/publication/326294915_Sandalwood farming in India problems and prospects. June 2018 [accessed 25 June 2021].

S Diwanji, Gold Production in India 2012-2018, https://www.statista.com/statistics/667473/india-gold production-volume/. May 2019 [accessed 23 Jan 2022].

A J Vinayak, The Hindu, December 2018, https://www.thehindubusinessline.com/economy/agri-business/areca-arrivals-down-by-3-in-karnataka-apmcs-in-2018/article25843191.ece. [accessed 31 January 2022].

Coffee Board, Indian Ministry of Commerce & Industry. https://www.indiacoffee.org/coffee-statistics.html. [accessed 12 May 2021].

Lightning Source UK Ltd.
Milton Keynes UK
UKHW010635150222
398721UK00001B/100